FIFTY YEARS OF CHANGE ON THE U.S.-MEXICO BORDER

D0721869

FIFTY YEARS OF CHANGE ON THE U.S.-MEXICO BORDER

Growth, Development, and Quality of Life

JOAN B. ANDERSON AND JAMES GERBER
PHOTOGRAPHS BY LISA FOSTER

UNIVERSITY OF TEXAS PRESS, AUSTIN

LIBRARY OF CONGRESS CATALOGING-IN-PUBLICATION

Anderson, Joan B.
    Fifty years of change on the U.S.-Mexico border : growth, development, and quality of life / Joan B. Anderson and James Gerber ; photographs by Lisa Foster.
        p.   cm.
    Includes bibliographical references and index.
    ISBN 978-0-292-71718-3 (cloth : alk. paper) — ISBN 978-0-292-71719-0 (pbk. : alk. paper)
    1. Mexican-American Border Region—Economic conditions.   2. Mexican-American Border Region—Social conditions.   3. Labor supply—Mexican-American Border Region.   4. Migrant labor—Mexican-American Border Region.   5. Industrial clusters—Mexican-American Border Region.   6. United States—Commerce—Mexico.   7. Mexico—Commerce—United States. I. Gerber, James.   II. Title.
    HC135.A774   2007
    330.972'1—dc22

                                                                2007026612

CONTENTS

PREFACE AND ACKNOWLEDGMENTS

The regions along the border between the United States and Mexico have experienced rapid demographic and economic growth since 1950. Growth has proceeded on its own terms, almost without regard for the ups and downs in relations between the two nations, and for both nations it shows the increasing influence of factors on the other side of the border. In as symmetrical a manner as possible, we discuss the nature and dynamics of this growth and what it has meant to the lives of border dwellers on both sides of the border. To compare the quality of life in the different parts of the border region, we develop a Border Human Development Index (BHDI), which is constructed in a way that allows cross-border comparisons.

We define the border region as all the counties (U.S.) and municipios (Mexico) that touch the U.S.-Mexico border. Most of the analysis in this book is based on data at the county and municipio level from the U.S. and Mexican censuses of 1950 through 2000. The data are presented in summary form here; detailed county and municipio data are available on an associated Web site, http://latinamericanstudies.sdsu.edu/BorderData.html.

A book of this sort owes to many. We thank David Molina, Paul Ganster, and an anonymous reviewer for their helpful comments. We also thank our many colleagues in the Association for Borderlands Studies who commented on parts of the book they heard at the annual ABS conference and at other venues. Especially helpful to us in deepening our perspective were the comments of Michael Patrick, Jorge Carrillo, Eduardo Mendoza, James Pick, Jim Peach, Tom Fullerton, Roberto Coronado, Bill Gilmer, Jesus Cañas, Keith Phillips, and William Gruben. We would also like to acknowledge the help we received from Ilian Emmons, Ivonne Jimenez,

Julie Miller, and Juana Purchase, all of whom provided careful and accurate work in assisting with the data gathering; cartographer Harry Johnson, for creating the maps; Lisa Foster, for taking most of the photographs; and Ying Jiang, who formatted the data tables published on the Web site related to this research. Portions of Chapters 7, 8, and 9 appeared in slightly different form in an article we published in *Journal of Borderland Studies*, "A Human Development Index for the United States–Mexico Border" (vol. 19, no. 2, Fall 2004, pp. 1–26); we are grateful to the editors for granting permission to reuse the material here. We are especially appreciative of the funding and other support received from the Transborder Institute at the University of San Diego and the Center for Latin American Studies at San Diego State University. Thank you, all! Needless to say, any errors of omission and commission are our own.

FIFTY YEARS OF CHANGE ON THE U.S.-MEXICO BORDER

THE UNITED STATES–MEXICO BORDER

Communities along the United States–Mexico border have a great deal in common, including a shared history, two deserts, rapid population growth, thriving tourism, and deepening economic integration. Day-to-day life for people living along the border is shaped by these common elements, plus the distinctive feature of an international border that divides families, friends, and businesses. The challenges posed by an international boundary that draws into proximity two vastly different countries while simultaneously dividing local communities of great similarity represent a complex mix of economics, politics, culture, and language. Directly or indirectly, the international boundary affects the daily life of nearly everyone living near the border through its impact on economic and political relationships, family and social ties, and the shared natural environment.

Throughout this book, we use the terms *border area* or *border region* as a linguistic shorthand; in fact, the U.S.-Mexico border comprises many regions. In an effort to discern the nature of the borderland, however, we will look first to a more general description. Culturally, the U.S.-Mexico border marks the intersection of cuisines, music, and languages from North America and Latin America. Economically, the border separates a developed country and a developing country, with one of the largest cross-border income gaps in the world. Nevertheless, in every economic and demographic category, the local and regional disparities are less than those between the two countries as a whole: whereas the Mexican border region is wealthier than Mexico as a whole, the U.S. border region is mostly poorer than the rest of the United States, thus bringing communities on either side of the border closer together than the enormous economic differences at the scale of the nation would suggest. The relatively smaller economic differences and greater similarities at the level of communities straddling the border make the border area unique.

Most public attention on U.S.-Mexico relations is focused on Washington, D.C., and Mexico, D.F. The latest statements from ambassadors, the personal relations of the presidents, or position papers on national migration policy capture most of the headlines, but beneath these high-level contacts and debates is a vast array of person-to-person contacts, most operating far outside the notice of the respective capitals or the major media. These contacts occur within the business and social networks of families that live on both sides of the border, of friends and colleagues who work, shop, socialize, and collaborate across the border, and of businesses that draw materials and labor from either side of the border to produce goods and services that are sent to local and distant markets. Borderlanders take note of the latest blowup in U.S.-Mexico relations and the policy maneuvers of political insiders in border states and the national capitals, and then they go about their activities as before.

The irony of the border is that it is the source of most of the integration between the United States and Mexico, but the national attention of both countries is focused elsewhere, as if the national capitals were in control. National policies are not unimportant, but those policies do not determine the enormous current of activities that is carrying the United States and Mexico toward a deeper level of integration. Rather, integration is rooted in the shared histories, migration and demographic changes, foreign investments, businesses, local governments, and the decisions of millions of families and friends engaging in activities that require border crossing. This ocean of local activity is largely beyond the control of national policy makers, who are viewed by many borderlanders as incompetent at best, and often positively harmful.

Within the border region there is a high level of recognition that national governments impede border relations at least as often as they enable them. At times this interference is by design, as when border crossing is intentionally slowed in order to interdict drugs or to search for other contraband, but at other times it is an unintended consequence of policies, as when border restrictions prevent twin cities from efficiently moving emergency responders and their equipment from one side of the border to the other. (*Twin cities* is the term given to a pair of cities, one Mexican, one U.S., that lie on either side of the border. This pairing of cities occurs along the entire length of the border. For example, Brownsville and Matamoros are twin cities, as are San Diego and Tijuana.) A problem for borderlanders is that they are a long way from Washington, D.C., and Mexico, D.F., and often are unable to make their needs known to national policy makers, who tend to view the border as a law enforcement and security problem and only rarely as an economic development challenge and opportunity.

It is beyond the scope of this book to offer a catalog of all the issues affecting the daily lives of borderlanders. However, within the limited domain of economics and demography, eight major issues set the terms of cross-border relations. These issues or areas of concern are not exclusively economic or demographic, but they spill into those arenas and therefore are relevant to our discussion of the current history of economic development along the border. In what follows, we briefly take up each of these issues: (1) trade and investment, (2) barriers to border crossing, (3) migration, (4) cross-border labor, (5) the environment, (6) poverty and income distribution, (7) exchange rates, and (8) governance and cross-border collaboration.

TRADE AND INVESTMENT

Much of the economic and demographic growth of the border region over the past fifty years has been fueled by two intertwined economic factors: trade between the United States and Mexico, and investment in manufacturing plants on the Mexican side of the border. The United States is Mexico's number one trading partner, and by 1999, Mexico had passed Japan to become the United States' second largest trading partner in total volume of trade.

Growth in both trade and investment came as an indirect response to the debt crisis that hit Mexico and much of the developing world beginning in 1982. Up until the mid-1980s, Mexico's economic development strategy looked inward, set strict limits on foreign investment, and emphasized investment in import substitutes over the production of goods for export. The Border Industrialization Program that began in 1965 was an effort to employ agricultural workers who were no longer allowed to enter the United States legally, but for many years the plan was relatively small and did not contribute significantly to Mexico's national economy. Beginning in the 1980s, with the pressure of the prolonged stagnation that resulted from the debt crisis, economic policy began to shift to an outward orientation. In 1986, Mexico became a signatory to the General Agreement on Tariffs and Trade, unilaterally cut its tariffs, and began to ease regulations on foreign investment.

Changes in Mexican economic policies attracted investment, and when the changes were institutionalized with the ratification of the North American Free Trade Agreement (NAFTA), Mexico went through a period in which it attracted a disproportionate share of the world's foreign direct investment in developing countries. Much of the investment was in manufacturing along the border, where proximity to the U.S. market created advantages, and in the mid-1970s through the mid-1990s, periodic peso devaluations increased the U.S.-Mexican wage differential and contributed to the growth in border industrialization. Jobs were plentiful in the cities on the border, and people from the interior of Mexico migrated there to take advantage of the new opportunities.

The impact of these changes did not stop at the border but spilled across to the U.S. side as well. Mexican demand for consumer goods stimulated growth in the U.S. border retail sector, while transportation services expanded to handle the increase in commerce, infrastructure was built to accommodate part of the growth, and affiliated manufacturing and warehousing activities stimulated the economy of the U.S. border region.

BARRIERS TO BORDER CROSSING

In 1853 the first man-made barriers, consisting of a series of cement obelisks, were constructed along the border to demarcate it. In the 1930s, Border Patrol observation towers were built, then removed two decades later, in the late 1950s, when U.S. ambassador to Mexico Robert Hill declared them an insult to Mexico. In 1975, Congress approved the construction of chain-link fencing between the two most used border crossings, San Diego–Tijuana and El Paso–Ciudad Juárez. These fences, dubbed the "tortilla curtain" amid strong negative reactions, were completed in 1978.

In the 1990s, contradictory U.S. policies with respect to Mexico led to freer trade in goods and services and the freer movement of capital, on the one hand, in concert with more restrictive labor movements on the other. Around the same time that NAFTA was signed and implemented, the United States instituted programs to "protect its borders" and stem the flow of undocumented workers. Operation Hold the Line was inaugurated in 1993 in El Paso, and in 1994, Operation Gatekeeper was set up to control the western end of the border, followed by additional initiatives in other parts of the border region. In addition to increases in the size of the Border Patrol, the programs included high-tech detection equipment and higher and stronger border fences. The porous chain-link fences of the 1980s were replaced with high steel walls, which were then doubled, and the areas between the fences were lighted at night. After September 11, 2001, U.S. border security and inspections increased dramatically. Under the Homeland Security Bill, double walls were expanded to triple walls near major urban areas. Crossing the border, especially by car, slowed to a crawl at the busiest border crossings and increased the opportunity costs of economic and social interaction.

MIGRATION

The United States as a nation is deeply divided over the issue of migration. U.S. workers worry that Mexican migrants depress wages, while employers and consumers enjoy the higher profits and lower prices that low-wage migrant labor provides. Mexico badly wants an escape valve for its restless and unemployed, and border residents cannot escape the fact that they live in two very different nation-states. While Mexican migration into the United States is a national issue, both because migrants go to all parts of the country and because migration policy is a federal responsibility, most migration law enforcement takes place in the border region. After passage of the Immigration Reform and Control Act (IRCA) in 1986, enforcement gradually became much less focused on work sites and more on restricting entry at the border, using methods that included the construction of higher, less porous walls, the installation of infrared lights, the creation of no-man zones, and expansion of the Border Patrol to 12,000 agents.[1] The increased cost of crossing from Mexico into the United States without documents sent migrants out of large urban areas and into the mountains and deserts, where they were much more vulnerable to both natural and criminal elements. Between 1994 and 2003, more than 2,300 bodies of Mexicans who had died while attempting to cross into the United States were found, representing a significant increase in the death rate associated with attempting to cross the border.

The unfortunate reality of the border region as the location of migration policy enforcement serves to strengthen the perception in Washington, D.C., and Mexico, D.F., that border matters are primarily law enforcement issues and sources of diplomatic tensions. An unintended consequence is that economic development issues, infrastructure, cross-border integration, and cultural vitality receive less attention than they deserve. Perhaps the best that can be hoped for in the short run is that the United States and Mexico will find an approach to migration that results in many fewer economic refugees dying in the deserts and mountains, and that the issue of migration will cease threatening good relations between the countries.

Freeway sign in San Diego County.

CROSS-BORDER LABOR

During 2002, an estimated 7.7 percent of the economically active labor force of both Tijuana and Mexicali worked in the United States. Using 2000 census figures for the size of the economically active population, an estimated 34,697 residents of Tijuana and 22,114 residents of Mexicali crossed the border from one to five days a week to work in San Diego and

Imperial County. Figures for the Texas border region are smaller but still significant. For example, the share of the labor force in Ciudad Juárez that worked in the United States (most likely El Paso) was 3.6 percent, equivalent to 17,404 people, based on 2000 population estimates. These workers are not undocumented immigrants but rather people who live on one side and work on the other, many complying with all the rules for entering and working in the United States.

Based on data from the Mexican Survey of Urban Employment, in 1998, 14 percent of the 35,943 transmigrant workers were U.S. citizens and another 33 percent had U.S. work permits (green cards). Another 43 percent of the cross-border workers had a tourist or other visa, and 10 percent had no visa. In other words, slightly more than half the workers were undocumented. In Tijuana and Mexicali in 1998, the average salary of cross-border workers was slightly above $1,000 per month, almost three times the average earnings of workers who remained on the Mexican side. However, at the eastern end of the border the average salary for cross-border workers was $663, just over twice the average earnings of workers in Matamoros.[2]

Cross-border employment runs in the other direction as well, but even less is known about U.S. workers commuting to Mexico than about residents of Mexico working in U.S. border cities. Managers of foreign-owned manufacturing plants, some of whom are U.S., Japanese, or Korean citizens, are an important component of the daily north-to-south flow of workers, but so are college professors teaching in Mexican universities, lawyers employed by Mexican law firms, and other professionals and business people who earn enough to live on the northern side of the border.

ENVIRONMENTAL ISSUES

There are two major sources of environmental stress in the border regions. One is the increase in emissions and industrial wastes associated with increased industrial activity, the environmental side effect of economic development. The other is the environmental effects associated with the rapid growth of population, including urban sprawl and congestion, increased motor vehicle use, increased waste generation, and increased depletion of natural resources. The rapid growth in both industrial output and population presents a number of environmental stresses related to water supply and quality, air quality, sewage disposal, industrial waste disposal, and wildlife preservation. These environmental stresses are not unique to the border but rather are the side effects of economic growth, with the difference that pollution is not contained by international boundaries. Rivers

Life in a Texas *colonia*.

polluted with sewage and air currents laden with particulates flow across international boundaries without going through border checkpoints.

Since polluted water and air do not respect international borders, the environmental issues associated with the surge in Mexican border industrialization have not been confined to the Mexican side of the border. Sewage overflows from Tijuana have contaminated beaches in Southern California, and Southern California's polluted air blows over Tijuana, while raw sewage dumped into the Rio Grande at Nuevo Laredo has contaminated drinking water on both sides of the border, and pesticides from the agriculturally rich Imperial Valley flow into Baja California. Adding to the problem is the fact that the border regions are relatively fragile, semi-arid to arid environments that lack the resources, including sufficient water, to keep up with the demands for infrastructure to accommodate rapid population growth.

Binational efforts are required to meet the environmental challenges of this rapidly growing border. While some institutions have been developed to carry out these efforts, so far they lack sufficient funding to meet all the pressing demands. At the time of the NAFTA agreement, estimated environmental infrastructure needs were between $5 and $12 billion, but by 2005 the North American Development Bank, charged with lending to communities for infrastructure development, had lent less than half a billion, which was divided between the two countries. To meet the environmental needs of the border regions, both nations will need to contribute much more in the way of financial and human resources.

POVERTY AND INCOME DISTRIBUTION

Poverty is a fact of life on both sides of the border. On the U.S. side, the proportion of families that fall below the official poverty line is greater than the national average, and along the Texas border, in the *colonias* (neighborhoods lacking some or all the basic services of electricity, water, sewage disposal, and paved roads), poverty is very visible. In the United States, poverty rates are highest at the eastern end of the border and lowest at the western end. By contrast, poverty rates on the Mexican side are lower than the national average but higher than on the U.S. side, and are still a huge problem. The availability of discarded materials from the U.S. side of the border to turn into functional salvage—old garage doors used for house walls, old tires for steps and retaining walls, used clothing and recycled appliances—makes the lives of the Mexican border poor a little easier.

In the United States, income inequality is also greater along the border than it is nationally, with the worst inequality located in Texas border counties and a tendency toward less inequality in the western half of the border region.[3] As is true for the United States as a whole, income inequality along the border is worsening over time. In Mexico, development has long been hampered by a highly unequal distribution of income, but income distribution in the Mexican border states is more equal and median household income is higher than in Mexico as a whole. The trend in income inequality during the 1990s appears to show a slight decrease in inequality in the Mexican border states, though it remains above the level of inequality found on the U.S. side.[4]

EXCHANGE RATES AND EXCHANGE RATE FLUCTUATIONS

In most places, the dollar is accepted on both sides of the border. Some places in Texas also accept pesos, but that is the exception rather than the rule. The relative stability of the peso until 1976 made exchange rates a non-issue until inflationary finance and then the debt crisis of 1982 led border residents to begin to worry about the value of the peso. Devaluations of the peso were a common feature of macroeconomic volatility in Mexico for the twenty years between 1976 and 1995. Exchange rate volatility has a large impact on border residents, although it is largely unnoticed outside of border cities. Retail sales are estimated to have fallen 80 to 90 percent in some Texas border stores when the peso was sharply devalued in 1982, and the overall impact on Texas border cities was greater than the impact of the steep U.S. recession of 1981–1982.[5] U.S. border retail and visitor industries are especially affected by slowdowns in border crossings brought on by large peso devaluations because all of the U.S. border metropolitan areas have historically had larger than average retail sectors, reflecting the fact that they serve a larger population base than their own urban area.

Residents in the larger Mexican border cities are also squeezed at home by devaluation as landlords, electricians, plumbers, and other service providers demand payment in dollars, or in constant-dollar-value pesos. That is, when devaluation hits, dollar-denominated goods in the United States become more expensive and Mexican rents go up in order to keep the dollar value constant. Perhaps more important, Mexican incomes are squeezed as the higher cost of imported goods leads to a price inflation that historically has not been offset by a corresponding increase in wages. Hence, the value of inflation-adjusted income declines, and residents of Mexico are made worse off. This decline in real incomes hits the border region particularly hard, since a large number of people regularly cross into the United States to make purchases. As evidence, two separate surveys of Baja California south-to-north border crossers found that shopping was one of the primary reasons for journeying to the other side.[6]

GOVERNANCE AND COLLABORATION ACROSS THE BORDER

Both Mexico and the United States are federal systems of state and local governments. In the United States, state and local governments have a relatively wide scope of action, along with revenue streams to finance their activities. Mexico's thirty-one states are subdivided into municipalities, or *municipios*, which are similar to counties in the United States and include both urban and rural areas. Municipios in Mexico are not nearly as independent as U.S. cities and counties, nor do they have substantial revenues, since urban planning and funding are traditionally federal responsibilities and there is no such thing as a municipal bond market where local governments could raise money for infrastructure or other capital projects. Although Mexico is decentralizing many of its public administration functions, its municipios are not likely to transform into the equivalent of U.S. counties, and significant differences in federal, state, and local functions will persist. Another important fact is that governors, mayors, and their administrations serve only one term in Mexico. This undermines continuity in policy making and limits the development of social networks among public officials.

Despite the resource gap and the differences in decision making between U.S. and Mexican cities, a number of notable examples of successful collaboration exist. Given the immediacy of many cross-border issues such as public safety, health care, emergency response, and environmental protection, twin cities along the border have had to find ways to collaborate, even when it did not come easily. The asymmetry in decision making and resource availability often makes collaboration difficult, and the legal status of many cooperative agreements is questionable, but necessity often wins out in the crush of day-to-day operations. The key, as the authors of a recent study of comparative borders pointed out, is for both sides to know what they want and to approach their respective national governments with clear and consistent ideas.[7] In this regard, some parts of the border are further along than others.

IS THE BORDER A REGION?

The purpose of this book is to explore the economic and demographic changes that have occurred in the U.S.-Mexico border region over approximately the last fifty years. Throughout the book, we speak of the border region as if it were a single, geographically and economically coherent region. We recognize that it is no such thing. What distinguishes our area of interest is the presence of an international border, but the border region is divisible into a number of different geographic and economic regions. For example, the Lower Rio Grande Valley is about as different from the Tijuana River Valley (which unites San Diego, California, with Tijuana, Baja California) as the Midwestern state of Iowa is from the state of Guanajuato in central Mexico. Nevertheless, the impact of economic integration and the presence of an international border make it useful to look at the entire border as an area or region of analysis. As a compromise, we have included detailed county- or municipio-level data in a data appendix on the Web site that accompanies this book (http://latinamericanstudies .sdsu.edu/BorderData.html), and throughout the book we point to differences within the regions.

This focus does not resolve a number of additional problems, however, as it still remains to determine how "deep" the border is. That is, how far into the United States and Mexico do border influences extend? This is an area of investigation for future research. Given the state of border studies, any definition we might offer now would be somewhat arbitrary;

consequently, we have adopted a definition that includes the twenty-five U.S. counties and thirty-eight Mexican municipios that touch the border. There is an element of convenience in this definition, as it follows the major data collection units of both countries and permits use of the U.S. and Mexican decennial censuses taken between 1950 and 2000 as the primary data source. The census data are supplemented by additional data where necessary and possible, but in all of the following chapters, we strive to maintain analytical symmetry between the United States and Mexico. There are a few exceptions, such as in Chapter 3, where we felt compelled to try to explain the reasons for the differences in the policies of U.S. border states (primarily Texas and California) toward Mexico, and in Chapter 7, where we had to use different variables in discussing income and poverty. Much of the previous research on the border has taken an exclusively Mexican or U.S. perspective and has ignored the other side, or else it has been limited by asymmetry in data and information sources. Although the two nation's censuses are not identical in scope or format, they overlap in their information, and consequently they do provide a rough equivalence between Mexican municipios and U.S. counties. The data appendix on the Web site provides an extensive set of border data, arranged symmetrically, and allows examination of much of the raw data we used in forming our analysis.

Our hope is that this work will provoke more quantitative analysis to be done to illuminate the historical patterns and contemporary trends of the border region. Given the historical trajectory of U.S.-Mexico relations and the degree to which contemporary integration is rooted in a deeply persistent trend, a closer examination of the economics of the region where integration is most advanced and most profound is warranted. Historians, fiction writers, sociologists, cultural geographers, and others have contributed enormously to our understanding of the border between the United States and Mexico. With this work, we hope to add an economic perspective to this growing body of knowledge.

▨ ▨

CHAPTER 1

ALONG THE UNITED STATES—MEXICO BORDER

For most of its nearly 2,000 miles, the United States–Mexico border is a permeable barrier of desert rock and sand. In a few places urban landscapes appear, with multiple fences and controlled gates of entry, while along the eastern half of the border the open space is divided by the Rio Grande. Through most of its western half, the boundary between national sovereignties is little more than a simple fence running across the two great deserts connecting northern Mexico and southwestern United States.

The residents of this region share far more than natural landscapes. Their regional histories and life stories, cuisines and music, cultural habits and language are shared experiences for a large segment of the border population, and, like the natural environment, these common traits compose an older stratum of social and economic history that runs deep beneath the surface of contemporary population growth and economic change. This older layer was laid down before the border was created, but it has survived the overlay of separate national identities and large flows of immigrants through its constant renewal by the natural tendency of people to cross over to the other side. Marriages, families, schools, churches, and jobs link people across the border and are responsible for much of the shared experiences, histories, and cultures. People track back and forth, commuting to work, shopping and eating out, visiting friends and family, and engaging in the normal activities of everyday life. This ebb and flow makes the border a kind of tidal zone of nationalities, neither completely Mexican nor completely of the United States, but a blend of the two.

EUROPEAN SETTLEMENT IN THE BORDER REGION

The border separating the United States and Mexico was created in 1848 by the Treaty of Guadalupe Hidalgo at the end of the Mexican-American War, or, as Mexicans prefer to call it, the War of North American Invasion. The treaty left the western half of the border without a clear definition until the Gadsden Purchase resolved the issue in 1853. For $10 million, the United States purchased approximately 30,000 square miles south of the Gila River and west from El Paso to California. The long stretch of the border between Texas and Mexico is defined by the Rio Grande (called the Río Bravo in Mexico), from the river's mouth on the Gulf of Mexico between Matamoros (Mexico) and Brownsville (Texas) all the way upstream to West Texas, where the river separates El Paso from its Mexican twin, Ciudad Juárez. West of El Paso the border is a line drawn in the sand and rocks of the vast Chihuahuan and Sonoran deserts that stretch across northern Mexico and southwestern United States. The border cuts through the Laguna–San Pedro Mártir mountains on the eastern edge of San Diego–Tijuana and ends in the Pacific Ocean at Border Field State Park.

Archaeological evidence suggests that the border region has been occupied for at least 10,000 years. River crossings on the Rio Grande, some still in use until the aftermath of September 11, 2001, date back several millennia, while a native population of Amerindians continues to live throughout most of the border region. Spanish explorers trekking from Florida to California were the first Europeans to arrive in the borderlands. The earliest to arrive—Alonzo Pineda in 1519 and Diego Camargo in 1520—laid claim to the territory surrounding the lower Rio Grande. A few years later, in 1527, Álvar Nuñez Cabeza de Vaca was shipwrecked in the Gulf of Mexico and spent eight years wandering westward across Texas and New Mexico, perhaps as far as eastern Arizona. Explorers and gold seekers were followed by Franciscan and Jesuit missionaries looking for converts among the indigenous peoples. The Jesuits made the first contact with the border region in 1591, and in 1598 Franciscans established missions in New Mexico. The most notable was the Jesuit priest Eusebio Kino, who began his explorations and founding of missions in 1687, continuing until his death in 1711. A string of missions were built in the region, some still operating today as churches, others destroyed by time or by the indigenous peoples of the border.

In 1749, more than 200 years after the first expeditions, Camargo and Reynosa were established in the Lower Rio Grande Valley, followed by Mier in 1753 and Laredo in 1755. The Rio Grande was a suitable transpor-

West end of the border: Border Field State Park, California.

East end of the border: Playa Bagdad, Tamaulipas.

tation waterway, and shipping eventually ran 150 miles or so up the Lower Rio Grande Valley to the town of Roma. This gave commercial advantages to the territory that was to become the eastern border and enabled its early settlement. By the nineteenth century, the frontier along the Rio Grande and the wild desert areas across the center of the North American continent were dotted with a string of military posts, railroad watering stops, and missions. For all of its history, this arid territory remained sparsely inhabited until the population explosion of the last half of the twentieth century.

OVERVIEW OF THE BORDER'S LANDSCAPE, HISTORY, AND ECONOMY

As one moves along the border from west to east, the landscape is dominated by two large deserts. The Sonoran Desert stretches south from California and Arizona, down into the Baja California peninsula and along the eastern edge of the Gulf of California into the Mexican state of Sonora. The Chihuahuan Desert is larger and touches the Sonoran Desert in southeastern Arizona, from where it spreads across southern New Mexico and western Texas on into the Mexican states of Chihuahua and Coahuila and then farther south into central Mexico. Mountains block the Sonoran Desert from the sea and the coastal cities of San Diego and Tijuana, while the Chihuahuan Desert is blocked from the eastern edge of the continent by the moist Caribbean air that bathes the Gulf Coast. About two-thirds of the border's landscape is dominated by the Chihuahuan and Sonoran deserts, giving it a rugged and wild appearance.

As with the natural environment, much of the border region is united by a shared culture that often turns preconceptions of the United States and Mexico upside down. Tijuana's gleaming skyscrapers rise above opulent mansions that surround a local golf course, while on the outskirts of several border cities in Texas, neighborhoods survive without running water, sewerage, or electricity. The challenge to common stereotypes occurs because the border is a mixture of both countries, a place where many people are bilingual and bicultural, with income and expenditure patterns and family and social networks that greatly depend on "the other side."

Along the California Border

At the western end of the U.S.-Mexico border are the twin cities of San Diego and Tijuana. This is the largest and richest population concentra-

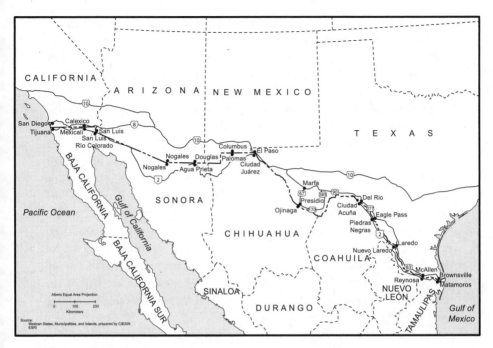

MAP 1.1. The U.S.-Mexico border.

tion in the border region, home to 4 million of the 12.2 million people who inhabited the border region in 2000. The average income in both San Diego and Tijuana is higher than their respective national averages, and both have the highest incomes and lowest poverty rates respectively of the U.S. counties and Mexican *municipios* that touch the border. (A municipio is an administrative unit below the level of the state. Municipios are similar to U.S. counties, and each one has urban and rural areas within it.) The main border crossing between the two cities is one of the busiest in the world, a distinction that it shares with the El Paso–Ciudad Juárez area, in Texas and Chihuahua.

Rapid population growth on the border began with World War II. In 1950 San Diego was a navy town, while a good part of Tijuana lived off its ability to cater to the desires of homesick sailors passing through San Diego. Tijuana's reputation as a "sin city" dates back to the Prohibition era, when it became a place for U.S. residents to acquire alcohol and gamble at the casinos and racetracks. Eventually, as with most places catering to tourists looking to escape the rules and constraints imposed at home, Tijuana developed a sex industry that continues today as part of both the formal and informal economy. With its lower drinking age (eighteen in Mexico, twenty-one in California) and legal prostitution, Tijuana bars and clubs are full of young San Diegans and Tijuanenses on Friday and Saturday nights, and a southern suburb, Playas de Rosarito, is a destination for students on spring break.

Despite these vestiges from the past, economic activity in both San Diego and Tijuana is no longer concentrated on the U.S. Navy or on tourists indulging in guilty pleasures forbidden at home. San Diego's economy has diversified beyond the military and defense industries into biotechnology, wireless communication, digital media, and other high-tech research and development sectors, while Tijuana has added four- and five-star hotels, upscale shopping centers, and an enormous manufacturing sector.[1] Throughout much of the 1980s and 1990s, the explosive growth in Mexico's export industries, in particular the border assembly and manufacturing sector known as the *maquiladora* industry, attracted both huge sums of foreign investment and workers from the interior of Mexico. The vitality of the maquiladora and its ability to generate jobs in Mexico account for a large share of Tijuana's rapid population growth.

To the east, San Diego and Tijuana are separated from the vast Sonoran Desert by the Laguna Mountains on the U.S. side and the Sierra de San Pedro Mártir on the Mexican side. On the northern side of the border, the small mountain communities of Jamul, Boulevard, Jacumba, and the Campo Indian Reservation dot the landscape, while to the south are the towns of Tecate and Rumorosa. Tecate, the largest community in the mountains, has the only official border crossing, along with a brewing industry and a beer to which it lends its name. Deeper and higher into the Sierra de San Pedro Mártir of Mexico is the Parque Nacional de Laguna Hanson, the oldest national park in the hemisphere.

East from Tecate, Mexico, and Jacumba, United States, the rugged mountains descend sharply into deep canyons on their eastern flank, where the occasional palm oasis can be found growing in the rocky creek beds, the latter mostly containing only seasonal water. The valley beyond the mountains is the western edge of the Sonoran Desert, but irrigation with water from the Colorado River has turned it into a fertile plain of winter vegetables, animal feed, olives, and other horticultural products. While it is but one valley, the international border has given the northern and southern halves different names. Both Imperial Valley in the north and Mexicali Valley in the south are economically dominated by the city of Mexicali, the capital of the state of Baja California. With more than 750,000 residents, according to the 2000 census, Mexicali has significant farming, food processing, and maquiladora manufacturing. It is also the source of most of the labor force that works in the fields and manages the farms in California's Imperial Valley, and it is an essential source of demand for the goods on display in the retail shops of the U.S. towns of El Centro and Calexico. Mexicali is a case where the Mexican city is more cosmopolitan than its U.S. twin city.

Arizona and Sonora

An hour's drive to the east of Calexico-Mexicali is the Colorado River and the cities of San Luis Rio Colorado, Sonora, and Yuma, Arizona. San Luis is a product of the *bracero* farm worker program that was implemented during World War II to overcome labor shortages in the United States by allowing Mexican workers to enter on temporary work permits. San Luis is still home to many farmworkers, but now it also has a number of maquiladora manufacturing plants. Twenty-six miles north of San Luis, the Colorado River crossing at Yuma has been called the gateway to California since the time of Father Kino, the Jesuit priest who explored and established missions in that area in the late 1600s. As with nearby U.S. and Mexican towns, Yuma's economy is mostly agriculture, but it is also supported by tourism and is a major destination for the seasonal migration of retired "snowbirds" who flee the harsh weather of the northern United States and Canada during the winter months.

East of Yuma and San Luis, tall saguaro cacti dot the beautiful Sonoran Desert landscape. Between the Colorado River and the Sonoita border crossing 120 miles further east is Mexico's El Pinacate Biosphere Reserve. The reserve sits between the border and the northern shores of the Sea of Cortez (Gulf of California) and is noted for the sand dunes, black cinder cones, and red rock craters scattered around its still active volcanoes.[2] On the U.S. side of the Sonoita border crossing, Organ Pipe Cactus National Monument protects organ pipe and saguaro cacti, along with other exotic desert vegetation. Sonoita is a small town that survives by catering to the traffic that passes by, most of which is on its way to Puerto Peñasco, or "Rocky Point," as the residents of Phoenix call it. Puerto Peñasco, on the Sea of Cortez, is a fishing village and the closest beach to Phoenix.

East of Sonoita the region is rich with the history of its native people and the Jesuit and Franciscan missionaries who established a trail of churches in their quest for converts. A small rural border crossing between Sasabe, Sonora, and Sasabe, Arizona, lies between Sonoita and the twin cities of Nogales, Arizona, and Nogales, Sonora. The two Nogales—*ambos*

Nogales—are border twins, similar in many respects, including their poverty, and are divided mainly by the border fence that runs through the middle of what would otherwise be a unified city. Sixty miles to their north is the more affluent metropolis of Tucson, Arizona, which has the highest per capita income in the border region after San Diego and a higher proportion of Anglo, non-Spanish-speaking population.[3] Census data for 2000 show that 27.5 percent of the residents of Tucson's Pima County speak Spanish at home, while in Nogales' Santa Cruz County, the figure is above 80 percent. The economy of Pima County and Tucson revolves around the University of Arizona, an air force base, defense industries, and tourism. Mexican influences are everywhere, but the university and the air force ensure a turnover of people and a cosmopolitanism that is the exception rather than the rule for border cities.

East of *ambos* Nogales sits the copper mining town of Bisbee, Arizona, which is now mining tourists. Desert mountains in the borderlands are rich in minerals of various kinds, and mining has been a major economic activity, particularly in the sparsely inhabited mountain areas. The copper-rich mountains of southeastern Arizona and northeastern Sonora are the northern reach of the Sierra Madre Occidental, one of the two great ranges of Mexico. This range forms the boundary between the Sonoran and Chihuahuan deserts, the latter of which stretches eastward on both sides of the border until it meets the moisture of the Gulf Coast coming up the Lower Rio Grande Valley.

About halfway between Nogales and Bisbee and across the border into Mexico is the copper-mining town of Cananea, Sonora. Cananea is a lovely and cohesive community with a long history of worker organizing. In Cananea, the fruits of the copper mines have raised the living standards above those of most municipios of its size, and at times in the 1960s and 1970s the local economy produced incomes that were among the highest in Mexico. Cananea still has a lower proportion of people earning extremely low wages (less than two times minimum wage) than any other Sonoran border municipio and has one of the highest proportions of the population age fifteen and older who have more than primary school education.[4]

Fifty miles east of Cananea are the twin towns of Agua Prieta, Sonora, and Douglas, Arizona. Douglas, too, was originally a copper-mining town, and although the copper smelter is gone, the town retains a faded elegance from the mining boom in the form of the Gadsden Hotel, which continues to operate as it has since 1906. Its Tiffany stained glass mural in the high ceiling of its lobby and its graceful spiral staircase seem incongruous with a downtown that is now filled with used and bargain clothing stores catering to Mexican shoppers from Agua Prieta. Today, without copper,

Chihuahuan Desert.

the main economy of both towns rests on maquiladora manufacturing plants in Agua Prieta.

The Chihuahuan Desert: New Mexico, West Texas, Chihuahua, and Coahuila

From Douglas and Agua Prieta, the border region enters the Chihuahuan Desert and the states of New Mexico and Chihuahua, where the border finds its most rural part. New Mexico has three border ports of entry, only two of which permit commercial vehicle crossings. As in the other U.S. border states, policy makers in New Mexico hope to take advantage of the state's proximity to the second largest trading partner of the United States and have invested in improvements to the highways and inspection stations connecting it to Mexico. The Santa Theresa crossing is eleven miles west of El Paso and has the potential to create more transborder commerce while siphoning off traffic (and potential customers) from the congested border crossings in Texas. New Mexico has the least amount of border trade, however, and the sparseness of population in this region, together with the existence of more direct international transportation routes in other regions, just about guarantees that border trade will not become as important to New Mexico as it is to California, Arizona, and especially Texas. Nevertheless, the spillover from El Paso and Ciudad Juárez is potentially lucrative to a small state and a sparsely populated region, and the New Mexico economic development agencies are working to capture some of the trade flow.

The dry and rocky landscape of the Chihuahuan Desert explains the emptiness of the border between Douglas–Agua Prieta and El Paso–Ciudad Juárez, but despite the geography, humans have carved out a living in the area for millennia. In the northwestern corner of the state of Chihuahua, the archaeological site of Paquimé at Casas Grandes contains evidence of ancient habitation, while in the nearby village of Mata Ortiz, 300 artisans work the ancient Paquimé designs into contemporary pottery that is exported to the United States. In addition to the ceramic business, the availability of water has opened up other possibilities. Río Casas Grandes and well water supply a farm sector that produces the raw materials for a thriving food-packing and processing sector. Some attribute the agricultural bounty to Mormons who settled in the area, crossing the border to escape the U.S. ban on polygamy. They introduced modern farming techniques, including the cultivation of slopes, and contemporary crops of apples and peaches are turned into Sara Lee pies and other processed foods.

In the emptiness of the border between the metropolises of Ciudad Juárez–El Paso and the towns of Agua Prieta–Douglas, small communities provide a market center for the farms and rural residents. The dusty little town of Las Palomas, Chihuahua, is a pass-through for agricultural exports, especially chile products. On the U.S. side, Columbus, New Mexico, holds the singular distinction of having been invaded by a foreign army. In 1916, Pancho Villa and his forces spilled across the border during the Mexican Revolution. The fighters eventually became immortalized in Pancho Villa State Park, three miles north of the border.

The banks of the Rio Grande and the city of Las Cruces, New Mexico, interrupt the desert landscape with their riparian habitat and lovely pueblo-style architecture. Situated on the banks of the river at the base of the Organ Mountains, Las Cruces was founded in 1848 as a supply point

Ciudad Juárez and El Paso, divided by the Rio Grande.

for mining operations and the forts that protected trade routes to Santa
Fe. There are several legends about the origin of the name, "The Crosses."
One of the most intriguing is that Las Cruces marks the spot where the
first Europeans who traveled what is now called the Camino Real encountered three graves marked with crosses in a land inhabited only by non-
Christian indigenous people.[5] Today, its economy depends heavily on agriculture, defense spending (White Sands Missile Range is four miles south),
New Mexico State University, and a small but vital manufacturing sector
that has grown significantly over the past three decades.

Farther downstream on the Rio Grande sit the twin cities of El Paso,
Texas, and Ciudad Juárez, Chihuahua. Juárez is the larger of the two cities,
but both are sprawling urban areas that line their respective sides of the
river. El Paso was originally named El Paso del Río del Norte (the Northern River Pass) by the first Spanish explorers and was the first river ford of
the Rio Grande they encountered. Ysleta, an eastern suburb of El Paso that
was founded in 1682, along with the mission Nuestra Señora del Carmen,
is the oldest European settlement in Texas. On the Mexican side of the
river, Ciudad Juárez was named for the great Mexican hero Benito Juárez,
who saved the country from the French and reformed the legal system. The
combined urban agglomeration of El Paso and Juárez forms a metropolitan

area that is second in population only to San Diego–Tijuana. Although Ciudad Juárez and Tijuana had nearly the same population in 2000, with about 1.2 million people each, San Diego County's 2.8 million residents exceeded El Paso's 700,000 by a factor of four, so that the westernmost urban agglomeration is the larger of the two. El Paso has more economic, political, and social interactions with Ciudad Juárez than San Diego has with Tijuana. There are a variety of reasons for this fact in addition to the historical ones, and it illustrates a common tendency for border relations to deepen (but not necessarily to widen) as one moves from west to east along the border. A key explanation is that the cultural and economic distances between the U.S. and Mexican twin cities in the Texas border region are much less than in the case of San Diego and Tijuana.

Marta's story is typical of the Texas region of the border. She was raised in Juárez and married an El Paso man. She says she never liked *Pochos* (Mexican-Americans), but she married one and contributed four more, her children. For the last thirty years she has crossed the border every Thursday to attend La Costura (the sewing circle), a group of about eighteen women who have been friends since childhood. They used to recite the Rosary, crochet, play cards, and have wine tastings, but as they have aged, they just do the wine tasting. Tijuana and San Diego have their own Martas, but their presence is diluted by the much larger population of San Diego with its smaller proportion of Latinos.

Despite the deeper cross-border ties in the El Paso–Juárez region, it is the site of a major land dispute between the United States and Mexico that flared up when the Rio Grande changed course in 1864. This shift in the riverbed added 700 acres of Mexico to the United States and set off a hundred-year dispute. It was finally settled with the Chamizal Agreement, which restored much of the land to Mexico and turned both sides of the river into parkland. One can walk from the U.S. Chamizal Park to the Mexican Parque Chamizal by crossing the Bridge of the Americas.

El Paso–Juárez has five border crossings, two of them added since the signing of the North American Free Trade Agreement (NAFTA), to handle commerce and people. In addition to their role as major commercial centers for surrounding communities and as gateways for international trade, both cities have significant manufacturing sectors. Ciudad Juárez is heavily involved in maquiladora manufacturing, while El Paso also has its share of labor-intensive manufacturing. In El Paso as in Texas, long-run trends in manufacturing have run opposite to the national trend, and the number of workers has grown over the past thirty years. Growth has not always been steady, and the depression in the U.S. manufacturing sector in 2000–2003 was hard on El Paso, but the long-run performance of manufacturing has been remarkable on both sides of the border. El Paso also has an agricultural base, growing Egyptian cotton, pecans and other nuts, fruits, market garden crops, and dairy products.

East of El Paso–Ciudad Juárez, on the Mexican side of the border, are the farm communities of Guadalupe and Praxedis G. Guerrero. These small towns, with a few paved streets and local primary and secondary schools, serve as bedroom communities for Ciudad Juárez, which is less than an hour away. Their rural environment, away from the distractions and problems of the city, is worth the commute for some people. The Texas side of the border to the east of El Paso is also rural and poor. It is a region where two-thirds of the population do not speak English as their first language and one-third speak English "less than well," as the census puts it. Language and living conditions are similar throughout most of the rural parts of the Texas border, where Spanish predominates and many people live in poor neighborhoods called *colonias*. The word *colonia* means neighborhood, and in Mexico a colonia might be rich or poor, but in Texas the word refers to neighborhoods that lack at least one of the basic services of electricity, running water, and sewerage. Some colonias lack all three.

Texas law allows developers to subdivide and sell raw land that has no infrastructure of water, sewerage, or electricity. Lots are sold for low down payments and low monthly payments, making land affordable to the working poor. With low payments for the land and a trailer, one can work toward becoming a landowner, even if it means forgoing many conveniences and requires an hour or more commute to work. Over time, colonias organize and obtain services. Electricity, which is the cheapest to provide, arrives first, followed by water and finally a sewer system. This process can take ten to twenty years, but once services arrive, land values go up. People who choose this option of living without basic services for a long period of time place a high value on home ownership. As one woman put it, she wanted to be sure that her children had a roof over their heads in ten years.

Further to the east, population becomes sparser and cattle denser. Fort Davis, a nineteenth-century military post constructed for defense against Indian attacks, tells of the region's history, while the town of Fort Davis in the heart of the Davis Mountains was a strategic point on the San Antonio–El Paso road. Following the border as it turns south are the historic towns of Marfa and Presidio. Marfa, the seat of Presidio County, was founded in 1881 as a water stop for the Texas and New Orleans Railroad, while Presidio and its Mexican twin city, Ojinaga, became the crossing point for the nineteenth-century Chihuahua Trail. The railroad, which crosses the border at Presidio and heads north to Dallas, connects Ojinaga to Ciudad Chihuahua, the state capital, and then to the Pacific Coast at Los Mochis. Ojinaga and Ciudad Chihuahua were originally founded in the 1500s as Spanish forts, or *presidios*, on the far northern frontier of New Spain. Their economies today are based on agriculture from the surrounding river plains, which are reputed to be the oldest continually cultivated farmlands in North America. In the summer this area is the hottest region in both Texas and Mexico.

To the southeast of Ojinaga is the last border municipio in Chihuahua state, Manuel Benavides. Accessible only by dirt road, this rural municipio was also the site of a mission church. Its Sierra Rica was mined for copper, zinc, and lead in the 1800s, but now only small-scale farming remains. In this part of the Chihuahuan Desert, population and roads are very sparse. To the north, across the border and just beyond Presidio, is the adobe Fort Leaton (El Fortín), which was built in the 1700s and used as a trading post in the 1800s.

Ten miles further east is Redford, a natural ford in the Rio Grande. Archaeological evidence indicates that Redford has been used as an informal crossing for the last 10,000 years, but after September 11, 2001, the U.S. Border Patrol (now called the Customs and Border Patrol, or CBP) poured cement blocks to close the crossing. A U.S. highway hugs the border, winding along the edge of the Rio Grande through the 250,000-acre Big Bend Ranch State Park and revealing spectacular views of river and cliffs. Nearby, the little towns of Terlingua and Lajitas, the latter with a ford across the river that was first recorded by Spanish explorers in 1588, are old mining towns that have been revived as Old West resorts to attract tourists. Just beyond these two towns is the western boundary of Big Bend National Park, established to preserve 801,000 acres of northern Chihuahuan Desert. The park has 118 miles of U.S.-Mexico border along its southern edge, and until September 11, 2001, the border was an integral part of the park experience. At two points in the park, U.S. tourists could hire a boatman to row across the river to the Mexican villages of Santa Elena, in the state of Chihuahua, or Boquillas, in the state of Coahuila. The adobe villages offered hearty Mexican food, margaritas, a few handicrafts, and a boat ride back to the United States. The effect of September 11, 2001, was to close all of the informal border crossings and to isolate the Mexican towns so that they are accessible only by dirt roads from the interior of Mexico. Without the tourist business, Santa Elena and Boquillas are no longer economically viable.

North of Big Bend National Park are the towns of Alpine and Marathon. Alpine, the county seat, began as a water stop for the Southern Pacific

Railway, then a shipping point for sending cattle to market, and now is a weekend getaway destination for tourists from El Paso. Marathon was established as a commercial center to support Fort Peña Colorada, which was built in 1879 to protect the coming railroad from Apache attacks. The area reminded Marathon's founder, Captain Albion Shepard, of the rocky hills around Marathon, Greece, hence its name. Like Alpine, Marathon's economy revolves around its role as a place where park visitors can find tourist services. This section of the border is sparsely populated, as there are no paved roads close to the border on the Mexican side, and the area to the north and east of the park is mostly open space, occasionally punctuated by small towns such as Sanderson, Dryden, Pumpville, and Langtry. In many of these West Texas towns, the myths, stereotypes, and hard realities of the Old West were created. For example, in the town of Langtry, the infamous Judge Roy Bean dispensed his own brand of law from his saloon, the Jersey Lily, which is still standing and a landmark for visitors.

Beyond the Pecos River is the Amistad Reservoir, a joint effort between the United States and Mexico to end the periodic downstream flooding of homes and farms. The eighty-five-mile-long reservoir, known as Lake Amistad (or Presa Amistad), lies directly on the border, so that visitors can cross between countries by driving across the dam. In addition to flood control, the lake provides opportunities for water sports and outdoor recreation, particularly for the twin cities of Del Rio, Texas, and Ciudad Acuña, Coahuila, located at the base of the lake.

Del Rio–Ciudad Acuña to the Rio Grande Valley

Del Rio and Ciudad Acuña both date from the 1870s and 1880s. Del Rio boomed in the 1880s as a result of railroad construction and is still a major shipping center for wool and mohair, as well as a port of entry from Mexico. Laughlin Air Force Base sits nearby and adds economic revenue to the local economy, along with the Alamo Village movie set, one of the largest in the United States. The set was originally built for John Wayne's *The Alamo*, but its frontier environment made it a good location for other westerns, among them *Lonesome Dove, Streets of Laredo*, and *How the West Was Won*. Ciudad Acuña, across the Rio Grande in Mexico, has also seen several movies made, including *El Mariachi, Desperado, Like Water for Chocolate*, and *Lone Star*. Ciudad Acuña began life in 1877 as a military post, but within a decade the military had been replaced by ranchers, who called the place Congregación Las Vacas (Cow Congregation). During the Mexican Revolution the town was renamed after the revolutionary poet, Manuel Acuña, but some local old-timers still call it Las Vacas. In addition to being an agricultural center, Ciudad Acuña has maquiladora manufacturing plants. Its social center is the main plaza and cathedral, located close to the border. While Del Rio on the Texas side has grown slowly and residents do not have a sense of big changes, Ciudad Acuña has experienced a large influx of people from the interior of Mexico looking for jobs and a better life on the border. Long-time Ciudad Acuña residents complain that they no longer know people. As one woman put it, "When you went to the plaza for a celebration you knew everyone. Now you only see a few people you know, and the rest are all strangers."

Mexican Highway 2, which follows the border but discontinues east of El Paso, begins again at Ciudad Acuña and continues along the border to the Gulf of Mexico. The border in this region runs mostly south and slightly east, down the horn of Texas. An hour's drive from the twin cities of Del Rio and Ciudad Acuña is the next pair of twins, Eagle Pass, Texas, and Piedras Negras, Coahuila. Piedras Negras, about twice as large as Ciudad Acuña, also began as a military post. As the closest border to San Antonio, Texas, and with a north-south railroad, the Piedras Negras–Eagle Pass gateway is the most important border crossing in the state of Coahuila. Piedras Negras, whose name, Black Rocks, refers to an exposed stratum of coal, claims to be the home of the nacho, but maquiladora manufacturing and coal mining are its main sources of economic support. The town's two-decade-long boom in border manufacturing has greatly expanded local commerce, as evidenced by the two new shopping centers that were recently added to an existing one and by the steady immigration of single men in search of work from the interior of Mexico.

Across the river from Piedras Negras, Eagle Pass developed around Fort Duncan, founded in 1849 as a stopover for Forty-Niners headed to the Gold Rush in California. During the Civil War, the fort was a Confederate stronghold and Eagle Pass was a center of commerce for exporting Confederate cotton and importing Mexican supplies from Monterrey, Mexico, for the Confederate Army. Before the arrival of Europeans, the region was heavily populated with indigenous groups, and it still has a large number of Kickapoo Indians. This legacy has resulted in a portion of the population being trilingual in English, Spanish, and Kickapoo. The only casino operating right on the border is on the Kickapoo reservation, a few miles east of Eagle Pass.

As Mexico Highway 2 heads mostly south and a little east along the border, it travels through the small, rural municipios of Guerrero and Hidalgo. Guerrero, less than an hour from Piedras Negras, is a bedroom community for Piedras Negras, as well as the site of the historic Misión San Bernardo. The highway passes through a narrow strip of the state of Nuevo Leon that touches the border. A new border crossing at Colombia, a small Mexican village that lies right on the border, provides another direct link between the important industrial city of Monterrey, Mexico, and the state of Texas, and is expected to grow as U.S.-Mexican ties deepen and expand.

Further to the southeast are the twin cities of Laredo and Nuevo Laredo. Given their strategic geographic position as the closest border crossing to Monterrey, Laredo and Nuevo Laredo are the leading ports between the United States and Mexico. Laredo was founded in 1755 as a ranching center by a Dr. Tomás Sanchez of the Royal Spanish Army. It was organized around a central plaza, but very quickly spilled across the river to form what is present-day Nuevo Laredo. The twin cities were a single community until they were divided by the international border in 1848 and the southern half became Nuevo Laredo. Before the Civil War, Laredo expanded from a small ranching center to a freight center, and during the Civil War it became a forwarding center for Confederate cotton, which was then shipped downriver on the Mexican side via Mier and Camargo to Matamoros and out to the gulf at Playa Bagdad. It has the distinction of being the only Texas community to have been under seven flags, including as the capital city of the short-lived (285 days) Republic of the Rio Grande, which was carved out of Texas between the Nueces and Rio Grande rivers. During the 1880s, Laredo became the junction of four railroads, making it a central point for commerce and trade across the international border. The Pan-American Highway was routed through Laredo in 1935, by which time it was known as "the gateway to Mexico." Laredo's historic role as a commercial center and gateway between the two countries continues, as 40 percent of the land commerce between the two countries crosses through Laredo–Nuevo Laredo. In 2004, nearly 1.4 million trucks crossed the border from south to north through Laredo, and a similar number passed in the opposite direction.[6] This amounted to approximately one-half of the total truck traffic through all Texas border crossings. Throughout Laredo's history, Mexicans have always been the majority ethnic group, making Laredo, according to one cultural geographer, the "most demographically Mexican medium-sized city in the United States."[7] In 2000, 94 percent of the population was Hispanic (mostly Mexican), and 91 percent spoke Spanish at home. There are four Spanish-language newspapers, and Laredo's cultural blend and pride in its Mexican heritage are unique. As one resident claimed, in describing the Mexican culture and U.S.

infrastructure, "living in Laredo is like living in Mexico, but the plumbing works."

Laredo's twin, Nuevo Laredo, was founded in 1848 when the newly formed international border separated it from Laredo. Now twice as large as Laredo but without the historic sites, it is a key tourist destination for the residents of nearby San Antonio. While maquiladoras are important to Nuevo Laredo's economy, the city is less dependent on them than are other midsized Mexican border cities, as its relatively diverse economy also generates income from tourism, farming and cattle ranching, import-export operations, and transportation, in addition to manufacturing.

As the Rio Grande angles south from Laredo–Nuevo Laredo, it passes through an area that is rich in history. Many of the towns were founded around 1750, while others date to the first half of the nineteenth century, when steamboats navigated the river. Modern highways follow the river closely on each side and are designated as "Los Caminos del Río Border Heritage Project." This project includes funds (so far insufficient) to restore and maintain historic buildings in these towns that predate the U.S. Revolutionary War.

Forty-five minutes south of Laredo–Nuevo Laredo are the little towns of San Ygnacio, Texas, and San Ignacio, Tamaulipas, settled in 1830 as a ranching outpost for Viejo Guerrero. San Ygnacio is the site of a customs house, built for the steamboat trade that began in the late 1840s, while the original town of Guerrero (called Revilla back in 1750 and now called Guerrero Viejo) was founded in 1750 as a ranching settlement. In 1953, the residents of Guerrero, Tamaulipas, and Zapata, Texas, were relocated downstream to accommodate the reservoir created by Falcon Dam. Like the Amistad Reservoir located upstream, Falcon Lake was built to provide irrigation water and prevent flooding, and it now also serves as a binational recreation area with a border crossing on the dam. The town of Zapata was not named for the Mexican revolutionary war hero Emiliano Zapata but rather for Colonel José Antonio Zapata, who lost his life in 1839 while fighting to establish the Republic of the Rio Grande.

South of Falcon Lake, and near a ford across the Rio Grande, lies the town of Mier, founded in 1753. Mier is a pleasant town of 6,788 inhabitants, narrow cobblestone streets, eighteenth- and nineteenth-century architecture, and a church, Nuestra Señora de la Purísima Concepción de Mier, built in 1798 on its central plaza. Mier's population has not changed much in recent years as all of the local population growth has gone to

Nuestra Señora de la Purísima Concepción de Mier.

Ciudad Miguel Alemán, fifteen miles to the south. "People here still know each other" is how one resident put it. The municipio of Miguel Alemán broke off from Mier in the 1950s and is connected to its U.S. twin city, Roma, Texas, by a suspension bridge across the Rio Grande that was built in 1927. The suspension bridge is the only one on the Rio Grande and is a National Historical Landmark in both countries. A newer bridge crosses the river upstream, but there are plans to restore the old bridge as a pedestrian walkway and tourist attraction.

Roma was settled in 1770 and became a thriving river port during the nineteenth century, when it was the most northerly port on the Rio Grande for commercial shipping. Above Roma, the river shallows permit only small watercraft. Roma's historical setting and architecture have made it the site of a few movies, including ¡Viva Zapata!, and its riverside historical district is part of the Caminos del Río Heritage Restoration Project. The Manuel Guerra store is considered a prime example of the architecture of Heinrich Porscheller, a German architect who designed many buildings throughout the Lower Rio Grande Valley during the nineteenth century, including the church on the plaza in Mier. Although it is rich in history, this part of the border region encompasses Starr County, which holds the distinction of being the poorest county on the U.S. side of the border and one of the poorest anywhere in the United States.

The Lower Rio Grande Valley

Downriver from Roma, Rio Grande City, Texas, was originally established as the Spanish colony of Camestolendas in 1768 and later became a ranching outpost for Camargo, Tamaulipas. Across the river, Camargo was founded in 1749 by the Spaniard José de Escandón. It was part of the nineteenth-century shipping economy on the Rio Grande, while its current population of 17,000 largely makes a living from brick making, farming, and ranching. A local quarry was the source of the molded bricks used by the architect Portscheller and still supplies local brick makers. Below Carmago is the hand-pulled ferry crossing between Los Ebanos, Texas, and Gustavo Diaz Ordaz, Tamaulipas, another farming center.

Downstream, toward the Gulf of Mexico, the string of small historic towns gives way to a large metropolitan area covering both sides of the river. In Texas, more than half a million people populate the cities of McAllen and Pharr, which are full of freeways and strip malls and have an economic base that includes seasonal tourists escaping the cold winters of northern states. Citrus orchards flush with pink Texas grapefruit, oil, railroads, and highway transportation services for U.S.-Mexican trade make up the bulk of the economy. Since the passage of NAFTA, offices of multinational companies have opened and new bridges have been built to connect McAllen, Texas, and its counterpart city, Reynosa, Tamaulipas. Reynosa, founded in 1749, was destroyed by a flood in 1800, and residents moved to the current site, directly across from the town of Hidalgo, ten miles south of McAllen. Reynosa, with 420,000 inhabitants (2000 census), is a large industrial city, with many auto parts and electronics stores and maquiladora operations, along with a huge PEMEX (the Mexican oil company) facility.

Nearly identical in size to Reynosa is the city of Matamoros, Tamaulipas, forty-five miles downstream. Originally a cattle ranch, its location near the mouth of the Rio Grande on the Gulf of Mexico enabled it to quickly develop into a major trade center. Matamoros prospered during the U.S. Civil War by supplying Confederate troops and exporting their cotton through the port of Bagdad on the Gulf of Mexico, just twenty-three miles east of Matamoros. The port, however, did not last, owing to the onslaughts of hurricanes, bandits, and pirates, and is now a beach resort. Matamoros is an important maquiladora manufacturing area and a rail terminus, and it also supports a significant tourist industry. It is known

Los Ebanos, the only remaining ferry on the Rio Grande.

for its strong labor unions and was the first of the border cities to reduce the work week in the maquiladoras from forty-eight to forty hours.[8]

On the other side of the river, Brownsville, Texas, is historically and economically connected to Matamoros. Founded in 1846 as Fort Brown, with the purpose of defending the U.S. claim to the Rio Grande as its southern border, it played an important role at the start of the Mexican-American War. Several of the original buildings from the fort are now part of the University of Texas, Brownsville. It is a major railroad and seaport, exporting agricultural goods and reexporting goods from Mexico, particularly the goods from the maquiladora industry in Matamoros. It also has a significant shrimp fleet, and attracts a large number of winter Texans and bird watchers, advertising more than 470 species of birds in the area. Along its eastern edge on the Gulf of Mexico are the beaches of South Padre Island, which, along with Playa Bagdad on the Mexican side of the border, marks the eastern end of the border landscape.

WHERE WE GO FROM HERE

This brief tour of the border is intended to give a sense of the place names, physical geography, and history and to provide a context for what follows. In the next chapter we turn to the demography of the border, with a broad examination of population movements since 1950, followed in subsequent chapters by a closer look at economic policy of U.S. border states (Chapter 3); trade, the environment, and labor (Chapters 4–6); and income, quality of life, poverty, and human development (Chapters 7–9). We conclude with an analysis of current tensions, including migration and border policy.

CHAPTER 2

POPULATION GROWTH AND MIGRATION

Oscar's parents are from Aguascalientes, in central Mexico. They migrated to Los Angeles in the 1960s, and that is where Oscar and one of his sisters were born. After a few years of trying to get comfortable in a sprawling American city, the family decided to move back to Mexico, where they felt more at home and could raise their family in the traditions they knew best. They chose the bustling city of Tijuana, but this too was hard, as the lower salaries in Mexico meant that their standard of living suffered. After a couple of years it was back to the United States, this time to San Ysidro, a border neighborhood in the city of San Diego, just across the Tijuana River from the city of Tijuana. San Ysidro offered the best of both places, with its American wages and Mexican lifestyle, its nearness to friends and family in Mexico, and its American schools and other urban amenities.

Even though San Ysidro is one of the poorer neighborhoods of San Diego, Oscar and his family thrived in its bilingual, bicultural environment. When it was time for college, Oscar went to a local university and earned a bachelor's degree while working for a nonprofit organization that assists small and medium-sized enterprises in southern San Diego County. Many of Oscar's clients are Latino entrepreneurs, and his ability to move effortlessly on both sides of the border allows him to offer them a wide variety of services and contacts.

BORDER DEMOGRAPHICS

Families like Oscar's are not uncommon in the border region. Many borderlanders, or *fronterizos*, move back and forth between the United States and Mexico while they raise their children and earn a living. The frequency of their moves can make it hard for their children to attain an academic mastery of either language, and they grow up bilingual and bicultural but without the formal skills of either a well-educated Mexican or a well-educated U.S. resident. These kids are classified as "partial bilinguals," and they present their school systems with special challenges, but, as Oscar's case illustrates, many others are proficient and comfortable in both languages and cultures.

Population Trends

Oscar's family is not uncommon for another reason: when they settled for good, it was in the border region. From San Diego–Tijuana in the west to Brownsville-Matamoros in the east, population growth in the Mexico-U.S. border region has been explosive over the past fifty years. From 2.4 million people in 1950 to 12.2 million in 2000, growth has averaged 3.3 percent per year in the combined border municipios and counties. This has resulted in a population doubling approximately every twenty-two years and in a total population increase of slightly more than 400 percent in the second half of the twentieth century. This rate of growth was faster than either the U.S. or Mexican national rate of growth, and as a consequence, border county and municipio populations became a larger share of their respective national populations. In Mexico, the share of the national population residing in the thirty-eight northern border municipios rose from 3.3 to 6.0 percent between 1950 and 2000, while the twenty-five border counties in the United States more than doubled their share as their population rose from 1.0 percent to 2.2 percent of the total national population. Figure 2.1 shows the population in the border region in 1950 and 2000. Box 2.1 describes the sources of data we used to describe the border region.

With respect to population growth on each side of the border, we note first that the Mexican border region population grew from 868,158 persons in 1950 to 5,877,738 in 2000. This was a 577 percent increase over the period, or an average increase of 3.9 percent per year. During the same period, the population in the U.S. border counties increased from 1,517,274 in 1950 to 6,312,252 in 2000, representing a 316 percent increase and a growth rate of 2.9 percent per year (Figure 2.2). Despite the more rapid growth rate in the Mexican border region, there are still about half a million more people in the U.S. border region. Conventional wisdom holds that Mexican growth rates are higher than U.S. rates. Figure 2.2 confirms this point, but

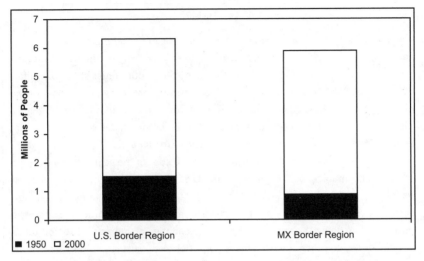

FIGURE 2.1. Border population in U.S. and Mexican border regions, 1950 and 2000.

it also shows that population growth in the U.S. border region has been the same as or higher than national rates in Mexico during most decades since 1950.

To get a picture of the dispersion of population along the border, Map 2.1 shows the populations of the U.S counties and Mexican municipios on the border for the year 2000. The concentration of border population, 44 percent of the total, in the California–Baja California border region stands out, as does the scarcity of population in the states that share the Sonoran and Chihuahuan deserts.

Population growth rates have varied widely along the border, from negative rates of growth in some rural counties and municipios, to zero growth in other locales, to moderate and rapid population growth in still other areas.[1] In general, rural counties and municipios have grown slower or even lost population, while urban areas, especially those with significant border crossings or important manufacturing development, have grown faster (Box 2.2). In recent years the trend has been for population growth to be concentrated in counties and municipios with three characteristics: a significant urban core or cores, manufacturing activity, and a border crossing. Between 1990 and 2000, perhaps influenced by the North American Free Trade Agreement (NAFTA), several municipios and counties experienced population growth of 50 percent or more.[2] The fastest growing of these was Ciudad Acuña, Coahuila, whose population nearly doubled, from 56,000 to 110,000 residents. On the other hand, the rural areas that lost population

BOX 2.1   DATA ON BORDER REGIONS

Throughout the book, we refer to the U.S. and Mexican border regions. For our purposes, the U.S. border region consists of the twenty-five border counties that touch the U.S. border with Mexico. These counties are in the four border states of California, Arizona, New Mexico, and Texas. The Mexican border region consists of the thirty-eight municipios (the Mexican equivalent of a county) that touch the border with the United States. They are in the six Mexican border states of Baja California, Sonora, Chihuahua, Coahuila, Nuevo Leon, and Tamaulipas.

Data for each border region as a whole are the sum of the values for each of the counties and municipios. For example, the U.S. border region population in 2000 was 6,312,252, which is the sum of the population in each of the twenty-five border counties in 2000. All percentage changes and ratios for border regions were calculated by adding the raw numbers for the counties or municipios to find totals for the border, and then the percentages or ratios were calculated. In the individual chapters data are presented in summary form, and usually only data for the border regions and national comparisons are provided. However, the online data appendices give detailed data for each county and municipio. The appendices are numbered to correlate with the chapter figures, which show aggregate representations of the more detailed data. The database is provided on the Web site http://latinamerican studies.sdsu.edu/BorderData.html, which has the detailed U.S. and Mexican population data for the trends graphed in Figure 2.1. Unless otherwise specified, the sources of the data cited in the book are the decennial population censuses conducted by the U.S. Census Bureau and the Instituto Nacional de Estadística, Geografía e Informática (INEGI) for the years 1950–2000.

We have attempted to collect comparable data for the two countries over time so that we can compare long-term trends in the two border regions and compare them to their national totals over a time span of fifty years. However, completely comparable data are not available for everything we wanted to study, in part because the level of economic development is very different in the United States and Mexico and has changed considerably over the fifty-year time period. For example after 1970 the U.S. Census Bureau stopped collecting data on literacy rates, considering it no longer to be an issue in the United States. Mexico collects very detailed data on the proportion of housing with piped-in water, types of sewage hookups, and so on, while the United States collects data only on the proportion of housing lacking complete plumbing. On the other hand, income and poverty data are much more complete on the U.S. side. We have tried to work with these differences to give the reader as clear a sense of comparison as is possible.

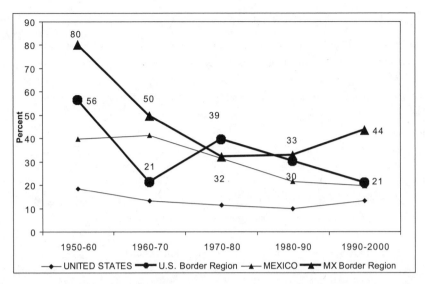

FIGURE 2.2. Percentage change per decade in national and border region population growth rates for the United States and Mexico.

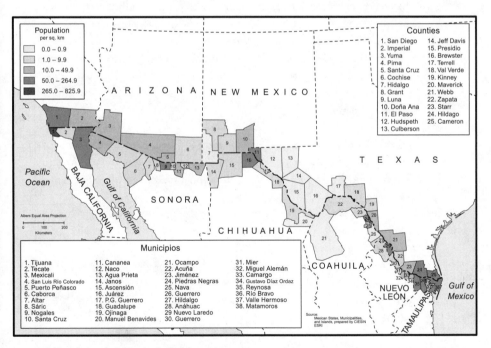

MAP 2.1. Population densities in the border regions.

BOX 2.2 CALCULATION OF GROWTH RATES

Annual rates of growth can be estimated in a variety of ways. The simplest way is to calculate the percentage change between each of the years of interest. This method only works, however, if there are observations for each year. For example, if El Paso's population is 682,000 in 2000 and 689,500 in 2001, then the rate of growth is equal to the percentage change between 2000 and 2001:

$$((\text{New value} - \text{Old value})/\text{Old value}) \times 100 = ((689{,}500 - 682{,}000)/682{,}000)$$
$$\times 100 = 1.1\%.$$

Mathematically, this is nearly equivalent to the difference in the natural logarithms of the two numbers, which is also often used to find rates of change:

$$\ln(\text{New value}) - \ln(\text{Old value}) = \ln(689{,}500) - \ln(682{,}000) = 1.1\%.$$

These methods do not work very well if we want to know an average rate over a longer period of time. For example, suppose that we only have data for 1990 and 2000. If we take the percentage differences using either of the methods above, we obtain the change over the whole period, which is different from the average yearly change between 1990 and 2000. It is possible to divide the percentage change by the number of years, but that only gives an approximation, since it does not take into account the compounding effect of growth. This problem is easily resolved, however, by using a formula that is the same one used to calculate compound interest.

$$\text{New value} = \text{Old value } (1 + g)^t,$$

where g is the rate of growth to be solved for and t is the number of years between the old and new values. For example, if El Paso's population was 595,350 in 1990 and 682,000 in 2000, then we can solve for its annual average growth rate by solving the following for g:

$$682{,}000 = 595{,}350\,(1 + g)^{10},$$
$$1.14554 = (1 + g)^{10},$$
$$\ln(1.14554) = 10 \times \ln(1 + g),$$
$$0.0135876 = \ln(1 + g),$$
$$\exp(0.0135876) = 1 + g,$$
$$g = 0.01368 = 1.368\%.$$

In words, the population growth rate was 1.368 percent per year, on average, between 1990 and 2000 in the El Paso metropolitan area.

or that had no population growth are in regions where there is no north-south border crossing infrastructure.

Population growth affects quality of life in both positive and negative ways. On the positive side, borderlanders who reflect on the changes in their communities frequently mention the advantages of paved streets that allow residents to travel beyond their homes (to work, school, and so forth) during big rainstorms. They also mention improved access to education, shopping, and entertainment. The residents of Piedras Negras, Coahuila, spoke about the changes over the last ten years as two new and large shopping centers were added to the existing one. With competition came lower prices, a greater variety of goods, and better quality. But not all the effects of population change are seen in a positive light. Some border residents feel nostalgic for a simpler, more intimate life. For example, a man from Matamoros, Tamaulipas, longed for the days from his childhood when he was able to hunt in the fields behind his house. Now the land has disappeared under paved streets and houses, and the hunting is gone. Others lament the increase in noise, traffic jams, and congestion, and complain that people in town no longer know each other. In Ciudad Acuña, a resident says, "In the old days when you went to the plaza for a fiesta you knew everyone. Now I only see a few people that I know." By way of contrast, in the Tamaulipas municipio of Mier, which recently celebrated its 250th anniversary, there has been very little population growth, and residents brag that the town still has the personal feel of a place where everyone knows each other.

Trends toward Urbanization

Population growth along the border has primarily occurred in the cities, with the result that both the U.S. and Mexican sides of the border are more urban than either nation as a whole (Figure 2.3). In 1950 the Mexican border was 65 percent urban, while Mexico as a whole was a little above 40 percent urban.[3] The U.S. border at mid-century was only slightly more urban than the nation as a whole (36 percent versus 32 percent), but from 1950 to 2000 the rate of urbanization exceeded the national rate, so that by 2000, 92 percent of the U.S. border population lived in urban areas, compared with 79 percent for the United States as a whole. The same pattern is observed in Mexico, where the Mexican border region reached 93 percent urban population by 2000, compared with 75 percent in Mexico as a whole.

Not only are urbanites the overwhelming majority of border residents, but they are highly concentrated in a few areas. For example, 2.8 million of

Urban and rural: downtown San Diego and a Texas ranch.

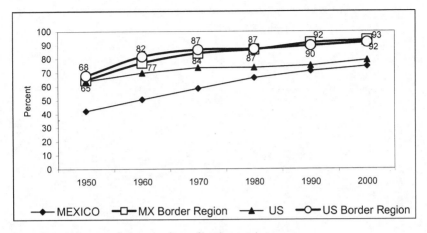

FIGURE 2.3. Urban population as a share of border population, 1950–2000.

the 6.3 million U.S. border residents (44 percent) live in San Diego County, while 2.4 million of the 5.9 million Mexican border residents (41 percent) live in Tijuana or Juárez. The border population is so urban and so concentrated in a few areas that in 2000, the six largest twin city agglomerations held nearly 60 percent of the total population.[4] On the other hand, a few counties and municipios did remain 100 percent rural (meaning no town with a population greater than 2,500 people) throughout the period. In the United States, five counties in Texas (Hudspeth, Culberson, Jeff Davis, Terrell, and Kinney), and in Mexico, five municipios spread across three states (Sáric and Santa Cruz in Sonora, Manuel Benavides in Chihuahua, and Guerrero and Hidalgo in Coahuila), remained rural.

Fertility Rates

Fertility rates in both the United States and Mexico decreased substantially between 1950 and 2000 as a result of economic, social, and educational improvements. Empirical studies consistently show that fertility rates decrease as family income rises, as the level of education rises, and as the proportion of the population living in urban settings rises.[5] Consequently, the rising urbanization rates in both nations and their border

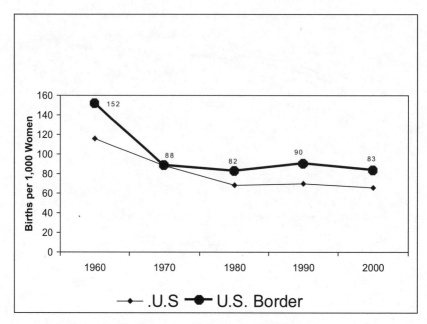

FIGURE 2.4. National and border region U.S. fertility rates: births per 1,000 women ages 15 to 44, 1960–2000.

regions may account for some of the decline in fertility rates. Even more important, increasing levels of income and educational attainment in both countries have contributed to the trend. In addition, an increase in types of and access to birth control options has played a role.

Census data on fertility for the United States and Mexico are not strictly comparable because they use different definitions of fertility. National and border region fertility rates in the United States are shown in Figure 2.4. These are the average number of births per 1,000 women aged fifteen to forty-four in the census year. Nationally, between 1960 and 2000, the number of births per 1,000 women of childbearing age fell from 116 to 66, with most of the drop occurring between 1960 and 1970. The introduction of the birth control pill occurred during that decade and gave women greater control over their reproduction decisions. After 1970, the fertility rate continued to decrease slowly at the national level, but it remained fairly flat in the border region. Between 1960 and 2000 the border region had consistently higher fertility rates, which still declined from 156 to 83 births per 1,000 women. Income and educational attainment levels in the United States are higher nationally than in the border region (see Chapter 7), which explains much of this difference.

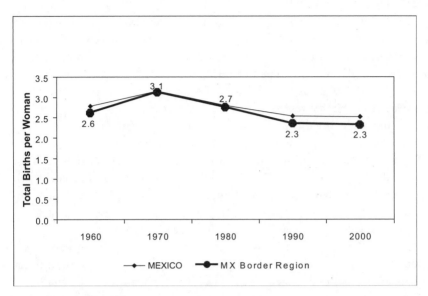

FIGURE 2.5. Total fertility rate in Mexico, 1960–2000.

The Mexican census reports a different, more comprehensive measure of fertility, total fertility rate. The total fertility rate is the average number of live births to all females aged twelve and older. When the total fertility rate equals 2.1, the population has a zero growth rate, excluding migration. As shown in Figure 2.5, the Mexican total fertility rate in 1960 was 2.8, while the rate in the Mexican border region was 2.6. The total fertility rate actually increased between 1960 and 1970, mainly due to improvements in prenatal care and a drop in infant mortality. Between 1970 and 2000, however, fertility declined substantially, decreasing by 22 percent nationally and by 29 percent in the border region. By 2000, rates had fallen to 2.5 nationally and 2.3 in the border region. Over most of the period from 1950 to 2000, Mexico's border region had a fertility rate that was lower than the national rate. This observation is consistent with the greater urbanization of the border, along with its higher income and education levels and the greater economic opportunities for women.

The Demographic Transition

Demographers use the term "demographic transition" when they discuss the long-term population changes that accompany economic growth and modernization. The term refers to the transition that takes place as countries move from high birth rates and high death rates to low birth rates and low death rates. Virtually all of the world's high-income industrial societies passed through this transition and have relatively stable populations. That is, their birth rates and death rates are low, so the overall rate of population growth (not counting migration effects) is slightly positive (birth rates greater than death rates) or slightly negative (death rates greater than birth rates).

Most of the middle- and low-income countries of the world are still in the transition period, however, with population growth rates that tend to be much higher than rates in the high-income countries. The reason for their higher rates of population growth is that death rates typically fall much sooner than birth rates as improved sanitation and modern medicine, including doctors and pharmaceuticals, become available at fairly modest levels of national income. Falling death rates do not immediately lead to falling birth rates, however, as birth rates are also sensitive to social and economic changes, including increases in education, rural to urban migration, and increases in economic opportunities, especially for women. As birth rates eventually begin to fall, the gap between the low death rate and the high birth rate narrows, and the overall rate of population growth comes down.

The demographic transition is important because it has a significant impact on migration, wages, and employment. For example, Mexico's overall rate of population growth peaked between 1960 and 1970, while the country was in the middle of a demographic transition and was experiencing high birth rates and low death rates. By 2000 the population growth rate was down to 2.0 percent a year, largely as a result of the decline in the average number of children per woman.[6] Figure 2.6 illustrates this pattern in a general way. When birth rates are evaluated against death rates in Mexico, the difference widens from thirty (46 − 16) per 100,000 population in 1950 to thirty-four in 1960. For the next data point, 1970, the difference falls to thirty-two. Thereafter there is a consistent decline, representing Mexico's passage through its demographic transition.

Youth Dependency Ratios

The dependency ratio is closely related to fertility and population growth and is a key demographic indicator, since it measures the proportion of the population either too young or too old to be in the labor force. Dependency ratios can be constructed in several ways, each of which gives an approximation of the share of the population unable to contribute to market production. A common way to construct the dependency ratio is to calculate

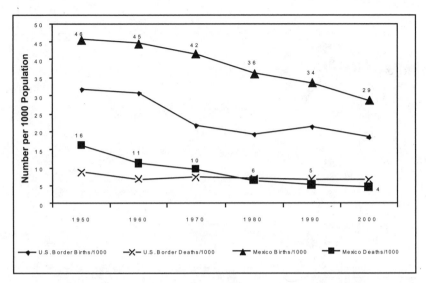

FIGURE 2.6. The demographic transition for Mexico nationally and the U.S. border region, shown as number of births per 1,000 population graphed against number of deaths. Note consistent decline after 1970.

the numerator as the population less than fifteen years old plus those older than sixty-five, and the denominator as either the whole population or the working-age population (16–65). While the definition of too young or too old to work varies across countries and cultures, it is still accurate to say that regions or countries with higher dependency ratios have fewer workers available to produce goods and services and consequently will have lower living standards than a region or country that is the same in every other way but has a lower dependency ratio.

The youth dependency ratio is similar to an overall dependency ratio except that the numerator includes only people too young to work (usually aged fifteen or younger). The youth dependency ratio given in Figure 2.7 is the ratio of the population under fifteen to the population aged fifteen and older. The youth dependency ratio is strongly affected by fertility rates and infant mortality rates, since a fall in infant mortality rates increases the youth dependency ratio, while a fall in fertility rates decreases the youth dependency ratio, all else equal. Both infant mortality rates and fertility rates fell in the United States and Mexico between 1950 and 2000, but fertility rate decreases had the largest effect, and youth dependency ratios fell in both countries, especially in Mexico. In 1950, the

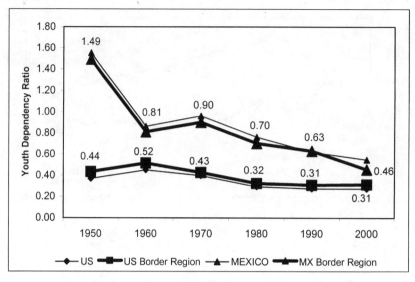

FIGURE 2.7. Youth dependency ratios in Mexico and the United States, 1950–2000.

Mexican youth dependency ratio was 1.55 (55 percent more population younger than fifteen than older than fifteen), while it was 0.37 in the United States (Figure 2.7). By 2000 the youth dependency ratio in Mexico had decreased to 0.55, while in the United States it had declined to 0.27. The decrease in the youth dependency ratio in Mexico was dramatic, while in the United States the youth dependency ratio increased between 1950 and 1960 as a result of the postwar baby boom and declined slowly thereafter.

Trends in the youth dependency ratios in the border region have closely followed the national trends, although the U.S. and Mexican sides have different relationships to their national levels. In Mexico, the border region's youth dependency ratio is lower than in the nation as a whole, while in the U.S. border region it is higher. Texas and New Mexico have the border counties with the highest ratio in the U.S. border region, and in the Texas border region the ratio of 0.39 is not much different from the border municipios of Baja California and Chihuahua (0.44).

The decline in youth dependency ratios in Mexico and its border regions is an important positive long-run trend. On the one hand, it means that a larger share of the population is able to work, so that even if there were no increases in worker productivity, average incomes would rise. In addition, the decline in youth dependency ratios means that there is a slowdown in the increase in the size of the labor force. Consequently, the pressure to create large numbers of new jobs for new entrants into the labor force should moderate, and with it some of the downward pressure on wages.

Net Migration

Population growth is due to both natural increase—the difference between births and deaths—and to net migration, which is the difference between in-migration and out-migration.[7] Migrants like Oscar's family came to the border from the interior of Mexico hoping for higher wages and a better life, and there are literally millions of similar stories in the border region. A shoeshine man tells of arriving in Matamoros from Torreón more than twenty years ago. He planned to cross into the United States, but he never found a good way to cross, so he continues to shine shoes in Matamoros. Another man tells of no work at home in San Luís Potosí, forcing him to the border, where he became a successful merchant, owning three retail stores. He describes how much he misses San Luís and how beautiful it is compared to Nuevo Laredo.

Unlike these two men and Oscar's parents, Juan grew up on the border, in Miguel Alemán, Tamaulipas, across the river from Roma, Texas. This is an old, historic area, settled by Europeans in the mid-1700s. Miguel Alemán and Roma are connected by a bridge and are at the end of the navigable portion of the Rio Grande. Juan remembers that it was no big deal to cross the bridge and walk into the United States when he was a child. Everyone in Miguel Alemán had a tourist card, and he used to walk across the bridge after school to buy an ice cream. He later married a woman from Roma whom he met at his cousin's graduation party. The cousin had attended school on the U.S. side of the border. Eventually Juan married and moved to the U.S. side. This is another fairly common pattern, like Oscar's family's move from Tijuana to San Ysidro (San Diego). One Mexican migrant from Nogales, Sonora, to Nogales, Arizona, stated that after thirty years, "everyone in Nogales, Sonora, moves to Nogales, Arizona," and new migrants from the Mexican interior take their place in Nogales, Sonora.

Anthropologist Tamar Wilson surveyed an unskilled, working-class neighborhood in Mexicali on residents' reasons for moving to Mexicali.[8] Forty-three percent did so because there were more jobs in Mexicali (high unemployment rate or crop failures in their place of origin) or the jobs paid better. Another 39 percent came in order to work across the border. Seventeen percent were pushed out of their previous homes by poverty, and the remaining 1 percent, one man, was in Mexicali because he had been deported there from the United States and decided to stay.

Anglos, too, have been attracted to the border, migrating from the Snow Belt to the Sun Belt for a better quality of life and better jobs. An El Paso man named Dick is one such example. Dick was born and raised in New England, but in the 1940s, during World War II, he was stationed at the base outside El Paso. He loved the area, which he saw as the last frontier of the Old West. After the war he returned to New England, married, and had a successful career, but when it came time to retire, he and his wife moved from New England to El Paso. They bought a lovely home in a gated community that has many other retired couples and made El Paso a permanent home. Other retirees, the so-called snowbirds, come to the border just for the winter, usually arriving soon after Christmas and returning to their homes in the north in the spring, living in mobile homes or condominiums while at the border. In Texas, these part-time residents are often referred to by the more welcoming term of "winter Texans."

Box 2.3 details the method we used to calculate net migration. Trends in population growth, natural increase, and net migration for the United States and Mexico and their border regions are shown in Figures 2.8, 2.9, and 2.10. The growth rate due to natural increase has declined in both countries and in their border regions. The population growth rate due to migration is another matter, however. On the U.S. side, net migration into the border regions has accounted for a very large share of the overall border population growth rate, particularly in California and Arizona. After 1980, migration to the Texas and New Mexico borders takes on a similar importance. In Mexico the picture is less clear, since the Mexican censuses did not measure birth and death rates at the municipio level until 1990, so there are no figures for border municipios before that. In 1990, migration was less a factor in population growth of the border region than natural increase. By 2000, however, migration had taken over as the main driver of population change, particularly in Baja California, Chihuahua, and Coahuila.

Net migration tells the percentage of population growth resulting from the movement of people, but it does not break that movement into foreign versus domestic movement (except for national level data, where migration is from foreign places by definition). In the border regions, however, it is also useful to consider the percentage of population that is foreign born and the percentage that comes from another state within the country. Trends in the proportion of the population born in other states of Mexico and the United States are shown in Figure 2.11, and trends in the

---

BOX 2.3   CALCULATING NET MIGRATION

Population change can be broken into two major components: natural increase and net migration. Natural increase is the difference between births and deaths. If the number of births is larger than the number of deaths, the resulting difference adds to population; conversely, if the number of deaths is larger than the number of births, the population decreases. This part of population change is called natural increase or decrease. Net migration is the difference between the number of persons moving into an area and the number moving out, regardless of whether the people are coming from (or going to) other parts of the same country or a foreign country. A positive net migration means that more new people have come into the area from other places than have left the area going to other places. A negative net migration means that more people have left than have come in. Since it is harder to numerically count movements of people (especially within a country) than it is to count births and deaths (both of which are customarily registered), net migration is often calculated as a residual, what is left over after the natural increase (or decrease) in population has been accounted for. In other words, net migration is the population change minus the natural increase:

Net migration = Total population change − (Births − Deaths).

For example, the total population change for San Diego County between 1990 and 2000 was 333,700 people. There were 466,870 births and 184,343 deaths. Therefore, natural increase accounted for 282,527 of the additional people. The other 48,173 additional people came from a positive net migration. In percentage terms, the total population change was 13.2 percent, of which 11.3 percent was due to natural increase and 1.9 percent was due to net migration.

---

proportion that is foreign born are shown in Figure 2.12. In both countries the proportion of the border population that was born in a state other than the current state of residence and the proportion born outside the country are higher than the national averages. In the U.S. border region, the proportion born in other states fell from almost 20 percent above the national level in 1960 to just about equal to it in 2000, although the region has far more international migrants than the nation as a whole. In light of the history of the U.S. border and its bicultural, bilingual reality, it should not be surprising that many of the international migrants come from Mexico. In the Mexican border region, the percentage born in another state is much higher than the national average and is rising. The

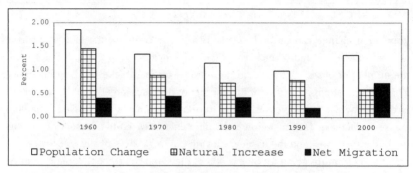

FIGURE 2.8. Percent natural population increase and net migration in the United States, 1960–2000.

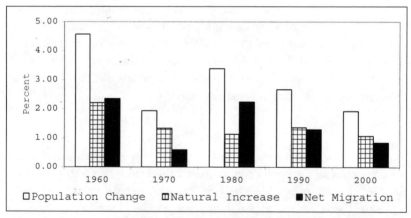

FIGURE 2.9. Percent natural population increase and net migration in the U.S. border region, 1960–2000.

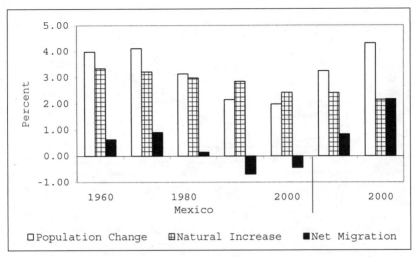

FIGURE 2.10. Percent natural population increase and net migration in Mexico and the Mexican border region, 1960–2000.

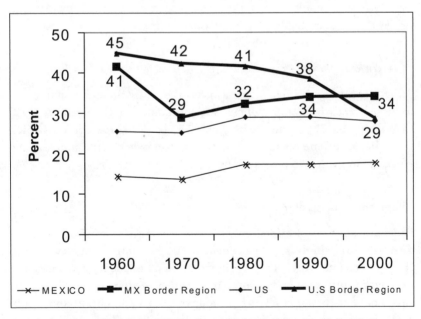

FIGURE 2.11. Share of population born in other states, in Mexico and the United States nationally and their border regions.

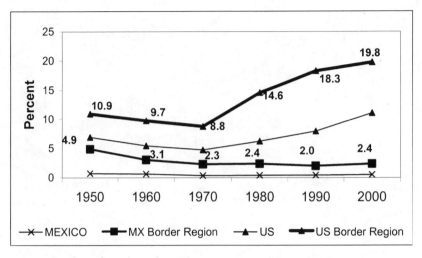

FIGURE 2.12. Share of population foreign born, in Mexico and the United States nationally and their border regions.

percentage foreign born is also higher than it is for the nation as a whole, but it is less than 5 percent of the population, compared to 20 percent of the population foreign born on the U.S. side. In the United States, and especially in its border region, the trend is positive, while in the Mexican border the trend is stagnant or slightly decreasing.

MIGRATION AND THE BORDER

Strictly speaking, Mexican migration to the United States is not a border issue since migration policies are formulated at the national level, in Washington, D.C., and Mexico, D.F. The border is the point at which the policies become operational, however, even when immigrants to the United States travel to places far away from the border.

Economic Analysis of Migration

Economic analyses of migration usually consider three broad areas or factors. Not surprisingly, supply and demand are two of the factors, while the third is social networks. In the context of migration, demand refers to the demand for migrants and is sometimes called "demand-pull." In reality, this is not one thing but refers to a group of factors that pull migrants into a migrant-receiving area. Demand-pull factors include wage levels and employment opportunities, as well as noneconomic factors such as better health and educational opportunities for their children. Migration supply refers to the supply of migrants and is sometimes called "supply-push." In a symmetrical way to demand-pull, the supply-push factors refer to any economic or noneconomic force that causes people to leave their homes. Low wages and a lack of economic opportunity are one set of factors, but revolutions, political oppression, and natural disasters, especially drought and crop failures, all play a role.

In addition to these two groups of factors there are network effects that stem from the presence of a group of migrants who send information back to their communities and families. In most cases, when migrants leave their homes, they do not move at random to another region or country. It is hard to get started in a new life, and migrants typically rely on family or community members who have gone before them to help them get started. Migrants already in the new region or country can provide a temporary place to live, information about jobs and job contacts, and other useful information about the culture and society of their adopted home.

These three effects—demand-pull, supply-push, and networks—do not distinguish between authorized and unauthorized migration. In economic terms the mechanisms are the same, although the costs of migration are usually higher for unauthorized migrants, which implies that the supply-push and demand-pull factors must be correspondingly stronger. Similarly, the three effects do not distinguish between domestic (within-country) migration and international (across national borders) migration. Again, the cost of international migration is generally higher, but from an economic perspective that does not alter the relevance of the three effects.

Supply-push and demand-pull factors are particularly sensitive to economic conditions. In the case of U.S.-Mexico migration, economic conditions have been fundamental to the observed pattern. Over the last ten to fifteen years, the average manufacturing wage in the United States was seven to ten times greater than the average manufacturing wage in Mexico.[9] In the United States, when the minimum wage was $5.15 per hour, it averaged 41.5 pesos per day in Mexico, or about $0.50 per hour for an eight-hour day, using market exchange rates to convert from pesos to dollars.[10] The wage differences allow a Mexican worker to take his or her skills and education to the United States and earn seven to ten times more income than those same skills and education can generate in Mexico. This differential serves as a very strong demand-pull force.

Much of the discourse on immigration in the United States assumes that Mexicans migrate in large numbers because they lack jobs. In fact, most migrants have jobs that they leave behind when they migrate, implying that the problem is more complex than a simple failure to create jobs. In particular, it is the quality of jobs—salaries and other components—

that are at issue. As long as wage differences remain large, Mexican migration to the United States will be a fact of life. Ironically, Mexican economic development might be the strongest supply-push factor at work in the generation of emigrants. Economic development fosters large-scale, across-the-board changes, which in turn create high levels of uncertainty. When there is no unemployment insurance, disability insurance, or other elements of a social safety net, families can reduce their economic uncertainty and risks by sending a family member or two to the United States, where they can earn an income that may eventually prove crucial to the family's well-being. In this respect, migration is a form of insurance that helps guard against unforeseen harmful events.

Although Mexican economic development and U.S.-Mexican wage differentials may be the primary causes of out-migration from Mexico, labor market rigidities are also a supply-push factor. This observation gains support from the World Bank Doing Business Index, which ranks 155 countries.[11] In 2005, the United States was ranked the third easiest country to do business in, while Mexico ranked seventy-third, slightly above the median, just below Italy and ahead of Argentina and China. However, in the sub-index that measures the costs of hiring and firing workers, Mexico ranked 125 out of 155. These rigidities may contribute to limiting the size of the formal labor sector, but it is unlikely that eliminating them would have much effect on migration as long as the wage differential remains and as long as uncertainties and structural changes are generated by Mexican development. In the border region, the lack of jobs is clearly not an issue, since many border manufacturing plants have posted permanent help-wanted signs since the early 1990s, with the exception of the slowdown that occurred in 2001–2003.

Unauthorized International Migration

National policies are important to the border because the vast majority of the resources devoted to the enforcement of migration laws are located on or near the border. Consequently, initiatives in the 1990s by the United States to control the border created changes throughout the border region. For example, Operation Hold the Line in the El Paso Border Patrol Sector (1993), Operation Gatekeeper in San Diego (1994), Operation Rio Grande in the Brownsville area of Texas (1997), Operation Safeguard in Arizona (1999), and numerous post-September 11, 2001, border enforcement actions all resulted in significant increases in the number of Border Patrol agents and in efforts to deter unauthorized immigration.[12] Invariably, the side effects of these efforts make life a little more complex and sometimes a lot

Migrants waiting to cross at Ciudad Acuña.

more difficult for the residents of the border regions of the United States and Mexico.

Operations Hold the Line and Gatekeeper are concentrated in the two largest metropolitan areas on the border, El Paso–Juárez and San Diego–Tijuana. The intention of these and other border operations is to reduce the flow of unauthorized migrants entering the United States by increasing the costs of unauthorized migration through tougher enforcement of border crossing restrictions. The length of the border and its extreme remoteness in places make it impossible to intensively patrol every part, so resources are concentrated in the metropolitan areas where undocumented migrants prefer to cross. Migrants' preference to cross in metropolitan areas is economically sensible: the physical challenges are less, and the availability of transportation and jobs reduces the costs of migration.

Ordinarily, an increase in costs reduces the demand. That is, if it is more expensive in terms of time, money, and effort, fewer people will choose to migrate, which is the intention of U.S. policy. In effect, however, there is no evidence of a reduction in the flow of undocumented migrants entering the United States from Mexico. In fact, Massey, Durand, and Malone, using data from the Mexican Migration Project, have shown that the probability of a Mexican migrating to the United States has not fallen, but the probability of that individual returning to Mexico has decreased, owing to the increased costs and risks of crossing the border.[13] It is no longer cost-effective to work in the United States and return to a family in Mexico with the expectation of easily returning again to work.

The push factors of low wages and a large pool of underemployed workers in Mexico continue despite the manufacturing boom in the Mexican border. These push factors are combined with the substantial pull factor of plentiful jobs at wages seven to ten times higher in the United States, making migration an attractive proposition for many Mexican citizens. Given that high walls and tough border enforcement cover only a small percentage of the almost 2,000-mile-long border, the impact of increased border enforcement is to detour would-be migrants into the deserts and mountains, where their chances of being stopped are less but the physical threats to their safety are greater. In fiscal 2005, more than 450 migrant deaths were reported along the border, mostly a result of the brutally hot summer of the Sonoran and Chihuahuan deserts, but also from exposure to extreme cold and snow during the winter.[14] A major effect of this heightened border security has been to shift Mexican migration from migration for purposes of work in the United States to permanent migration.

As the border has become increasingly militarized, antimigrant sentiment in the United States has continued to grow. After the September 11, 2001, attacks, security at the U.S.-Mexican border was increased even more, and political tensions increased to new heights. The issue of undocumented workers crossing the border became even more politicized and partisan. Private U.S. citizens started vigilante-style border patrols such as the "Minutemen" patrols, and the border has become an even more dangerous place for both residents and migrants. At the same time, other volunteer citizen groups began providing water and food caches at stations located along migration corridors in the deserts.

Binational Mobility

Although there is no evidence that the various Border Patrol operations or the post-September 11 enforcement efforts have resulted in a decline in the number of undocumented migrants entering the United States from Mexico, there is evidence that these initiatives have made life more difficult for border residents. For example, the towns of Jacumba, California, and Jacume, Baja California, are located to the east of San Diego and Tijuana, on a pine- and brush-covered mountain plateau that separates the coastal region from the Sonoran Desert. These small communities are interconnected through a web of family, social, and commercial ties. Although there is no officially designated border crossing, it was always easy for residents to walk or drive to the other side of the border to visit family members and friends and to shop at the small grocery store in Jacumba. As Operation Gatekeeper in the San Diego area pushed would-be migrants further east, the residents of Jacumba and Jacume saw an increase in border crossings by strangers, followed by an increase in Border Patrol activity. In response to the spillover of migrants from the San Diego urban area, the Border Patrol closed parts of the border with a metal fence. This did not completely seal the border, however, as the floodplain between the two towns was left unfenced, partly because of the cost of erecting a permanent barrier in an area subject to periodic flooding. Both U.S. and Mexican laws prohibit people from crossing the border at unofficial sites, but the residents of Jacumba and Jacume agreed that Border Patrol agents usually looked the other way when the local townspeople walked to the other side.

After September 11, 2001, U.S. federal policies hardened, and no one was allowed to cross, even though Border Patrol agents personally knew many of the locals. To get to the other side, residents now must drive an hour west to the nearest official crossing in Tecate, wait in line, then drive east. Some of the residents of Jacume, Mexico, are U.S. citizens with jobs in and around Jacumba who choose to live in Jacume for a variety of reasons, including living costs and ties to their extended families. The commute to work is no longer a few minutes but has become hours in each direction. Use of the public phone in Jacumba to call relatives in the United States is no longer practical while international calls from Mexico remain expensive, even though the distance called may be only a few hundred yards or a few miles. The store in Jacumba lost about 40 percent of its customers, and families and friends are no longer able to visit and socialize as they used to do regularly.

This story is repeated at multiple points along the border. At a ford in the Rio Grande at Redford in Presidio County, for example, two brothers have farms, one on each side of the river. All their lives they have crossed back and forth to help each other with the farming. Now it is a thirty-mile trip to cross the river at the Presidio-Ojinaga crossing. Another example is the town of Boquillas across from Big Bend National Park, which used to depend on visits from tourists at the National Park. There are many similar tales, as border citizens have suddenly discovered that their lives are more complicated and restrictive and their economic, social, and family ties are more difficult to maintain.

Former informal crossing to Boquillas in Big Bend National Park.

The Reality of Binational Citizenship

There are two realities when it comes to migration. There is the local border reality, but there is also an international Mexico-U.S. reality. These two realities share some similarities, but in general, the internal imperatives are very different. Most people, regardless of where they live, recognize the need for security. Whether the insecurity comes from "coyotes" (people smugglers), who abandon hapless migrants in the desert, from drug and gun smugglers, who wreak havoc on peaceful communities, or from international terrorists, citizens in both the United States and Mexico share a desire to live in communities that are free from the threat of violence or terror brought on by illegal cross-border trafficking.

At the same time, many areas along the border are places where residents are bilingual and bicultural, where cross-border family life and social networks are the norm and local commerce serves both sides of the border on a daily basis. The manner in which border control policies are enforced and intensified often strikes border residents as devoid of common sense. Border Patrol agents who ignored local residents walking or driving to the other side before September 11, 2001, suddenly began acting as if the residents of Jacume or Boquillas were international terrorists. The local border reality is binational, and this characteristic does not fit well with the international reality of antiterrorism or with federal policies that originate in centers of power thousands of miles away.

The United States asserts its right to control its border, but it mostly looks the other way once migrants make it into the country. Private business interests in the United States want access to unskilled and semi-skilled Mexican labor, and they maintain pressure on the federal government to ensure that undocumented migrants working in the United States are infrequently deported. The result is a U.S. policy based on an ineffective but disruptive show of force at the border and very lax enforcement at work sites inside the country. For its part, Mexico depends on the tens of billions of dollars earned by its citizens and remitted back to Mexico. It also enjoys an escape valve of migration north as a solution to its failure to create a sufficient number of high-quality jobs within Mexico.[15] Hence, Mexico has no incentive to try to stem the flow of migrants.

The United States and Mexico are at an impasse over the issue of migration, and not surprisingly, there is probably no easy way to finally resolve it in a manner that satisfies everyone. Perhaps the best that can be hoped for is that both sides will at least look for a way to lower the level of tension and seek to amicably manage migration. In particular, three goals seem reachable. The first goal should be to reduce the number of deaths. Death rates of approximately one person per day are a cruel and avoidable reality. The second goal should be to manage the problem of labor flows in such a way that it does not constantly threaten to blow up into a major political problem, either inside the countries or between them. Demagogues in both countries try to gain strategic political advantage from this issue, with the result that U.S.-Mexico relations are made much more difficult than is necessary and local border communities have a much harder time achieving goals that require cross-border collaboration. The third goal should be to recognize the border as a bicultural world whose social, commercial, and spiritual well-being requires an easier cross-border flow of local residents.

It is easy for the United States to point a finger at Mexico for its failure to achieve sufficient economic development to close the economic gap that is driving migration. But large out-migrations are a common feature of economic development, and if the United States were serious in its desire to slow migration, it could follow the example of the European Union, which contributes economic development aid to its poorer members in order to bring those countries' economies to a level equal to the rest of the members. Well-focused aid for economic infrastructure, including education and border-crossing infrastructure, would both slow the rate of Mexican migration and increase markets for U.S. businesses. For its part, Mexico could work toward reducing rigidities in the labor market and enable wages to increase as labor productivity increases.[16] Until Mexico and the United States have a set of policies that work to close the wage and development gaps, migrants will continue to be pulled to the United States. No matter how many fences are erected, or how many Border Patrol agents are stationed at the frontier, or how much it disrupts the lives of border residents, migrants from Mexico will find ways to enter. The minimum goal for both countries should be to manage this reality, so that people do not die trying to cross and the issue of migration does not damage the lives of borderlanders or U.S.-Mexico relations.

■ ■

CHAPTER 3

U.S. BORDER STATES AND BORDER RELATIONS

The North American Free Trade Agreement (NAFTA) was signed and rati-
fied in 1993 and implemented on January 1, 1994. Along the border there
was a flurry of activity as state and local chambers of commerce, business groups, and public officials began to prepare for a more open Mexican
economy. On the U.S. side, fears of competition from relatively low-wage
Mexican workers were offset by the anticipation of export and outsourcing
opportunities, particularly in Texas and California, the two most populous
states and the two with the largest quantity of exports going to Mexico.

Commerce aside, however, not all was well in the border states. At the
start of 1994, Californians were still worried about the effects of a national
recession that lingered in the state several years after the recession had
ended in the rest of the country. The lengthy recession caused large state budget deficits, which in turn prompted an angry public debate over the relationship of the deficits to the cost of providing schools, health care, and other
social services to immigrants. Ultimately, an opportunistic Governor Pete
Wilson was able to split the electorate and ride a wave of anti-immigration
feeling to reelection in a vote that was widely viewed as anti-Mexico.

In the same year, Texas governor-elect George Bush gave a number of
speeches tying the state's economic future to Mexico and explicitly reject-
ing California's immigrant bashing.[1] Throughout the state, Texans signed
up for classes "sponsored by community colleges, chambers of commerce
and government agencies, to help . . . turn themselves into Mexicans."[2]
Media exaggeration, perhaps, but along the border, local symbols and politics exhibited a similar pattern. In the Gulf Coast city of Brownsville, legal arguments were made on behalf of the city to appropriate the official

designation of "NAFTA Home Port," while the Pacific Coast city of San Diego rejected the idea of a binational, joint-use border airport with its neighbor, Tijuana.[3]

WHAT LIES BENEATH THE DIFFERENCES?

California and Texas are the two most populous states in the United States. Both share a border with Mexico, and both have significant Mexican American minorities. Both were Spanish colonies and part of Mexico's empire after its independence, and their place names, colonial architecture, cuisine, and literature all reflect Latino, specifically Mexican, influence. The question naturally arises as to how one state could be perceived as anti-Mexico while the other tied its future to collaboration with Mexico. To some extent, these perceptions are media creations, but beneath the marketing and public relations efforts are some fundamental demographic and economic realities that shape state policy and, as a consequence, have significant implications for border communities and their citizens. Border populations and state-level economic incentives are critical to understanding differences in the political responses of communities to cross-border relations, since these two variables interact in ways that create both doors and walls between U.S. border communities and their counterparts in Mexico.

State Policies

Differences in state policies toward Mexico are paralleled by differences in border community relations. For example, Rodriguez and Hagan focus on Laredo–Nuevo Laredo and El Paso–Ciudad Juárez, where an extensive network of cross-border relations exists.[4] Among the examples cited are joint urban planning (such as Urban Plan of Los Dos Laredos), joint environmental planning, guides to the cities' histories, shared construction of international bridges, joint training of nurses and public safety officials, and many other initiatives. In addition, Texas state policy offers in-state tuition to Mexican citizens attending state universities located on the border, and in El Paso, Laredo, and Brownsville, this is a powerful draw for students from Mexico.

California, by way of contrast, has essentially two border communities, San Diego and Imperial counties. San Diego County, which comprises the city of San Diego and seventeen additional city jurisdictions, is the largest metropolitan area in the border region and, judging from the origins of its population, the most cosmopolitan of border counties. Imperial County is a mixture of suburbs and agricultural fields and is overshadowed from across the border by the much larger urban area of Mexicali, Baja California.[5] Cross-border relations are very different in the two California communities, and although San Diego offers numerous examples of collaboration in higher education, civic organizations, and local public administration (such as public safety, health care, and fire protection services), cross-border community relations in general are much less developed. One recent study offers a pessimistic view in which cross-border problems remain unaddressed until they become unavoidable, but also much more intractable and difficult to resolve.[6]

Between California on the western border and Texas in the east, Arizona and New Mexico fill intermediate roles. Their relatively smaller populations and the fact that their borders span the Sonoran and Chihuahuan deserts make them less visible in U.S.-Mexico relations. Nevertheless, Arizona's common border with the major agricultural export state of Sonora and its proximity to Sinaloa, a major producer of winter vegetable crops, have created significant incentives to cultivate closer ties with Mexico and to capture a larger share of the transportation and trade jobs generated by Mexico's exports of vegetables, beef, and other agricultural products. Even New Mexico, which has the least amount of cross-border trade, both in absolute terms and relative to its total trade, has invested in border crossing infrastructure to capture some of the congestion that is spilling out of the El Paso–Ciudad Juárez metroplex.

History and Ethnicity

One assumption we make is that the Latino origin populations in U.S. border cities and states are central to relations with Mexico. That is, a population that speaks Spanish and identifies itself with Mexican culture is critical to cross-border relations, even if the degree of identification is less than complete. Consequently, it is useful to look at the size of the Latino population and its settlement patterns.

In 1850, the 14,000 Mexican Americans in Texas, called Tejanos, made up only about 7 percent of the state's population.[7] Texas was a "failed frontier" in the eyes of Spain and Mexico, and both nations had trouble attracting settlers. There was no gold or silver, and no great Native American civilizations seemed to exist. By comparison, on the eve of the Gold Rush, California's population is estimated to have been about 15,000 people total, exclusive of Native Americans, with about half that total (7,000) considered

Californios (that is, Mexican citizens). According to Wright, "California displayed a culture predominantly Hispanic-American; the language was Spanish, the religion Roman Catholic."[8] The Gold Rush changed everything in California, and even though the first miners came from Sonora, a tidal wave of humanity swept over the gold fields and quickly changed the state into a cosmopolitan frontier with a predominantly Anglo culture. The gold fields quickly became inhospitable to foreigners, and although Spanish remained important to the daily life of many Californians (for example, the state constitution was drafted in both Spanish and English), the Californios were pushed aside, at first by the new immigrants and then by legal challenges to their landholdings.[9]

Texas Latinos, or Tejanos, were not overcome by a tidal wave of immigration as were Californios, but they were subject to the same ethnic and political pressures, including the denial of property rights that confronted Mexican Americans in the nineteenth and twentieth centuries. In other words, the idea that Anglo-Mexican relations are more harmonious in Texas than in California is relatively new. Martinez, for example, chronicles a long list of conflicts, and Larralde and Jacobo in their discussion of Juan Cortina and the Cortinista rebellion assert that "Texas law practically encouraged intimidation and dispossession of the Mexicans."[10]

Figure 3.1 shows the Latino origin population from 1970, when the Census Bureau began to measure it, to the recent census in 2000. As can be seen, differences between California and Texas in the size of their Latino populations were not very great, and by 1990 the difference had disappeared altogether. This fact argues against the idea that border relations in Texas are better because the state population of Latinos is larger, or that it has been significantly larger throughout history.

If the size of the state Latino population does not seem to carry a lot of explanatory power, its location may. Several scholars have noted the concentration of Tejanos along the Texas border region and have tried to classify the area as a distinct cultural region. For example, Arreola identifies at least seven cultural regionalizations of south Texas Latinos in the scholarly literature between 1948 and 1984.[11] Jordan's "Hispanic borderland" seems the most comprehensive description of a swath of counties on the southern border of Texas.[12] Quantitative analysis supports the idea of a relatively concentrated Latino population. As Figure 3.2 shows, the Texas border has long been heavily Latino, accounting for two-thirds of the state Latino population in 1970, with this share increasing to 72 percent in 2000.

Overall, the proportion of population in the U.S. border region that is Latino increased from 29 percent in 1970 to 48 percent, or almost half the population, in 2000. Three border counties, all in Texas, were more than

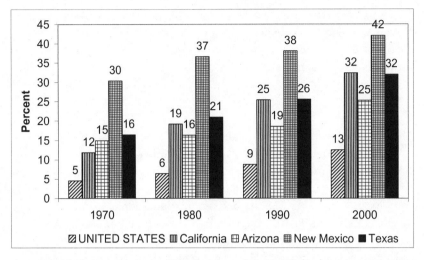

FIGURE 3.1. Hispanic population as share of total population in U.S. border states, 1970–2000.

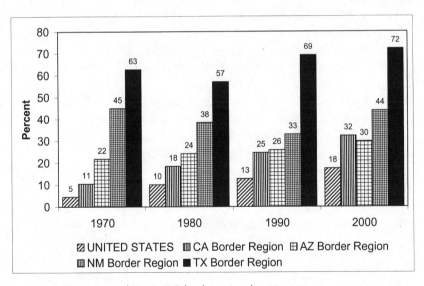

FIGURE 3.2. Hispanic population in U.S. border regions by state, 1970–2000.

90 percent Latino in 2000: Webb County (Laredo) was 94.3 percent Latino, Maverick County 95 percent, and Starr County 97.5 percent. Like Texas, Arizona shows a slow, steady increase in the proportion of the Latino population, while the proportion in New Mexico actually declined during the 1970s and 1980s, returning to its 1970 level by 2000. Back in 1970, the California border region was only 11 percent Latino, but that proportion tripled over the next thirty years. The 10 percent of Texas counties with the great-

est Latino population have a larger share of the total Latino population (81 percent) than the equivalent set of California counties (71 percent).[13] By 2000, the Arizona border region, with a 30 percent Latino population, had the lowest proportion.

Language

The high proportion of the Latino population also means a higher proportion of the population with a mother tongue other than English. The U.S. border region is an area with a much higher proportion of bilingual speakers than the nation as a whole, and this proportion has been increasing. By 2000, 45 percent of the U.S. border region population claimed a language other than English, mainly Spanish, to be their first language, and 20 percent spoke English "less than well," according to the census. Figures 3.3 and 3.4 show the increase in English as a second language and the proportion speaking English "less than well" in the border region of each border state. In the Texas border region in 2000, 72 percent did not have English as their first language and 33 percent spoke English "less than well," suggesting that 40 percent or more of the population is bilingual.

Spanish is the primary language of a majority of Texas border residents in all but two rural counties, Jeff Davis and Kinney. In Maverick, Webb, Cameron, Hidalgo, and Starr counties, which include the cities of Laredo, McAllen, and Brownsville, English is not the mother tongue for more than 80 percent of the population. Even New Mexico cannot rival the Texas border in its use of Spanish as the primary language. In contrast, in the California and Arizona border regions, the population speaking English as a second language increased to 32 percent and 30 percent, respectively, by 2000. In New Mexico this proportion actually declined from 53 percent in 1970 to 33 percent in 1990, then rose again to 44 percent in 2000. This very high incidence of bilingualism, which is rare in the rest of the United States, adds a cultural richness to the region. As one El Paso woman explained: "Speaking only one language is like being vanilla ice cream. Being bilingual is like being Cherry García, and who wouldn't prefer Cherry García?"[14]

Ethnic Concentration

In sum, there are no significant differences in the size of the Latino origin population in California and Texas, but there is both qualitative and quantitative evidence that the Latino population is more concentrated along the border in Texas than it is in California.[15] The importance of

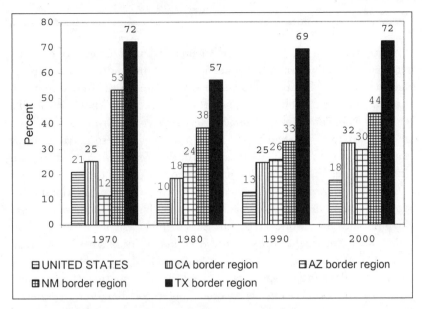

FIGURE 3.3. Share of population with English as a second language in U.S. border states, 1970–2000.

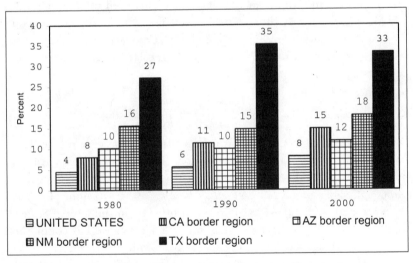

FIGURE 3.4. Share of population speaking English "less than well" in U.S. border states, 1980–2000.

shared ethnicity and language cannot be overestimated as an explanation for the perception of relatively deeper border integration among the communities that share the Rio Grande as a common divide between the two nations. In a practical and obvious way, ethnicity and language can facilitate communication, making cross-border cooperation easier between local public authorities, civic groups, and ordinary citizens. In addition, a shared language and culture offer a greater likelihood that cultural assumptions and historical points of references are shared across the border as well. For example, Canada's standing as the closest U.S. ally and trading partner is partly a result of its location, but also partly a result of its shared history and language. Similarly, observers of the European Union's progress have noted the advantage to integration that accrues after one or two generations of bureaucrats have worked in a multilateral environment where they have been able to develop language skills and social and professional networks across the EU's member states.

Mexican Americans fulfill a key function in local cross-border relations. Their cross-border networks of family, social, and professional ties facilitate understanding, cooperation, and the construction of public and private networks. Writing about cross-border collaboration in Laredo–Nuevo Laredo and El Paso–Ciudad Juárez, Rodriguez and Hagan comment that "it was clear that persons saw their inter-city solidarity to be a product of local relational styles and local problem-solving approaches, owing nothing to formal, federal, agreements between the United States and Mexico. Especially in Laredo–Nuevo Laredo, many respondents commented that the high level of transborder relations between their two cities was, for the most part, based on informal relations and interpersonal contacts."[16]

Political Representation

Ethnic identity affects politics in direct ways. In the case of the Texas border counties, the larger concentration of Latino population leads to more elected officials of the same ethnicity. According to the 2002 *National Directory of Latino Elected Officials,* Texas accounted for 1,965 (44.0 percent) of the 4,464 Latino elected officials in the United States.[17] The figure includes federal and state office holders as well as county and municipal officials, elected judicial and law enforcement officials, school board and other elected education officials, and special district officials, such as those for hospital or irrigation districts. Insofar as Texas has more than four times as many counties as California, the presence of more local governments implies that there are more opportunities to hold office. Nevertheless, the share of the total population that is Latino is nearly identical in Texas and California, yet the former has more than twice as many Latino elected officials—1,965, compared with 904 in California.

TABLE 3.1 *Latino Elected Officials in U.S. Border States, 2001*

	California	Arizona	New Mexico	Texas
Population				
State	34,501,130	5,307,331	1,829,146	21,325,018
Border	3,008,563	1,186,862	258,471	2,024,798
Latino elected officials				
State	871	304	589	1,923
Border	66	67	60	721
Population per Latino elected official				
State	39,611	17,458	3,106	11,089
Border	45,584	17,714	4,308	2,808

NOTE: Figures in table represent city, county, and special districts, including elected members of the judiciary, but not state and federal office holders.

SOURCES: NALEO (2002); U.S. Census Bureau (2001).

Table 3.1 shows that in the four U.S. border states, the variation in the number of Latino elected officials is much greater in the border region than at the state level, particularly if population weights are used. On a per capita basis, comparing the border region and state, the data range from 3,106 persons per Latino elected official (New Mexico) to 39,611 (California). In the border regions, however, the range is 2,808 (Texas) to 45,584 (California). In the case of Texas, approximately 38 percent of its Latino elected officials are in the border region, where less than 10 percent of the total population resides. By contrast, less than 8 percent of the Latino elected officials in California come from the border region, where just under 9 percent of the total population resides. Once again, the location of the Latino population is important in explaining patterns. The relatively higher concentration of Latinos in the Texas borderlands and their relatively greater diffusion throughout California determine that political representation by Latino elected officials is much greater in the Texas border regions than it is in either the rest of Texas or California.

These data support the hypothesis that border relations in Texas are likely to encounter fewer difficulties based on language, ethnicity, or a lack of understanding of cultural contexts of decisions and values. Local elected officials in the border region still must learn the institutional structure of the other side, and although speaking the same language does not guarantee this result, the cultural distances between local elected officials in the border region of Texas are much less than the distances that must be traversed by officials in San Diego or Tucson. For this reason alone, it should not be surprising to find greater cross-border collaboration at the eastern end of the border than at the western end.

ECONOMIC MATTERS

The economic relationship between Texas and Mexico is remarkably close, rather like the relationship between Michigan and Canada. For example, the share of state exports sent by Michigan to Canada and by Texas to Mexico is a nearly equivalent share of each state's gross state product.[18] Although official measures of state exports are not necessarily an accurate guide to the value of goods produced in the state and exported, the point remains that Texas plays a role in U.S. relations with Mexico that is similar to the role played by Michigan (and the auto industry) in relations with Canada. The margin by which Texas exports dominate exports from any other state in trade with Mexico is remarkable and cannot be due to measurement issues alone.[19] State leaders have not consistently realized the importance of trade with Mexico, and during boom periods, when oil prices or cotton production have been high, the proximity of a large developing country has not always seemed advantageous. The current path of deeper integration with the Mexican economy began after the oil price collapse of 1982 and the state recession of the mid-1980s, as U.S. national policies began to promote greater competitiveness and attention to world markets.[20] Before the early 1990s, it is difficult to find many references to trade with Mexico in the Texas business press; after the negotiations over NAFTA became serious, the opportunity presented by a large emerging market became too obvious to ignore.

Relative Income

To get a sense of economic crisis and boom at the state level, Figure 3.5 shows personal state income in Texas and California from 1970 to 2002, relative to average U.S. personal income. A value of 100 indicates that state income is equal to the national average. Figure 3.5 is divided into three periods, beginning with the oil boom of the 1970s and early 1980s. During the first period, per capita incomes in Texas were rising relative to the U.S. average, while in California there was no trend up or down. This was followed by the collapse of oil prices and the resulting economic adjustment, which coincided with the "Lost Decade" of development in Latin America. The collapse of the oil market, together with tough anti-inflation policies in the United States, sent ripples through the Texas economy, causing a

Sign in McAllen, Texas.

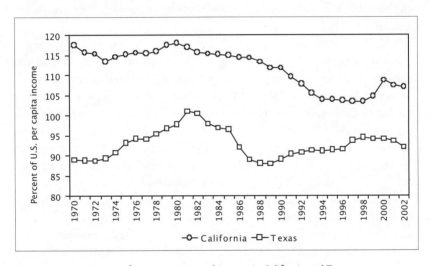

FIGURE 3.5. Comparison of per capita personal income in California and Texas, 1970–2002.

collapse in the real estate market, declines in the construction and financial sectors, and a major recession and restructuring. The recovery in Texas began shortly after the collapse of oil prices in 1981, but another collapse, this time in real estate markets in the mid-1980s, continued to push down relative state income. By 1989, when Mexican president Carlos Salinas de

Gortari announced he was opening negotiations with the United States to create a free trade agreement, state income had fallen to less than 90 percent of the U.S. national level. California was also affected by the national recession, but its average income level began a much more gentle decline toward the national average.

The third period began around 1990, when a long period of expansion started in Texas, despite a relatively mild national recession in 1991. For the state, this was a period of slow convergence toward the U.S. national average income, increasing trade with Mexico, and deepening cross-border ties that lasted until 1998. For California, the third period was seriously negative, as the mild national recession of 1991 turned into a steep decline at the state level. The end of the cold war precipitated a dramatic economic restructuring as defense firms consolidated and many high-wage jobs disappeared. In addition, a national financial crisis in the banking industry, along with inflated real estate prices at the state level, led to a painful adjustment, with negative effects on construction, real estate, and financial services. To add a final dose of pain, a multiyear drought in the Central Valley hurt agricultural production and employment. The state economy did not begin its recovery until 1995, but by then the decline in California's fortunes had created a scar that showed up in various anti-immigrant measures.[21]

In the mid-1980s, as Mexico attempted to address its own crisis brought on by the collapse of oil prices and the rise in world interest rates, it became a newly opened market on the southern border of Texas. Mexican president Miguel de la Madrid (1982–1988) tried to turn Mexican trade policy away from an inward orientation that had been in place since the 1930s, but the pressures of the debt crisis prevented success. In 1986, Mexico joined the General Agreement on Tariffs and Trade (GATT), and in 1989, President Salinas (1988–1994) announced the opening of negotiations to create a free trade area with the United States.[22] Mexico's abandonment of its long-held protectionist policies had a two-fold benefit for the United States and especially for the state of Texas. The state is located on the main trade corridor between Mexico and U.S. manufacturing centers. Not surprisingly, most overland trade between the two nations flows through Laredo and other ports of entry in Texas, and as a consequence, transportation and allied trade services became an unusually large share of the state economy as trade with Mexico grew. Between 1990 and 1999, the state experienced a growth rate in transportation services that was nearly 75 percent greater than the expansion of the same sector nationally, while state wholesale trade grew about 46 percent more than its national counterpart.[23] A second advantage was the spillover of manufacturing. As northern industrial cities such as Monterrey, Matamoros, Saltillo, Reynosa, Nuevo Laredo, and Ciudad Juárez expanded production, the manufacturing sector in Texas grew along with it. This required structural adjustments in manufacturing as some sectors shrank (for example, apparel manufacturing in El Paso), but total manufacturing employment and production grew dramatically, particularly in comparison with the U.S. national experience. In the 1990s the United States lost 630,000 manufacturing jobs, but the state of Texas gained 109,848 jobs.[24]

Job growth in Texas was fueled by several factors, including the unilateral lowering of trade barriers in Mexico, but also the growth in Mexican manufacturing on the border, as discussed more fully in the next chapter. Three of the five cities that collectively have more than 50 percent of the firms and workers in U.S.-origin Mexican maquiladora firms are directly on the border with Texas—Ciudad Juárez, Matamoros, and Reynosa.[25] U.S. firms and other nations' firms looked to Mexico as a production site where they could take advantage of relatively low wages and close proximity to the large U.S. market. In the new environment of openness, Mexico became a highly desirable location for producing goods to be sold into the U.S. market. The growth of Mexican manufacturing was difficult for some U.S. workers, however, as it shifted parts of production south of the border. Nevertheless, the growth in manufacturing on the Mexican side of the border had a positive net impact on manufacturing employment in the adjacent U.S. border cities, as the analysis by Hanson clearly shows.[26] Needless to say, job growth in the United States has not directly offset job loss, since it is in different locations and different industries.

Trade Dependency

Despite the caveats given earlier about state export statistics, it is safe to say that Texas is responsible for more exports to Mexico than any other state. Given its location close to Mexico's most industrial northern city, Monterrey, and also given that it is the midpoint on a line between central Mexico and the U.S. industrial heartland, foreign trade originating in Texas is concentrated on Mexico. Table 3.2 shows the trade pattern for all U.S. border states. In 2000, 46 percent of the exports originating in Texas went to Mexico, whereas only 5 percent of New Mexico's trade was with its southern neighbor. One-third of Arizona's trade was with Mexico.[27]

In dollar terms, Texas's Mexican trade is more than 2.7 times greater than California's exports to Mexico, even though California is number

TABLE 3.2 *Trade Patterns of U.S. Border States, 2000*

	California	Arizona	New Mexico	Texas
Total trade with world (millions)	119,640	14,334	2,391	103,866
Trade with Mexico (millions)	17,515	4,651	127	47,761
Percent of state trade with Mexico	14.6	32.4	5.3	46.0
No. 1 trade partner	Mexico	Mexico	Korea*	Mexico

*By 2004, Mexico had become New Mexico's chief destination for its exports.

SOURCES: U.S. International Trade Administration (n.d.); U.S. Census Bureau, *TradeStats Express* (http://tse.export.gov).

two in state trade with Mexico. This is a remarkable concentration of trade, particularly since Mexico is a developing country. Although it is not uncommon for developing countries to export the bulk of their goods to a high-income country, it is rare for the reverse to occur. In general, developing countries are unable to absorb a large share of the output of rich country markets, which have a wide variety of other rich country markets they can sell their goods to. In part, trade between Texas and Mexico is based on the state's strategic location, but it is also partly due to the growth of manufacturing along Mexico's northern border. Computers and electronic products, transportation equipment, and electrical equipment, both appliances and parts, made up 49 percent of state exports to Mexico in 2000.[28] Although precise numbers are unknown, a large share of this trade is intrafirm or intra-industry, between plants in Texas and Mexico. Growth in the maquiladora industry has supported the development of this trade and has enabled firms to remain competitive through the use of plants in Mexico.

Maquiladora manufacturing is also strong on the California border, with a large number of plants in Tijuana and Mexicali. In fact, the development of San Diego as a location center for wireless communication development and production may in part be due to its proximity to cheap assembly labor in Tijuana. However, since this area is the southwestern corner of the United States and the northwestern corner of Mexico, it does not have the advantage of being a major trade corridor. From California's perspective, it is more important that it is located on the Pacific Rim. From the time California became a state, its trade with Australia, Japan, China, and other population centers across the Pacific has figured more prominently in the state's economy than its trade with Mexico. This picture has changed somewhat with the recent growth in California-Mexico trade, together with Japan's stagnant economy during the 1990s, but the state remains more concentrated on Asia than on Latin America. Consequently, the regional and global economic integration that occurred through the 1980s and 1990s had different meanings for California and Texas. Because of this difference in orientation of their economies, it is not difficult to understand why governors in Texas cultivate relations with Mexico, while California's leadership tends to look west, across the Pacific Ocean.

Economic Distance

Discussions of Mexico-U.S. border relations usually frame the issue in terms of the asymmetry of political power and differences in culture. These are important dimensions, but they are often confused with obstacles to cross-border collaboration stemming from the asymmetry of economic development. That is, economic distance caused by differences in the level of economic development can pose serious obstacles to cross-border collaboration. The specific effects of economic distance are difficult to quantify but must include a higher degree of mistrust and lack of confidence in cross-border partners. This can run in both directions. Those on the Mexican side may experience a sense of exploitation or of being patronized by their richer counterparts across the border. Those on the U.S. side may tend to focus on lack of enforcement of rules and regulations, corruption, and a lack of transparency in the design of systems and policies. Papademetriou and Meyers show that border dwellers around the world worry about corruption, rule transparency, and follow-through on commitments by their counterparts on the other side.[29] Although many of these concerns have a cultural or linguistic element, there is often an economic one as well. For example, the perception of order in an urban landscape is partly a cultural phenomenon related to architecture and the built environment of roads, parks, sidewalks, and other constructed elements. The perception of order is also economic, since less-well-off cities have less to spend on graffiti and litter removal, the delivery of clean water, paving of roads, and other urban amenities.

Table 3.3 illustrates the degree of economic distance between border counties and municipios, grouped together by state. All values are per person, and Mexican values are converted to U.S. dollars at purchasing power parity exchange rates, which take into account the differences in prices.[30] There are several striking features to the data in Table 3.3. First, the ratio of per capita income between the nations as a whole is greater than that for the whole border region. The average per capita income in

TABLE 3.3 *Ratio of GDP per Person, U.S. Border Counties and Mexican Border Municipios (U.S. Dollars, PPP Basis)*

	1970	1980	1989	1999
U.S.: Mexico	3.15	2.81	3.66	4.07
U.S. border: Mexican border	2.22	2.20	2.45	2.40
California: Baja California	2.31	2.37	2.88	2.85
Arizona: Sonora	1.55	1.77	1.97	1.92
New Mexico: West Chihuahua	3.51	3.86	2.47	2.66
West Texas: East Chihuahua	1.91	1.62	1.56	1.58
East Texas: Coahuila, Nuevo Leon, Tamaulipas	1.33	1.35	1.60	1.56

NOTE: PPP = purchasing power parity estimates for an average of each state's border counties and municipios.

SOURCE: Authors' calculations; see Chapter 7.

the United States was four times greater than the Mexican average, compared to 2.4 times higher in the border region in 2000. Second, the ratios have increased slightly over time, although not in every locale. Third, and perhaps most striking, is the relatively smooth decline in the ratios from west to east. The California border is the richest border region, and even though Baja California is a relatively prosperous Mexican region, the ratio is almost three to one. Moving east, the U.S. side of the border becomes progressively poorer, and the ratio of incomes falls to around 1.6 to one by the time the Texas border region is reached.

This analysis does not prove anything about border relations, but it does suggest that even if cultural issues such as language and ethnicity are set to one side, the residents of the Texas border are much less different, economically speaking, relative to their counterparts in Mexico than are residents of the California or Arizona border regions. These numbers represent averages, with the usual caveat that if they are relatively accurate estimates, there is still a great deal of variation in individual incomes. Nevertheless, they confirm general impressions of the border that differences between Texas and Mexico are not nearly as great as the differences elsewhere along the U.S.-Mexico border.

CONCLUSION

In their recent collection of essays on borders around the world, Papademetriou and Meyers conclude that it is common for border communities to influence border conditions and national border policies.[31] The key, however, is that they must first know what they want. What this chapter shows is that communities in California and Baja California will have a more difficult time developing mutual understanding and agreement on a common future. Collaboration at the western end of the border runs up against numerous barriers in the form of cultural, linguistic, economic, and administrative differences between border cities. These barriers make it less likely that Californians and Baja Californians can reach agreement about the operation of the border and the many ways it inserts itself into the lives of both communities. In the case of Texas, however, the story is somewhat different, as many of the factors that interfere with collaboration in California are sources of strength, and state planners increasingly recognize this fact.

■ ■

CHAPTER 4

TRADE, INVESTMENT, AND MANUFACTURING

Transportation costs play a major role in both domestic and international commerce. In general, water transport is usually the cheapest way to move goods over long distances, and air transport is most suitable for high-value, low-bulk items that need to reach their markets in the shortest possible time, yet the vast majority of U.S.-Mexico trade is hauled on the ground by trucks and trains. Although two-thirds of U.S. merchandise trade with the rest of the world is via water and air, and only one of the top five international gateway ports for the United States is a land-based port (Detroit), most goods shipped between the United States and Mexico move along the north-south highway corridors connecting the two countries through one of the many land-based points of entry.[1] Not one of the top five U.S. ports of entry for commerce is critical to trade between the United States and Mexico; the border crossings between the two countries service only binational trade. The most significant ports of entry are Laredo–Nuevo Laredo, El Paso–Juárez, and San Diego–Tijuana.

Since the mid-1980s, trade between the United States and Mexico has grown more rapidly than the total trade or the gross domestic product (GDP) of either country, and consequently, each has become a relatively more important trading partner for the other. In Mexico's case, trade with the United States dominates its overall trade relations. For example, in 2005, Mexico shipped more than 85 percent of its total exports to the United States.[2] U.S. exports are diversified across a much larger number of countries, but Mexico has grown to be the number two most important purchaser of U.S. products, second only to Canada. Though trade between the United States and China captures more headlines and has grown more rapidly over the past few years, as of 2005 it had not surpassed Mexico in

Presidio, Texas.

the value of its trade. However, at current rates of growth, China could overtake Mexico in 2006 or 2007, at least for merchandise trade.[3]

Along with a dramatic increase in trade since the mid-1980s, foreign direct investment (FDI) flows have also grown in size and importance. FDI is intimately linked to trade, since a significant share of cross-border trade is intrafirm trade.[4] Many of the manufacturing plants that have sprung up along the Mexican side of the border during the past twenty-five years are either U.S.-owned or a joint venture between U.S. and Mexican partners, although an important but minor share is owned by Japanese, Korean, Taiwanese, European, and other interests from outside North America. For example, Sony, Panasonic, Samsung, Toyota, and quite a few other electronics and auto firms have manufacturing plants in northern Mexico, often in close proximity to a twin city plant along the U.S. southern border. FDI flows from Mexico to the United States are less frequently cited but are a significant part of the border economy, since Mexican investments in the United States are mainly in counties near the border.[5]

A majority of U.S. exports to Mexico originate in border states. In 2005, for example, more than 60 percent of all U.S. exports to Mexico originated in one of the four border states, Texas, California, Arizona,

Anti-NAFTA sign, Customs House, Cuidad Acuña.

and New Mexico. Further, nearly 42 percent of U.S. trade with Mexico originated in Texas, while another 14 percent originated in California. Thus, two border states supplied 56.5 percent of total merchandise exports from the United States to Mexico.[6] Similar estimates are not available for Mexican border states, but insofar as more than 45 percent of all exports by Mexico are from export-processing plants (maquiladoras), 80 percent of which are located in border states, it can be inferred that Mexican border states play a disproportionately large role in Mexico's total exports to the United States.[7] In sum, much of the economic activity linking the United States and Mexico is based in border states where the proximity of markets and the differing strengths of the U.S. and Mexican economies create a desirable combination of characteristics for locating many types of production.

SHIFTING NATIONAL POLICIES

During the four decades immediately following World War II, Mexico tried to develop its national economy by protecting its national industry with high tariffs and restrictive quotas. These policies limited foreign investment and sheltered domestic manufacturers from foreign competition. The goal was to build an industrial base through government support for the manufacture of goods that could be substituted for imports. Import substitution industrialization (ISI) policies were the conventional wisdom of the 1950s, 1960s, and 1970s and were widely practiced throughout Latin America and the developing world. Encouraged by the United Nation's Economic Commission for Latin America and the Caribbean (ECLAC), ISI policies featured high levels of protection for domestic markets, a deemphasis on trade as a beneficial activity, and direct government support for specific industries. In the late 1960s, the Republic of Korea, Taiwan, and a few other countries began the shift toward export promotion policies, and in the 1970s ISI policies came under intense criticism from economists, who conducted detailed empirical analyses of specific country experiences.[8] The international debt crisis that began in 1982 when Mexico declared it was unable to make payments on the interest and principal it owed foreign banks and governments set off a series of crises that further intensified the criticism of ISI policies and eventually led to their abandonment. In Mexico and throughout Latin America, the period after 1982 is characterized as a time of crisis and falling incomes during which many of the economic policies of the previous forty years had to be revised. High levels of foreign debt required a steady inflow of foreign currency to fulfill payment obligations, but with export sectors that had been neglected by four decades of ISI policies, Mexico and the rest of Latin America lacked the competitive manufacturing base they needed to produce exports.

The debt crisis that began in 1982 coincided with the election of a new president in Mexico. President Miguel de la Madrid (1982–1988) began a fundamental reexamination of development policies that would ultimately lead to the dismantling of ISI policies in favor of a more open, export-oriented trade policy. Moreover, the changes were not limited to trade but affected every aspect of economic planning and policy making. As de la Madrid and his successors, Carlos Salinas (1988–1994) and Ernesto Zedillo (1994–2000), grappled with the economic stagnation of the 1980s and the legacy of ISI policies, they implemented dramatic changes in agricultural policies, banking and finance, and foreign investment controls, and privatized a large number of state-run enterprises. Taken together, these changes amounted to a rejection of Mexico's state-led, ISI-based economic development strategy in favor of a market-led, export-oriented strategy. This historic policy shift was felt along the entire border with the United States, and in many ways it created the contemporary border economy. The signing of the North American Free Trade Agreement (NAFTA) was another important development, but in essence, the changes anticipated under NAFTA were begun nearly a decade earlier with the shift out of ISI.

Of direct relevance for the border economy, Mexico's dismantling of its inward-oriented ISI policies in the mid-1980s fundamentally altered the incentives for locating production closer to the border rather than near Mexico City or other major Mexican markets such as Guadalajara. For individual firms, transportation costs play a key role in location decisions. Firms must consider both the costs of transporting materials and parts to a factory and the costs of getting the final product to the market. Because production processes in many industries have minimum size requirements for maximum efficiency, there is a limit to the number of plants that can be built if a firm wants to achieve an efficient scale of production. Within an economic policy framework that emphasizes production for the national market, these two considerations—transportation costs and efficiency in the scale of production—led a disproportionate number of manufacturers to locate their plants in or around Mexico City, Monterrey, and Guadalajara, the three largest domestic markets. And, as de la Madrid, Salinas, and Zedillo began the process of reorienting Mexico's economy toward international markets by dismantling protectionism and subsidies for import substituting industries, firms began to look abroad. At the margin of their decision making, the incentives to produce for the domestic market were much less, while foreign markets such as the United States looked relatively more profitable. To reduce transportation costs, however, the optimal location strategy became one of placing plants in a few locations physically close to the U.S. market. After that, manufacturing in the Mexican border region increased rapidly.[9]

With the implementation of NAFTA in 1994, a number of trade barriers between the United States and Mexico were immediately removed, while others began to fall more gradually. The net result was an immediate and sustained increase in U.S.-Mexico trade. For example, total merchandise trade (exports plus imports) between the United States and Mexico was $58.4 billion in 1990. By 2005, total trade was five times greater, or

TABLE 4.1 *Trade Concentration, 2005*

Direction of Trade	Share of Country's Total Exports or Imports
Mexico's exports to U.S.	85.7%
Mexico's imports from U.S.	53.6%
U.S. exports to Mexico	13.3%
U.S. imports from Mexico	11.3%

SOURCES: International Trade Administration (2005); INEGI (2003).

$290.2 billion.[10] In the process, Mexico's share of total U.S. merchandise trade grew from 7.1 percent in 1991 to 11.3 percent in 2005 (see Table 4.1).

In addition to increased trade, U.S FDI in Mexico increased significantly with the signing of NAFTA. U.S. FDI in Mexico averaged $1.6 billion annually between 1980 and 1993, compared to $8.6 billion between 1994 and 2005.[11] Changing trade policies and the signing of NAFTA encouraged other countries besides the United States to invest in Mexico, and overall FDI grew proportionately. The U.S. share of Mexico's inward FDI fluctuated from year to year but averaged 63 percent of the total from 1994 to 2005. Not all of this growth in FDI can be viewed as a result of NAFTA, however, since the robust U.S. economy of the late 1990s increased its investments worldwide, and de-privatization measures created many opportunities to purchase businesses in Mexico.

MANUFACTURING ON THE BORDER

The development of a manufacturing sector fueled by foreign investment is one of the most dramatic economic changes affecting the border in the last half-century. The new manufacturing plants, which are located largely on the Mexican side, have absorbed a steady stream of migrants from Mexico's interior, have created managerial-level jobs for graduates of expanding border universities, and have generated an increasing share of the total foreign exchange earnings of Mexico. The growth of manufacturing in Mexico's border region has spilled over onto the U.S. side, with many U.S. border cities adding some manufacturing jobs over the last two decades even as the United States as a whole lost manufacturing jobs. In sectors such as building materials and transportation equipment (autos and auto parts), U.S. firms became more competitive as production was integrated with Mexican firms in Monterrey, Mexico City, and the Mexican border.

TABLE 4.2 *Manufacturing Employment Shares, 2001*

Region	Percent of Labor Force in Manufacturing
United States	14.1
U.S. border	10.0
Mexico	19.0
Mexican border	34.6

NOTE: Data include all firms, maquiladoras, and others.

SOURCES: U.S. Department of Commerce (2002); INEGI (2005).

Nevertheless, the differences in the relative importance of manufacturing in border counties versus border municipios are a significant feature of the region. For example, in 2001, more than 41 percent of Ciudad Juárez's labor force worked in manufacturing, while directly across the Rio Grande, in El Paso, the figure was 11 percent. The same pattern holds for a number of other twin cities, such as Tijuana and San Diego, where the shares of the labor force in manufacturing were 26.1 percent and 7 percent, respectively.[12] Table 4.2 compares the relative importance of the total manufacturing sector in the border region with its importance nationally for both countries. Relative size is measured by the share of the total labor force that is in manufacturing.

As shown in Table 4.2, the Mexican border is dominated by its manufacturing sector, which absorbs one-third of its labor force, much more than is true for Mexico as a whole. In contrast, the U.S. border is slightly less oriented toward manufacturing than the United States as a whole, and much less so than the Mexican border region. This gives rise to a profound difference in economic structure between the U.S. and Mexican sides of the border.

The Border Industrialization Plan

There are multiple reasons for the growth of manufacturing in Mexico's border region. In 1964, the United States terminated a major guest worker program that had been started in 1942 as a way to fill labor shortages caused by World War II. Called the Bracero Program, the guest worker agreement granted temporary, usually seasonal, entrance for thousands of

Mexican men. This was not the first labor agreement between the United States and Mexico, but it left an important legacy in U.S.-Mexico relations and is still looked to as a possible model for future guest worker programs.[13] The program lasted more than two decades, until pressures from labor and civil rights groups prevailed and it was cancelled. U.S. opponents of the program argued that it depressed U.S. wages and employment while leading to the mistreatment of Mexican guest workers. In 1964, the United States unilaterally ended the guest worker program.

With the border suddenly closed to guest workers who had been crossing into the United States since the 1940s, the Mexican government responded with the creation of the Border Industrialization Program (BIP). This was an effort to provide jobs for the suddenly unemployed men concentrated on the border. The new program created an export-processing zone where firms could import tariff-free components and intermediate goods as long as the imports were assembled into a product that was exported out of Mexico. (Export-processing zones are described in Box 4.1.) The initial aim of the BIP was to create jobs, but over time this extended into a more comprehensive set of goals: increasing worker skills, generating earnings of foreign exchange for Mexico through the attraction of investment and sales of exports, the transfer of technology and know-how, and the development of managers with advanced business skills. Tariff-free "temporary" importation of capital and the elimination of all tariffs on imported components allowed U.S. firms and other foreign firms to take advantage of Mexico's relatively lower wage rates and the proximity of Mexican border cities to the large U.S. market. These export-processing firms, called *maquiladoras* or *maquilas,* also enjoyed advantages under U.S. tariff rules that allowed goods to be exported for assembly and reimported to the United States while being subjected to U.S. tariffs only on the share of the value that was added (mainly the value of the labor) in the exporting country.[14] In sum, both Mexican and U.S. tariff laws encouraged this new form of production in the border region.

Export processing such as that handled by Mexico's maquilas depends on the evolution of transportation and communication technology that took place in the second half of the twentieth century.[15] With advances in transportation and communications, multinational firms were able to create global factories capable of exploiting the cost advantages offered by different countries. This strategy required firms to divide the production process into discrete labor-intensive and capital-intensive steps. The capital-intensive processes, such as design, engineering, and machine tooling, are done in places rich in capital and skilled labor, such as the United

BOX 4.1   EXPORT-PROCESSING ZONES

Export-processing zones, or EPZs, are widely used by developing countries to attract foreign investment and to promote manufactured exports. EPZs usually offer foreign investors a variety of tax breaks and other incentives such as utilities or land, if they choose to locate in a specified area in the country. In the Mexican case, however, the geographic limits on investment that required firms to be at the border were eventually relaxed and firms could receive the import tax breaks regardless of where they located, so long as they complied with the rules (for example, that all of the output is exported). Since the signing of NAFTA, the rule that all products must be exported has also been relaxed.

Export-processing zones have a mixed record. In some countries they have succeeded in creating many new jobs while simultaneously improving labor conditions. In other countries the results are very mixed or even negative. At their worst, EPZs create zones where coercive techniques are used to keep workers in line, while factory conditions are unsafe and unhealthy. In these repressive cases, minimum wages may be nonexistent or not enforced, wages for women lag behind those for men, child labor laws are ignored, and workers are generally mistreated. At the opposite end of the spectrum, however, in countries where the EPZ rules are in line with international standards, workers are able to earn modest but decent incomes, working conditions are clean and safe, and the foreign investment proves to be a foundation for economic growth. Well-run EPZs can particularly benefit women in traditional societies, where the EPZ may provide one of the first avenues toward financial independence.

Successful EPZs depend on a number of related policies in the broader national environment. Exchange rates must be competitive and not overvalued, so that the country's exports are realistically priced in foreign markets. EPZs must also provide infrastructure that is both reliable and reasonably priced. This includes utilities and transportation and communications services. In addition, successful EPZs have a stable and transparent system of laws and protections for property rights. This attracts business by helping to ensure investors that disputes will be decided fairly and impartially, and that everyone is equal before the law.

If properly implemented, EPZs may help generate economic growth, but they are clearly not a very useful tool for the direct reduction of poverty. When they are located in isolated areas with greater poverty, firms are reluctant to invest, since the problems of transportation, utilities, and attracting a labor force are all more difficult. In addition, locating in rural or isolated areas limits the ability of firms to create linkages to the rest of the economy by acting as a source of demand for local inputs. In that case, EPZ production does not have many spillover effects, and one of their potential economic benefits cannot be realized. Moran's *Beyond Sweatshops: Foreign Direct Investment and Globalization in Developing Countries* (2002) is a good introduction to the topic.

States or Japan, while highly labor-intensive assembly processes are done in developing countries where there is an abundance of low-wage labor. The proximity of a country with abundant supplies of low-skilled labor to a country with abundant supplies of capital, highly skilled labor, and a large consumer market made the U.S.-Mexico border region an ideal location for production-sharing operations carried out by global factories.

A wage gap between the United States and Mexico was not the only requirement for the BIP to eventually take off. Also of importance was that the productivity gap between U.S. and Mexican workers and firms was less than the wage gap. This is easily illustrated with a hypothetical example. Suppose that workers in Mexico earn only one-fourth as much as U.S. workers, but the value of their production is one-tenth the U.S. level. In that case, it would not be profitable for U.S. firms to locate in Mexico, since the value of production (10 percent of the U.S. value) lags behind the cost of wages (25 percent of the U.S. wage). In other words, despite large wage gaps, it may be unprofitable to locate abroad. Consequently, another condition for the successful growth of manufacturing has been that the productivity gap between U.S. and Mexican firms be less than or equal to the wage gap. In our hypothetical example, Mexican productivity must be 25 percent or more of the U.S. level, if Mexican wages are 25 percent of U.S. wages.

A Profile of the Maquiladora Industry

During the first fifteen to twenty years of its existence, the maquiladora industry was relatively small and its growth was limited. Probably no one expected border manufacturing to take off and become a major engine of Mexican growth, least of all in the 1960s and the 1970s. But several events converged to make the industry a major recipient of foreign investment. Most dramatically and painfully, a series of devaluations of the peso lowered the dollar cost of Mexican labor to U.S. and other foreign firms. These devaluations began in 1976 with a financial crisis, and then appeared more dramatically in 1982 with the onset of the debt crisis, which put continued pressure on the peso and led to several devaluations in the 1980s. The devaluation of the peso set off an inflation relative to the dollar, which lowered Mexican labor costs in peso terms, since wages did not keep up with the price increases. In these years, the real value of the Mexican wage fell dramatically. In 1986, as part of its overall reforms of economic policy, Mexico announced that it was joining the General Agreement on Tariffs and Trade (GATT, the precursor of the World Trade Organization). This encouraged foreign investors to consider Mexico, since it raised expectations that they could use Mexico as an export platform from which they could sell to the rest of the world without running into sudden and arbitrary tariff increases or quotas. Domestic investors were encouraged to look at the border region since membership in the GATT represented a shift toward a more open economy and, at the margin, an increase in the incentives to produce for foreign markets. From the mid-1980s, the number of maquiladora plants and workers increased dramatically.

Figures 4.1 and 4.2, showing the number of maquiladora plants and maquiladora employment from 1970 to 2005, have two outstanding characteristics. One is the steady growth in the number of firms and workers from the mid-1980s to 2000. The second is the sudden downturn in 2000. After more than two decades of double-digit growth, the maquiladora industry went into a severe recession in October 2000. The downturn lasted until February 2002, by which time the industry had shed 26.7 percent of its jobs.[16] Casual analysis led many to believe that the era of growth had ended, since it was widely thought that China's negotiations to join the WTO and its accession in 2001 created a far more attractive environment for foreign investors than Mexico. China's negotiations and accession to the WTO undoubtedly had a negative impact on maquilas in some sectors in Mexico, particularly clothing. Other less noticed but important changes also contributed to the downturn. These included a reduction in U.S. tariff rules for clothing imports from Central America and the Caribbean in 2000 and a U.S. recession in 2001. Finally, the maquila sector was hit by a steep but temporary fall in worldwide FDI. The U.S. recession led to a temporary decline in the demand for maquila output, while the worldwide depression in FDI cut into the flow of new investment in the industry. At the time, much was written about the impact of China, but several of the other factors went unnoticed.

As a first step toward explaining the recession, and to throw some light on whether these are temporary or permanent effects, it is useful to divide the causes into cyclical and structural changes. Cyclical changes are short- and medium-run changes that are related to the business cycle and to temporary shifts in economic activity. Structural changes are permanent and represent changes in basic economic relations, such as the increased competition that came with China's entry into the WTO. The primary cyclical effect is the status of the U.S. economy. Since the lion's share of the industry's output is exported to the United States, a recession north of the border significantly reduces the demand for output from maquiladoras. Gruben and Gerber and Mundra provide two similar estimates for the impact of a U.S. recession on overall maquila employment.[17] In their

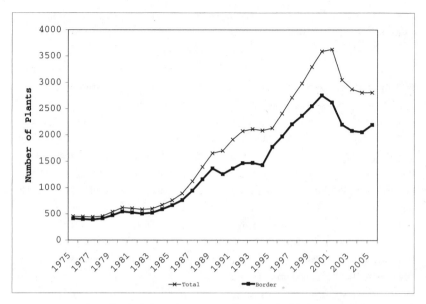

FIGURE 4.1. Number of maquiladora plants nationally and in the border region, 1975–2005.

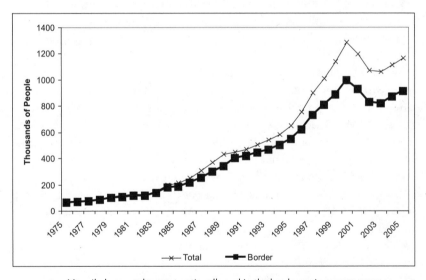

FIGURE 4.2. Maquiladora employment nationally and in the border region, 1975–2005.

econometric models, a 1 percent decline in U.S. industrial production is associated with a decline in maquiladora employment of approximately 1.25 percent. An additional effect was caused by the strengthening of Mexico's peso, which made it more expensive to employ workers in Mexico relative to Asia or the United States. The U.S. recession, together with the strengthening of the peso, is estimated to explain somewhere in the range of 65 to 75 percent of the job loss.

To develop some idea of China's impact and how it relates to the other factors, it is useful to look at the sectoral distribution of the maquila industry before and after 2000. In that year, the three sectors of clothing, electronics, and autos accounted for more than two-thirds of all workers and more than half of all plants (52.9 percent, see Table 4.2). Other sectors, such as furniture, food processing, mechanical machinery, chemical and plastic products, and services, were relatively less important, although the pattern varied somewhat by locale (see Table 4.3). After 2000, the biggest drop in employment and firms occurred in the clothing sector. Electronics also saw a decline but on a smaller scale, while the auto sector saw neither decline nor growth until around 2003, when it began to expand again. Clothing, the biggest loser of jobs, is also the sector most sensitive to wage differences and was the sector that experienced strong competition from both China and Central America. Electronics manufacturing varies greatly. Some electronic manufacturing is repetitive and uses large amounts of unskilled labor to make a standardized product, while other segments require vast amounts of capital along with scientific and engineering labor inputs. Automobiles are bulky and thus more sensitive to transportation costs, require an extensive network of suppliers, and use lots of capital in combination with skilled and semiskilled labor. This makes automobile production, with its just-in-time inventory systems, more difficult to locate across an ocean, no matter what the wage structure is like. The prognosis for the auto maquiladoras depends directly on the ability of Mexican-based manufacturers to increase the technical sophistication of their production processes and products. With economic integration proceeding rapidly across the globe, the only way for growth to continue is through more or less constant industrial upgrading.

Maquiladoras represent a large share of the total manufacturing in the border region, but in an absolute sense, about five municipios account for the majority of manufacturing jobs (see Table 4.4). These are, in order, Juárez, Tijuana, Matamoros, Reynosa, and Mexicali. They are spread across the border from the Pacific Ocean to the Gulf of Mexico, and all five of these regions have experienced extremely rapid growth in maquiladora manufacturing. As a group, they accounted for nearly 84 percent of the maquiladora jobs on the border in 2000, and about 10 percent of the total manufacturing jobs in Mexico.

With the failure over the long run of the Mexican economy to generate as many formal sector jobs as its population growth demands, the rapid expansion of border manufacturing in general, and of the maquiladora

TABLE 4.3 *Share of Employment by the Three Largest Maquila Sectors*

	Employees	Pct. of Total Workers	Firms	Pct. of Total Firms
Clothing				
Oct. 2000	293,576	21.8	1,113	30.5
Jan. 2006	167,169	14.3	506	18.0
Electronics				
Oct. 2000	357,174	26.5	567	15.5
Jan. 2006	257,538	22.0	432	15.3
Autos and parts				
Oct. 2000	250,635	18.6	255	7.0
Jan. 2006	271,127	23.1	312	11.1
Above three combined				
Oct. 2000	921,877	68.3	1,935	52.9
Jan. 2006	695,834	59.3	1,250	44.4
Total, all sectors				
Oct. 2000	1,347,803		3,655	
Jan. 2006	1,172,987		2,815	

SOURCE: INEGI (2006).

TABLE 4.4 *Growth and Employment in Manufacturing, Selected Mexican Border Municipios*

Region	Annual Growth Rate of Maquila Employment, 1990–2000	Share of Manufacturing in Total Employment, 2000	Total Labor Force (Economically Active Population), 2000
Juárez	7.4	46.2	483,469
Tijuana	12.1	32.5	450,608
Matamoros	5.6	39.9	165,214
Reynosa	10.9	36.4	168,926
Mexicali	11.7	25.4	287,208

SOURCE: INEGI (2005).

industry in particular, has partially filled a serious need. One consequence of such rapid growth, however, is that, beginning in the late 1980s, the existing labor force in many Mexican border communities became inadequate to fill the available positions. Excess demand for labor was visible in a number of ways as firms experienced high turnover rates among their

Permanent help-wanted sign on a maquiladora, Tijuana.

workers and put permanent help-wanted signs on their factories. To attract workers and to try to keep them, some companies began to supply their workers with simple consumer goods, such as shoes, or services such as transportation to work and day-care centers at work. Some firms sponsored sports teams and bought them uniforms, or they threw parties and gave various forms of bonuses if workers refrained from leaving to seek work elsewhere. Eventually, even higher wages began to enter the mix, with the result that the Mexican border region slowly became a relatively high-wage region in Mexico, comparable to Mexico City.

Neither Mexico's comparative advantage due to the availability of low-wage, unskilled or semiskilled labor nor the situation of low wages with relatively high levels of productivity adequately explains the geographic concentration of several key manufacturing sectors, including electronics and autos (including auto parts). Wages are lower in the south of the country and in many of the states midway between Mexico, D.F., and the border. The strong presence of manufacturing on the border indicates that the proximity of firms to a major market like the United States must also play a key role. Factors such as transportation costs, the need for close coordination of production processes, the use of just-in-time inventory control, and other market-related factors play important roles.

The development of the manufacturing sector has also led to the creation of economies of scale of the external variety. External economies of scale occur when each individual firm becomes more productive as the overall size of the industry grows. External economies as defined by Alfred Marshall stem from the ability of firms to share a common labor pool, a common supplier base, including nontraded inputs (legal, accounting, marketing, and so forth), and information about markets and trends.[18] Once established, external economies generate self-reinforcing factors that lead to more and more growth. For example, firms may locate in a region because there is a strong supplier base or an abundance of specialized service providers. Workers migrate from the interior of the country because jobs are relatively plentiful, and that signals to employers that there is an available industrial labor force and leads to even more investment in the region. This process, often referred to as regional agglomeration or geographic concentration, plays a significant role in determining the location of manufacturing industries and explains at least part of the process behind the growth of border manufacturing.[19]

Over time, the development of industrial centers in border cities such as Tijuana, Juárez, Reynosa, Matamoros, and other locales began to feed on itself as suppliers relocated in order to be near their markets. Workers migrated because they knew there was work, and investors saw possibilities for larger industrial developments. The presence of these manufacturing centers within an expanding urban environment has defined the most significant changes in the border over the past several decades. The growth of manufacturing is misunderstood and controversial. It has clearly brought both costs and benefits to the region. Among the benefits are higher incomes and jobs. The costs include congestion, pollution, challenges to traditional social arrangements, and increasing demands for scarce water, energy, and other resources. (The environmental impacts are discussed in Chapter 5.)

The Development of Second- and Third-generation Maquiladoras

During the 1980s, a number of researchers began to note that border manufacturing and the maquiladora encompassed a wide range of technological sophistication. That is, some firms used unskilled labor and crude machinery to make large quantities of very simple products while others used more skilled labor and expensive manufacturing equipment. Analysts began to talk of the first-, second-, and third-generation maquiladora, as if the maquiladoras were a kind of evolutionary chain that stretched from simple assembly to true manufacturing and then to research and development with constant innovation. The labels first, second, and third generation are metaphors for three different levels of sophistication, but none of these levels is precisely measurable. Essentially, the movement along the chain from the first to the second to the third generation represents industrial upgrading, or moving up the ladder of comparative advantage.[20] Carrillo and Hualde first defined these shifts in a consistent way, with first-generation plants corresponding to simple assembly operations using relatively unskilled, low-wage labor.[21] Although this type of production requires an industrial labor force (or must generate one), issues of quality control and technological complexity are minimally important. In the 1980s, some maquiladoras began moving toward organizational changes associated with Japanese manufacturing techniques, including work teams, quality circles, statistical quality control, modular production teams, and worker multiqualification.[22] Carrillo and Hualde designated this shift the second generation of maquiladoras, with the intention of singling out plants with a higher degree of decision-making autonomy, more advanced manufacturing technology, including automation or semi-automation, higher levels of participation by engineers and technicians, and a clear emphasis on product quality. Third-generation plants have characteristics that include an intensive focus on the use of information technology, along with the development of R&D capacity and advanced manufacturing capabilities.

Data on the number and relative importance of each of the three generations of maquiladora plants are limited. First-, second-, and third-generation plants coexist side by side, and once a plant of a particular type is built, it is doubtful that there is a tendency toward upgrading. Rather, the addition of second-generation and then third-generation plants appears to come with the construction of new plants. The television manufacturing industry illustrates this evolution, as it has grown from making wooden cabinets (the labor-intensive production of simple commodities) to flat panels, and then to digital and high-definition television sets.[23] A number of plants, for example Sony, Samsung, RCA, and Philips, have their own R&D, particularly in product design, and they manufacture under their own labels and those of other companies. For example, a Sony TV plant in Tijuana, a third-generation maquiladora with an R&D component, developed a cathode ray tube that is used in 70 percent of all Sony TVs sold in the United States.

In an attempt to measure the relative importance of each generation of manufacturing, Gerber and Carrillo estimated that about 40 percent of the electronics plants in three surveyed cities (Tijuana, Mexicali, and Ciudad Juárez) are first-generation plants competing primarily on the basis of

Maquiladora plant, Tijuana.

price. These plants utilize low-cost, relatively low-skilled assembly operations that are less focused on precision, quality, or technological advance-
ment.[24] Beyond this group, perhaps 20 or even 30 percent of the firms are
third generation, operating at the frontier of their industry, competing on
quality as well as price and using large amounts of constantly upgraded
engineering and technical expertise in their processes. That would imply
that another 30 to 40 percent of the firms are at the second-generation or
intermediate levels of sophistication.

The Role of the United States

One of the key characteristics of the maquila sector is that the existing
stock of foreign-owned maquilas is mainly of U.S. origin. For example, from
1994 through 2000, U.S. investment was 87.5 percent of the $13,229 mil-
lion that the world invested in Mexico's maquiladora sector. In addition,
U.S. investment is highly concentrated geographically along the border,
and specifically in five cities that house the majority of the maquilas.[25]
Various explanations have been offered for the use of the maquila sector by
U.S. investors. From the perspective of business strategy, the United States
International Trade Commission (USITC) has proposed a laundry list of

reasons for investment in border maquila manufacturing operations, all of which are aimed at lowering costs.[26]

Most explanations for U.S. investment in Mexico's border manufacturing can be covered under a general set of principles explaining FDI. John Dunning's ownership-localization-internalization (OLI) theory holds that in general, firms invest abroad for the combination of the three reasons given in the apt name of his theory. Firms own a valuable asset, such as a patent or a trade secret, that gives them an advantage in a particular product line. The choice of a location in which they can produce their product most efficiently depends on a variety of factors, from taxes and wages to transportation costs to the availability of supplies and labor and other critical factors that determine production and distribution costs. Finally, the firm decides to keep the production inside its own operation (internalization) rather than purchase the product from a supplier, again for a variety of reasons involving trade secrets, monitoring costs, and quality assurance, among others. In effect, management decides that the value of its asset (patent, trade secret) is greatest if it produces within its own firm rather than contracting out.[27]

THE COSTS AND BENEFITS OF MAQUILADORA MANUFACTURING

Since its inception, the maquiladora industry has generated controversy and energized both its supporters and its critics. Supporters point to benefits such as jobs and foreign exchange earnings, while critics raise concerns about environmental stresses, exploitation of workers, and the lack of spillover onto the rest of the Mexican economy. The environment is discussed in the next chapter. In the remainder of this chapter we look more closely at some of the benefits and costs of manufacturing on the border.

One of the primary benefits of the border maquiladora industry to Mexico is the large trade surplus it generates and, together with the foreign investment it pulls in, the foreign exchange it earns for the national economy. In 2005, the maquiladora industry had a trade surplus in excess of $21.6 billion while the rest of Mexico's manufacturing ran a deficit of $29.2 billion. Since around 75 percent of the industry is on the border, more than $15 billion can be attributed to border maquiladoras. Maquiladoras' level of net exports was not far below the value of Mexico's net exports of crude oil and petroleum products ($25.7 billion) and was far above the balance on tourism services ($5.2 billion).[28] The foreign exchange earned by the industry, both through its net exports and through its attraction of foreign investment, is vital for the country, since it enables payment of foreign debt and the importation of greater quantities of goods and services.

Another characteristic of the industry that is fundamentally positive has been its steady growth rate and the corresponding ability to provide jobs to a growing labor force. With more than a million workers, it has offered one of the most consistent employment opportunities over the last twenty years. Furthermore, many of the jobs—currently about 49 percent of the total—go to women in Mexico, who, outside of the professions, have traditionally had limited employment opportunities. Although the initial impetus for establishing the maquiladora industry was to create jobs on the border for Mexican men, throughout much of its history, the industry has employed women in larger numbers than men. This may have heightened social tensions, but without doubt it increased opportunities for women. Still, the insufficiency of day-care centers, harassment from sexist and abusive managers, the lower wages generally paid to female employees, and the glass ceilings that limit promotion within a plant, along with the fact that most female maquila workers do not see a corresponding reduction in their work at home, are serious issues. Although maquila work provides some financial independence, for many it is like having a second job on top of the one at home. Nevertheless, interviews with women workers indicate that in general, they revel in the financial independence and new opportunities the maquiladoras provide.[29]

Perhaps more controversial but still most likely a benefit is the transfer of technology and management practices to the Mexican economy. This point is less easy to capture with a simple set of numbers such as the trade balance or the number of jobs. The maquiladora industry began with low-wage assembly work, where the actual amount of technological spillover or other linkage to the rest of the Mexican economy remains small. Where technology and managerial transfer is taking place is primarily in the second- and third-generation maquiladoras, but precise estimates of the size and value of the technology transfer remain unavailable.

Foreign exchange earnings, jobs, and technology transfer are positive results but must be weighed against the potential negatives of industrial growth. Specifically, the border region is growing ever more congested as traffic, water shortages, deteriorating air quality, and a general lack of public infrastructure in the form of paved roads, water treatment, electrical power, housing, and schools challenge the quality of life for border residents. These are serious problems stemming from the rapid population growth along the border, much of which has been encouraged by the growth of the maquiladora manufacturing industry. Although it is possible for countries to grow rapidly without creating bottlenecks in infrastructure such as housing, water, power, and urban amenities, Mexico's border cities are typical of many places around the world where urban development has outstripped the provision of services. Industrial growth has pulled in a steady flow of immigrants from the interior, where jobs are scarcer, and in the process it has generated a set of challenges related to congestion and rapid growth. New residents need schools, water, power, parks, paved roads, sewer hookups, urban transportation, and communication systems. The rapid population growth beginning in the 1980s has put increased demands on highly centralized, underfunded urban systems and has stressed the environment.

From one perspective, this challenge of industrialization is far better than the challenge of no industrialization. Nevertheless, if the institutions of Mexico and the United States are unable to respond to the needs of a growing border region, and if breathable air, drinkable water, and other basic needs go unmet, then the quality of life can seriously deteriorate, even if some people's incomes might be higher as a result of the new industry. Both the U.S. and Mexican border cities are handicapped by their distance from their national capitals and by the tendency of those capitals to view the border as primarily a security or law enforcement issue rather than an economic development issue. This limitation on drawing public resources to the region for social and economic development as well as for environmental protection is an ongoing controversy that is likely to intensify in the years to come.

Another negative for some observers of the maquiladora industry is its lack of integration into the Mexican economy. According to this view, the maquilas are enclaves of U.S., European, and Asian manufacturing, with few linkages to the domestic Mexican economy. The primary piece of evidence in this claim is the share of intermediate inputs that are imported versus the share that are purchased nationally.[30] In 2003, maquilas obtained 97 percent of their material inputs from abroad and only 3 percent from national manufacturers, according to official data.[31] Some observers believe the 3 percent figure to be a gross understatement, but there is little doubt that linkages between the maquiladora and domestic Mexican manufacturing are disappointing despite considerable efforts by Mexican policy makers to induce an increase in the proportion of Mexican supplies. For reasons that are not entirely clear, many firms rely on suppliers from outside Mexico. In part, this situation may be related to the general problems faced by small and medium-sized enterprises in Mexico and the barriers to their development. Among other things, these barriers include

Maquiladora workers making wooden frames, Tijuana.

scarce capital and an unstable banking sector, bureaucratic obstacles to obtaining permits, punitive bankruptcy rules, and a lack of transparency in the legal system. Large firms usually have greater access to capital and to the legal and administrative resources they need to navigate the legal system and the bureaucracy. Hence, much of the investment comes from abroad, and those foreign firms often rely on their own supply networks when they seek parts and other intermediate inputs from small and medium-sized producers.

In the next chapter we consider the environmental impact of manufacturing in the border region. For many observers, the environmental impacts of manufacturing are one of the greatest threats and challenges to the border. We argue that border manufacturing, while not environmentally benign, is far from the most serious environmental problem in the region. Rather, the tremendous growth of cities and their seeming inability to keep up with the construction of urban services poses the greatest challenge to the border environment.

■ ■

CHAPTER 5

THE ENVIRONMENT

The maquiladora boom of the 1980s and 1990s and the accompanying population growth in the Mexican border region dramatically increased strains on the environment. The direct impacts of increased manufacturing activity include the generation of toxic wastes, chemical spills, pressures on water and wastewater treatment, air emissions, and other side effects of industrialization. Indirectly, the growth of border manufacturing increased the demand for labor and contributed to a rapid migration to the border region at a time when many regions of Mexico had fewer employment opportunities. Population in the Mexican border region increased by 31 percent in the decade of the 1980s and by a staggering 45 percent in the decade of the 1990s (see Figure 2.2). Rapid population growth generates its own set of environmental pressures, in particular those related to water quality, wastewater treatment, air quality, waste disposal, and wildlife preservation. Though not all migration to the Mexican border is related to border manufacturing, in light of the border's other attractions, not the least of which is proximity to the United States, the dynamism and job opportunities of border manufacturing acted as an irresistible magnet for many people in the interior of Mexico. The multiplier effect of factory employment generates jobs in retail, construction, government, and all other areas of economic activity, creating employment and acting as a pull factor in attracting migrants to Mexico's northern border.

Rapid population growth on the U.S. side also increased demand for energy plants, intensified U.S. use of shared water resources, put millions more cars on the roads, and generated environmental impacts that spill over into Mexico. Americans complain about sewage overflows from

Tijuana that have contaminated beaches in Southern California, but at the same time Southern California's air pollution flows into Baja California, and pesticides and other farm chemicals often pollute the water flowing south into Mexico. Polluted water and air do not respect international borders, and the environmental pressures associated with growth on one side of an international boundary are not constrained by that boundary. In the U.S.-Mexico border region there is no escape from environmental cost sharing.

BORDER FEARS AND HOPES

In the run-up to the signing of the North American Free Trade Agreement (NAFTA), various governmental and nongovernmental organizations (NGOs) provided estimates of what it would cost to address all the environmental issues in the U.S. and Mexican border regions. The estimates varied greatly, but most were in the $5 billion to $12 billion range.[1] It is probably safe to assume that no one knows for certain what the costs are, in part because there is no consensus as to what would constitute adequate cleanup, restoration, and conservation. It is also probably safe to assume that what most people would consider a reasonable set of actions would require billions of dollars in expenditures.

Before the Clinton administration could seek passage of NAFTA, it was forced to take into account environmental concerns. These concerns were embodied in the side agreement to NAFTA called the North American Agreement on Environmental Cooperation (NAAEC). The major concern for supporters of NAAEC was that polluting firms would migrate to Mexico, where lower standards or lax enforcement might permit them to use less expensive, more pollution-intensive production processes. In other words, Mexico would become a pollution haven where firms could pollute more freely. Herman Daly succinctly captured this view in his 1993 debate with the noted trade economist and proponent of free trade, Jagdish Bhagwati.[2] Daly's position was that free trade creates an environmental "race to the bottom" by allowing firms to relocate production in countries that do not enforce environmental rules. According to Daly, this reduces their costs and gives them a competitive advantage. Further, even if they do not move, the threat of moving gives them an upper hand in seeking a reduction in environmental (and labor) standards and enforcement in the United States (or wherever they are located). Consequently, free trade and the movement of firms set off a competition among countries to see who can lower their environmental standards furthest and fastest.

Bhagwati's position in this debate was that trade and foreign investment can raise living standards and that countries with higher standards are usually cleaner and less polluting. That is, environmental goods such as clean air and water can be analyzed like most (normal) goods, where demand increases as incomes rise. At relatively low levels of income, there may be trade-offs in which people select jobs over a cleaner environment, but as their incomes rise and basic material needs are met, normal preferences for a cleaner environment begin to take precedence. This is often referred to as the environmental Kuznets curve hypothesis, and it stands in direct opposition to the pollution haven hypothesis of Daly and others.[3]

Both the pollution haven hypothesis and the environmental Kuznets curve hypothesis have logical stories to support them, but neither has strong empirical support. Gallagher tested both hypotheses for Mexico in the NAFTA era and found little support for either.[4] In the case of the pollution haven hypothesis, pollution abatement costs are thought to be too small a share of overall operating costs to warrant moving operations to another country. Furthermore, branded multinationals are sensitive to international pressures and seek to maintain a positive image. The wide range of potential pollutants, from solid wastes to hazardous materials, sewage, and various industrial by-products, makes it unlikely that a common pattern such as the Kuznets curve would hold in the relationship between pollution and income. Hence, neither the most optimistic (Kuznets curve) nor the most pessimistic (pollution haven) views of trade and the environment have much empirical validity.

The meaning of this for the border and border manufacturing is straightforward. On the one hand, it is unlikely that manufacturing in the border region took off because manufacturers were trying to escape rigorous environmental standards in their home country. This does not imply that no firms moved to the Mexican side of the border as a way of escaping environmental regulations, nor does it mean that most firms operate according to best practices of environmental standards. Rather, it means that the firms that moved to avoid environmental regulations do not make up a large share of the manufacturing capacity of the border. Anecdotal evidence indicates that furniture manufacturing and metal plating in particular may have moved from Los Angeles to Tijuana in the 1980s as air quality standards in California rose, but as the research surveyed in Chapter 4 indicates, industrial upgrading in the border region is associated with a trend toward more advanced products and processes. These types of firms are almost always associated with higher environmental standards. For example, a 2002 survey of all automotive and electronics firms in three border cities—Tijuana, Mexicali, and Ciudad Juárez—showed that 18 percent of the firms have met ISO 14001 and 14002 environmental control systems standards.[5] Insofar as the International Standards Organization only began to set environmental standards in 1997 and certification is rigorous and voluntary, an 18 percent compliance rate is a positive sign for border manufacturers.

On the other hand, not all manufacturing firms are at the frontier of their industry, and not all industries have moved toward environmentally friendly production processes. Hence, there is no reason to expect that the environmental Kuznets curve will automatically begin to eliminate environmental problems as border incomes rise and border residents begin to push for more rigorous standards and a better environmental infrastructure. In all likelihood there will continue to be a steady stream of new problems related to industrial development and its associated population growth. If environmental conditions on the border are going to improve, the active intervention of private citizens together with local, state, and federal engagement will be required. In addition, addressing the current set of problems would require far more funding than has been available to date.

THE REAL ENVIRONMENTAL PROBLEMS OF THE BORDER

Border environmental problems are primarily a result of rapid population growth, which has worsened the air quality, put increased pressures on water resources, generated large amounts of residential and industrial waste products, and threatened biodiversity.[6] Each of these problems has multiple interrelated causes, and although species loss and other impacts may not be repairable, conditions can be significantly improved, and in some cases the damage can be mitigated where resources, both financial and human, are available.

Air Quality

Deterioration in air quality along the border is the result of both population pressures and added industry. Population growth generates a growing number of automobiles, trucks, and buses, and the lack of paved streets in the new neighborhoods increases the amount of dust in the air. Dust may seem benign, but it can become a toxic stew in places where homes lack connection to sewage treatment systems, or in rural areas where aerial and other pesticide spraying takes place. Lack of sewage connection means that dried fecal matter, household chemicals, motor oil, and other toxins are thrown up into the air, along with the dust particles that become airborne when vehicles drive on dirt roads in the new neighborhoods. In rural areas the same problems occur, plus pesticides and herbicides are mixed with the dust that is thrown up into the air by vehicles. Not surprisingly, border residents have relatively high rates of respiratory problems.[7]

Air quality is further degraded by some types of industrial activity. For example, the informal manufacture of bricks has been a problem in several places, including Tijuana, Tecate, and Ciudad Juárez. Increased manufacturing has also led to a dramatic increase in the number of trucks working in the border region carrying goods between the United States and Mexico. Between 1995 and 2004, the number of trucks crossing into the United States from Mexico rose from 2.9 million to 4.5 million.[8]

Water

Water scarcity is another critical environmental issue for the border regions, where the natural environment ranges from arid to semi-arid. Southern California, Arizona, and much of Baja California already exist on imported water, and El Paso–Juárez, Nogales, and other areas are overdrawing from their aquifers, leaving the future water supply in jeopardy. Mandated low-water-use fixtures, pricing water at its true value, metering all water, and implementing an aggressive leak prevention and repair program would all help to conserve water, yet not many of these policies are in place.[9] Complicating the issues are agreements between the United States and Mexico over shared surface water resources that are largely made at the national level rather than at local levels, while subsurface water stored in natural aquifers is controlled and regulated by state-level governments in the United States.

Joint use of surface waters is the responsibility of the International Boundary and Water Commission (IBWC,) which was constructed in its modern form in 1944. The IBWC is a binational agency with the mission to maintain the boundary between the United States and Mexico, to distribute surface waters according to international agreements, and to address some water sanitation issues. Despite some successes, the IBWC is widely criticized as nontransparent and ineffective, while joint conservation efforts on a large scale are beyond its mandate.[10] There are no local agreements to share surface water resources and the important issue of stored groundwater is beyond the scope of international negotiations.

An example of a water resource that could be more efficiently exploited if there were joint agreements is treated wastewater. The current system of only one source of piped, potable water for all uses is at best inefficient. For example, at present the cost of this treatment to meet California's standards is about $200 per acre-foot plus the cost of a distribution pipeline. Using gray water for landscape irrigation would free the currently used potable water for other purposes. Although in older buildings, this would require expensive retrofitting, in new dwellings it would not add much to the cost of construction and would save on future water bills. There is even more potential in industrial settings that require water in the manufacturing process and where on-site treatment for reuse can be cost-effective. This extends to municipal sewer "mining" to divert sewers' available flow into use for parks, road landscaping, golf courses, sports fields, and so forth.

The potential to partially address the problem of water scarcity through the increased use of gray water emphasizes the asymmetries of the border. Most U.S. cities and counties have environmental infrastructure, if not the capacity to use gray water. Mexican municipios, on the other hand, commonly have significant areas with little or no environmental infrastructure. Hence, the ability to use gray water is even more limited when there is not yet a municipal capacity to supply all households with potable water.

Residential Wastes

Migrants to the Mexican and Texas border regions often settle in new, marginal neighborhoods that lack urban services such as electricity, water, and sewer systems. For example, it is estimated that five acres of land per day are being developed in Tijuana just to keep pace with the population influx.[11] A sewer system is the most expensive service and the last to be installed, often not arriving until ten to twenty years after the birth of a neighborhood. (See Chapter 7 for a history of the development of a marginal neighborhood in Mexicali.) The lack of sewer systems means that more household waste goes untreated and can end up contaminating rivers and the water supply.

This problem is compounded by Mexico's highly centralized system of taxation, which provides far too few resources to border communities. Municipio infrastructure budgets per capita tend to be less than a quarter the size of those on the U.S. side, where most cities and counties have at least some environmental infrastructure. Nonetheless, a similar problem occurs where unincorporated areas, particularly in Texas, have appeared without zoning laws or the authority to impose taxes or levies for local infrastructure development.

During the 1990s, Mexican border communities made a major effort to provide more sewer systems. Between 1992 and 1995, Mexico spent $500 million for sewage plants, solid waste disposal systems, and nature preserves along the border. Mexican census data suggest that this resulted in a significant improvement in providing sewage systems to the border region, as the number of homes without sewage treatment decreased from 31 percent in 1990 to 14 percent in 2000.[12] With the large migration of people to the border region, this effort is barely keeping up with the absolute increase. Nevertheless, the strong binational effects of sewage on shared watersheds have resulted in cooperative efforts to build binational wastewater treatment plants to treat overflow sewage, such as the construction of the plant on the San Diego–Tijuana border in 1998. On-site pretreatment of industrial sewage can also substantially reduce contaminants entering the environment through water discharges and overflows. For larger firms, this occurs with increasing frequency.

Industrial Wastes

The issue of industrial waste disposal may be the most heated border environmental issue and one that was central to the debate over the signing of NAFTA. Many proponents of the pollution haven hypothesis have charged that industrial plants move their operations to Mexico to avoid stricter U.S. environmental regulations, while opponents of this view argue that multinationals adopt worldwide environmental standards and maintain those standards in their foreign plants, including those in Mexico's border regions.[13] Although the pollution haven hypothesis lacks evidence as a general rule, the increase in the total size of the industrial sector has led to a significant rise in emissions and industrial wastes. Urbanization, industrialization, and the developing regional economy have dramatically increased the scale of production and along with it the absolute quantity of some forms of pollution. Although large manufacturing plants and maquiladoras may be contributors, in general, they are much more likely to follow environmental laws.

In contrast, a major source of industrial pollution is small enterprises that are unregulated and unmonitored on the Mexican side of the border. Small metal plating firms, auto paint shops, backyard brick manufacturing, and a host of other toxin-generating activities have no enforceable regulations or waste collection and disposal facilities. For example, the small-scale brick industry in Juárez, which uses kilns that run on wood scraps, old tires, used motor oil, and other nonconventional fuels, was found to be the city's worst source of air pollution.[14] There are too many of these tiny enterprises and they are too small to show up on the regulatory radar screen. Population growth increases the demand for the environmentally damaging services of small, unregulated activities and supplies the informal labor that operates them.

One final complication with respect to managing industrial waste is that there are no official hazardous waste disposal sites in the Mexican border region and there is only one in Mexico, located outside the border region in the state of Nuevo Leon.[15] Under the 1983 La Paz Agreement, maquiladoras are required to return industrial wastes to their country of origin, but there are significant discrepancies between estimates of maquiladora-generated waste and observed Mexico-U.S. transboundary hazardous waste shipments.[16] The dimensions of the problem are also obscured by the fact that an increasing share of hazardous materials used in border manufacturing plants are of Mexican origin and outside the scope of the rules that apply to imported hazardous materials. It is unclear how NAFTA affects this, since the agreement called for the phasing out of the special tax exemptions received by the maquiladoras. Presumably, this would have an impact on the requirements to ship hazardous wastes back across the border, since maquiladoras would be like any other Mexican manufacturing firm, but so far Mexico has been able to maintain the maquiladoras' special tax exemptions through a series of complicated accounting rule changes. Nor are all the problems on the Mexican side. Tomaso and Alm quote the Dallas office of the U.S. Environmental Protection Agency (EPA) to the effect that regulatory agencies do not really know how much hazardous industrial waste is being generated by U.S. firms or how it is being disposed of.[17]

Endangered Wildlife

Border fences and the rapid transformation of untouched land into housing tracts are threatening the continued existence of some species as a result of the loss of cross-border wildlife corridors. Some of these corridors have been protected on the U.S. side of the border, but protection on both sides is needed to preserve the natural domains. Las Californias Binational Conservation Initiative, supported by major environmental groups in both the United States and Mexico, is working on the west end of the border where Tijuana's and San Diego's urban sprawls and the U.S. expansion of the border security fence are reducing the ecological value of thousands of acres of open space and closing the cross-border corridors. Cross-border efforts are under way to try to conserve these all-important arteries, following the model established seventy years ago when Canada and the United States connected Glacier National Park with Canada's Waterton Lakes National Park.[18]

BORDER ENVIRONMENTAL INSTITUTIONS

The International Boundary and Water Commission was the first binational institution with Mexican and U.S. representation. The institutional precursor of the IBWC dates back to the nineteenth century, but it took on its modern form in 1944 when it was given a mandate to maintain the boundary between the two countries and to develop agreements for sharing common surface water resources.[19] Because it dealt with water issues, it can perhaps be considered the first binational environmental institution, but it was not founded with the intention of addressing environmental problems. Nevertheless, it has taken on an environmental role as awareness of water issues has grown. Insofar as it was not conceived to perform this role and it functions as a relatively nontransparent, top-down organization, its effectiveness in addressing environmental issues has been very limited.

In the 1980s, activism over the issue of air pollution from Mexican copper smelters in Sonora generated public pressure for an agreement on air quality in the "Smelter Triangle." This led to the first comprehensive agreement on transboundary pollution, the Agreement on Cooperation for the Protection and Improvement of the Environment in the Border Area, also known as the La Paz Agreement after its signing in La Paz, Mexico, by U.S. president Ronald Reagan and Mexican president Miguel de la Madrid. The U.S. EPA and Mexico's Secretaría de Desarrollo Urbano y Ecología (SEDUE) were designated the national coordinators for the agreement.[20] The La Paz Agreement was a breakthrough because it was the first general statement on the importance to both countries of a healthy border environment. The agreement affirmed the need and the requirement that the United States and Mexico work together to address border problems, defined the border as 100 kilometers deep into each country, and singled out air, water, and land pollution as themes of concern. The agreement further required a minimum of one high-level meeting per year to review issues and activities. The La Paz Agreement also forms the basis for subsequent agreements, including the Integrated Environmental Plan for the Mexican–U.S. Border Area (IBEP, signed in 1992) and the two major follow-on agreements, the Border XXI Program (1996–2000) and Border 2012 (2002–2012).

The Border XXI program and its successor, the Border 2012 Program, carried matters further by setting a number of goals and specific objectives for reaching them. The Border 2012 Program Framework was developed after a series of consultations with states, local governments, tribal representatives, industry, NGOs, and interested citizens. Six themes became the focus of border issues: water, air, and land pollution, environmental health, chemical exposures, and overall environmental performance. The six goals and their objectives are listed in Table 5.1.

The goals and objectives of Border 2012 reflect the concerns of people living along the border. In general, they are the issues one would expect from a region that has experienced urban sprawl and population growth but lacks the infrastructure to handle it. Access to potable water, wastewater treatment and sewage connections and the assessment, monitoring, and improvement of environmental health are central concerns. Several of the issues are transboundary ones and cannot be effectively addressed on one side of the border alone but require coordination, notification, and joint investments to improve conditions. For example, the cross-border sharing of water resources as a result of the physical geography of the region means that safe drinking water, water for industrial and agricultural uses, and proper treatment of wastewater are mutual concerns, and that actions (or inaction) on one side of the border have consequences for the other side. Hence the emphasis on the development of information systems that can be shared and the development of institutional mechanisms for consultation and action.

Mechanisms and resources for binational action to address border environmental concerns were included under the auspices of NAFTA. Two institutions, the North American Development Bank (NADB) and the Border Environment Cooperation Commission (BECC), were established for the purpose of working together to evaluate potential solutions to border environmental problems and to provide access to funding. The institutions were created with separate yet interdependent missions so that each could develop specific forms of expertise in addressing border environmental problems. The role of the BECC is to evaluate the environmental integrity of proposed projects and to ensure community support for the project. The NADB's role is to assist projects approved by the BECC through the provision of partial funding and to assist in locating grants and loans to cover the rest of the project. The NADB also provides technical assistance to local communities that have not managed large projects requiring borrowed money, and it must certify the technical financial plan of projects it is involved with. Both the Border XXI Program (1996–2000) and Border 2012 (2002–2012) work with the BECC-NADB.

TABLE 5.1 *Goals and Objectives of the Border 2012 Program Framework*

Goal	Objectives
Reduce water contamination	Increase homes connected to potable source and wastewater treatment system. Assess surface water sources and improve their quality. Monitor and evaluate coastal waters. Assess water systems to identify opportunities for improvement.
Improve air quality	Reduce air emissions to meet each country's national standards.
Reduce land contamination	Improve infrastructure and institutions for treating hazardous wastes. Consolidate linking of U.S. and Mexican waste-tracking systems. Clean up three largest depositories of used tires. Develop a binational cleanup and restoration program for hazardous sites.
Improve environmental health in the region	Evaluate and track respiratory health in children. Evaluate methods of tracking water quality–related gastro-intestinal illness. Develop a binational method for reporting pesticide poisoning and reduce exposures. Build capacity through development of graduate programs and training of health care workers.
Reduce chemical exposures, either from accident or terrorism	Develop mechanisms for cross-border notification. Establish local joint-contingency planning for emergencies.
Improve overall environmental performance through compliance, enforcement, pollution prevention and environmental stewardship	Increase firms using environmental auditing systems. Identify most hazardous environmental risks to human health. Improve responsiveness to citizen complaints, compliance, and enforcement.

SOURCE: U.S. Environmental Protection Agency (2006).

TABLE 5.2 *BECC Project Certifications as of December 2005*

Projects	Total	U.S.	Mexico
Water and wastewater	67	45	22
Solid waste	13	4	9
Air quality	4	0	4
Conservation	21	20	1
Total	105	69	36

SOURCE: Border Environmental Cooperation Commission–North American Development Bank (2005).

TABLE 5.3 *NADB Financing (in millions of USD) as of December 31, 2005*

	Total	U.S.	Mexico
Projects requiring NADB financing	91	61	30
Projects with approved financing	90	61	29
Total project costs	2,347.9	1,024.1	1,323.8
Total NADB participation	703.8	360.4	343.4
Total financing contracted	658.0	324.6	333.4
Total financing disbursed	378.6	180.4	198.2

SOURCE: Border Environmental Cooperation Commission–North American Development Bank (2005).

Table 5.2 shows that the BECC had certified 105 projects as of the end of 2005, with sixty-nine of the projects in the United States and thirty-six in Mexico. Nearly two-thirds of the certified projects have focused on water and wastewater treatment. Table 5.3 shows the amount of funds disbursed by the NADB. As of the end of 2005, ninety-one projects with a total cost of $2.35 billion required NADB financing, and the NADB had disbursed $378.6 million of the $703.8 million it was expected to provide. Through 2005, despite Mexico having fewer projects, total project costs and the financing contracted and disbursed were slightly greater on the Mexican side of the border ($198 million for Mexico, compared with $180 million for the United States). From the projects funded it appears that the NADB is attempting to balance funding between the two counties. However, equal apportionment of expenditures between Mexico and the United States is probably not optimal, given that credit and access to financial capital are more constrained in Mexico and the needs for infrastructure improvements are greater. The greater needs in Mexico are reflected in the 2005 change to the definition of the border. The BECC-NADB institutions redefined the border region as extending 300 kilometers into Mexico and still 100 kilometers into the United States.

Assessment of the performance of the BECC and NADB is a moving target. Nevertheless, many observers have been highly critical of the slowness of the institutions. More than ten years after their creation, they have identified $2.35 billion in projects, but assessments made around the time NAFTA was implemented (1994) put regional needs in the $5–$12 billion range. The U.S. Government Accountability Office (GAO) cited estimates that $8 billion was needed for border environmental infrastructure over the first ten years of NAFTA.[21] A decade later, less than one-fourth of the needed amount had been identified, and actual BECC-NADB participation amounts to less than one-third of what the GAO identified.

The response of the NADB and BECC to these criticisms is that they have had to move slowly because their work requires more than project evaluation and financing. In addition, they see their role as essential to the development of human capital that can assess a situation, evaluate environmental needs, and propose a viable project, including mechanisms for financing it. That is, the NADB and BECC have responded to their critics with the defense that they are investing time and human resources in training community members and other nonexperts, since many communities in the border region have needs but lack the trained personnel to propose a viable project that addresses them. Furthermore, the NADB does not provide the entire amount of funding required, and it must loan at market rates of interest, which frequently puts the project out of reach of local communities with limited resources. To make a project feasible, communities often must blend grants with loans to make repayment of the loans feasible and to reduce the burden of debt repayment. This adds another level of complexity to projects, however, as most communities have been accustomed to grants but not loans, and they must train personnel to manage the loans, find grants to blend with the loans, and ensure a revenue stream to pay back the loans.

The reduction in border environmental problems is not simply an issue of environmental technology or environmental infrastructure but is also dependent on financial resources and the development of local human capital that can manage all the pieces of a project, from the proposal stage to financing, construction, and management. To date, funding for environmental infrastructure has been dismally low, especially in view of the estimates from the early 1990s of a $5–$12 billion deficit in border infrastructure. During the first ten years of NAFTA, NADB loans averaged $40 million per year, split between the two countries—hardly a visible drop in the bucket. Neither country is doing its share. At the same time, it is not the NADB that is to blame but its mandate to loan only at market rates. The small rural communities along the border tend to be poor communities with big needs that cannot afford the loans. They need grants of aid and, if loans, at lower, preferential rates. The environmental problems of the border will not be solved without both governments increasing cooperation and allocation of resources (cold, hard cash) to create adequate infrastructure to ameliorate the effects of rapid population and industrial growth.

LOOKING FORWARD

Forecasts of population growth in the border region indicate that the border population will increase to between 19.4 million and 24.1 million by 2020.[22] Even the more conservative estimate is a 60 percent increase over the estimated 2005 population. Nearly all this expected population growth will be in urban areas, where the ability of local governments to keep up with the energy, water, and waste treatment needs of their new residents is already overextended. Border residents have a much higher rate of respiratory problems and are water mining their aquifers to satisfy current needs. Untreated wastewater flows into watersheds in many areas, while sewage treatment is woefully inadequate. Clearly, the environmental challenges of rapid population growth are not going away and are likely to intensify.

There are no easy solutions to the environmental issues confronting residents and wildlife on the border, but two points should stand out. First, there is a great need for more funding. At the margin, another dollar spent at the U.S. border is likely to generate a much greater benefit than expenditures elsewhere in the United States, and whereas the Mexican side is relatively better off than many other places in Mexico, the rapid growth of Mexico's border population has turned it into a region that is vastly underserved by Mexican federal authorities. Meeting the goals of Border 2012 will require far more money from both sides than has been invested to date. The second point is that additional funding will probably be contingent on one of two possibilities—either an environmental catastrophe of some form or other or a coordinated, binational effort by border residents, their representatives, and their local governments. As Papademetriou and Myers have shown in a variety of contexts across a wide range of borders around the world, border communities can influence national policies, but first they must know what they want, and they must speak with a unified voice.[23]

■ ■

CHAPTER 6

FORMAL AND INFORMAL LABOR

Jorge and Gabriel are from different generations, but they each view the border as a place of opportunity. Jorge left his home town, Torreón, in the interior of Mexico to look for work in the border town of Piedras Negras. Piedras Negras was full of young men like Jorge who came to find work and better wages. Jobs were scarce and paid badly in Torreón, but Jorge knew he could find work in Piedras Negras because his cousins had migrated there and had kept him posted about job openings in the border manufacturing plants that were springing up. He knew that if he stayed in Torreón he would not be able to save the money he needed to open his own business, and the border looked like a place where he could earn enough to save something so that he could eventually return and have a better life. Twenty years before Jorge migrated, Gabriel came to the border, also to have a better life. Gabriel's dream, however, was to cross into the United States and to earn a better living on the other side. He chose Matamoros as his border crossing point, and while getting ready to cross over, he set up a shoeshine business on a corner near the market and began to earn a modest but steady income. Twenty years later, he still shines shoes in Matamoros.

The experiences of Jorge and Gabriel and their perceptions of the border as a place of opportunity are not very different from the pattern of events on the U.S. side. During each of the five decades between 1950 and 2000, both the Mexican and the U.S. border region added new jobs and workers at a pace that exceeded the respective countries' national average. In some decades the difference was striking. For example, between 1980 and 1990, the U.S. border region added workers at a rate that was nearly three times faster than the U.S. average, and in Mexico during the same decade, the rate was almost four times greater on the border. The 1980s were unusual in this regard, but in most of the years between 1950 and 2000, employment growth in the border region averaged between 40 and 80 percent higher than the national rate. In part this excess reflects the demographic and migration trends discussed in Chapter 2, since job growth responds to population growth. But without doubt, causation goes in both directions, as people migrate to where they think the jobs are. For both Mexico and the United States, the border has been one of those places of opportunity.

BOX 6.1 DEFINITIONS OF LABOR FORCE PARTICIPATION AND UNEMPLOYMENT RATES

Economists view the decision to work as a trade-off between leisure and income. The need for income induces people to give up leisure and to join the workforce. Customarily, economists do not include work done in the home without pay as part of the economic output of a society and therefore do not count it as work, even though it is essential for a family's survival and even though it produces private and social benefits. A complete economic analysis should also include home-based work. For example, in terms of the provision of services, there is no difference between child care when provided by a family member and when purchased from a nonfamily member. Nevertheless, the inclusion of household production is beyond the scope of our analysis, and we will focus instead on production outside the home.

The labor force participation rate (LFPR) is defined as the percentage of the total working-age population that is economically active, where economically active means that they are either working or actively looking for work:

LFPR = Economically active/Working-age population,

where

Economically active = Working + Looking for work.

In other words, the LFPR is the fraction of working-age people who are contributing or seeking to contribute to society's output of goods and services produced outside the home.

Unemployment is defined as the share of the labor force (economically active population) that is actively looking for work:

Unemployment rate = Looking for work/Economically active population.

THE LABOR FORCE PARTICIPATION RATE

International comparisons in labor force participation, such as those between Mexico and the United States, are difficult to make, because the definition of the "working-age population" tends to vary with income. (A formal definition of the labor force participation rate is provided in Box 6.1.) In particular, the minimum age for entering the labor force tends to move upward as incomes grow, the economy develops, and the age norm for school leaving rises. In the United States, for example, the minimum

With some relatively minor variations, both the United States and Mexico follow accepted international practices for measuring unemployment rates, with both countries using monthly household surveys. The Mexican household survey, called the *Encuesta Nacional de Empleo Urbano*, is currently conducted in the thirty-four most important urban areas. The omission of smaller urban places and all rural areas causes the measured rate to be slightly higher, since rural areas tend to have lower unemployment rates in Mexico. The U.S. survey, called the *Current Population Survey* (*CPS*), is national and includes places of all sizes, both rural and urban. The *CPS* is used to calculate a national figure, which in turn becomes one piece of information used by the Bureau of Labor Statistics and state and county labor offices to calculate state- and county-level unemployment rates. Table 6.1 summarizes the data sources.

TABLE 6.1 *Data Sources for Unemployment Estimates*

Level	United States	Mexico
Nation	Monthly national household survey (*Current Population Survey, CPS*)	Monthly household survey of the 34 largest cities (*Encuesta Nacional de Empleo Urbano, ENEU*)
City or county	National survey adjusted by local surveys of businesses, economic conditions, and employers	Same as above for monthly data; an annual survey (*Encuesta Nacional de Empleo*) includes rural areas and smaller towns, but only once a year

SOURCES: U.S. Bureau of Labor Statistics, (n.d.), *Local Area Unemployment Statistics;* INEGI (2005); Fleck and Sorrentino (1994); Martin (2000).

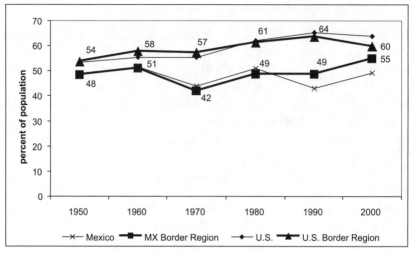

FIGURE 6.1. Labor force participation rates in Mexico and the United States nationally and in the border regions, 1950–2000.

age for entering the labor force was fourteen in census years 1950 and 1960 but sixteen from 1980 onward. In Mexico, the minimum working age is defined as twelve years old.

Figure 6.1 shows that over the whole period, labor force participation rates (LFPR) in the United States nationally and in its border region were higher than in Mexico. In 2000, the national differences between the LFPR in the United States and Mexico was about 15 percent (64 percent versus 49 percent), while in the border region the difference was only 5 percent (60 percent in the United States versus 55 percent in Mexico).[1] In other words, labor force patterns are reminiscent of other patterns: the U.S. border is below the U.S. average, the Mexican border is above the Mexican average, and the overall difference between the United States and Mexico is much smaller in the border regions than it is nationally.

Both countries exhibited a strong increase in LFPR during the second half of the twentieth century. As Figure 6.1 shows, U.S. rates rose from 53 percent in 1950 to 64–65 percent in 1990–2000. Although Mexico's case is less dramatic overall, after 1970 there was a strong increase in LFPR, both nationally and, especially, in the border region. Up until 1990, the re-ported LFPR in Mexico was lower in the border region than for the nation as a whole, but beginning in 1990, the border LFPR exceeded the national level. This result was undoubtedly due to the increasing employment, par-ticularly female employment, in the maquiladora manufacturing plants along the border. These plants offered lots of jobs and attracted large numbers of workers to the border, especially after 1980.

On the U.S. side of the border, during the 1950s and 1960s the U.S. border region had a slightly higher LFPR than the United States as a whole, but beginning sometime in the 1970s, rates began to fall below the national rate. In 2000, 64 percent of the national working-age population participated in the labor force, while 60 percent of that population did so in the U.S. border region. Both female and male LFPRs in the border region were below the national average, a fact that has two possible explanations. First, unemployment in the U.S. border region tends to be higher than the national average, so that some workers may become discouraged and drop out of the labor force altogether. Second, the U.S. informal economy is probably larger in the border region. Consequently, there may be more people working in an unrecorded cash economy, where they appear to be out of the labor force but in fact are not reporting their income and employment.

There are two likely reasons for the lower LFPR in Mexico than in the United States during the same time period. First, the definition of working age in Mexico includes young people ages twelve to fifteen, whereas these workers are not included in the U.S. data. Over the period from 1950 to 2000, we would expect to see a larger proportion of twelve- to fifteen-year-olds remaining in school, putting downward pressure on the measured LFPR. Second, the LFPR in Mexico is strongly influenced by the role of women. Mexican women participate in work outside the home at much lower rates than their U.S. counterparts (Figure 6.2). In 2000, the female LFPR for Mexico was 30 percent, whereas it was 57 percent for the United States. Again, the gap between U.S. and Mexican female LFPR in the border region is smaller (36 percent versus 52 percent) than the national gap, as employment opportunities for women in the Mexican border region are much greater than in Mexico overall. Large differences in the female LFPR are normal when one is comparing a high-income, industrial economy such as the United States to a middle-income, developing economy such as Mexico because in general, social and economic development are associated with greater participation by women in the market economy.

In fact, most of the trend toward increasing labor force participation in the United States and Mexico is a result of the increased female LFPR (see Figure 6.2). In the United States, the female LFPR was already rising before 1950, in part owing to the labor shortages during World War II, which drew women into the labor force and removed some of the social stigma of working outside the home. In the United States, by 1950 29 percent of working-age women and 26 percent of those living in the border region

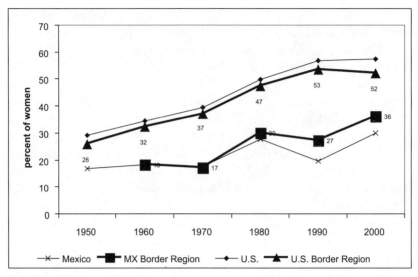

FIGURE 6.2. Female labor force participation rates in Mexico and the United States nationally and in the border regions, 1950–2000.

were working outside the home. This figure increased steadily to more than 50 percent by 1990. Meanwhile, in Mexico, the trend toward increasing female LFPR did not start until after 1970. Although the national and border rates were close to equal at that point, women's participation increased faster in the border region, most likely as a result of expanding employment opportunities for women in the maquiladoras. The 2000 rate of 36 percent in the Mexican border region was roughly equal to the 1970 U.S. border women's LFPR.

An important reason for the increase in women's participation in the labor force is the technological developments in housekeeping that have occurred, reducing the number of hours needed to care for the home and freeing women to do other things. This assist from labor-saving technology is often overlooked, since household production is not counted as part of the national output. In fact, labor studies frequently refer to women who do not work outside the home as having chosen leisure over work, even though caring for a home and family is real and necessary work. Further, our system of national accounts tracks recorded production but does not take into account the increases in efficiency and productivity in the household sector. Home appliances—vacuum cleaners and automatic washing machines—are counted as consumer goods instead of capital goods. Yet the development of labor-saving devices for the home expanded enormously during the twentieth century. The progression from washboards

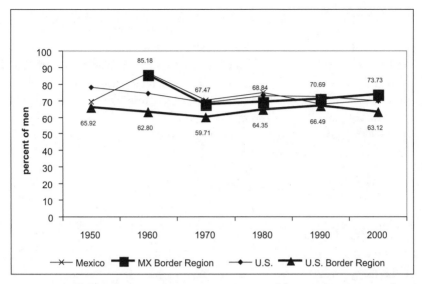

FIGURE 6.3. Male labor force participation rates in Mexico and the United States nationally and in the border regions, 1950–2000.

to wringer washing machines to automatic washing machines and from clotheslines to dryers has cut the time it takes to do the family laundry from one full day a week to a few hours. Vacuum cleaners, dishwashers, and better cleaning liquids, along with store-bought clothing and prepared foods, have decreased the number of hours per week that women need to take care of household chores.

In Mexico, especially in poor areas, home technology, including such things as running water, has been much slower to arrive. For example, in 1960, only 21 percent of Mexican houses had bathrooms with running water, and only 28 percent of houses had those amenities in the Mexican border region. By 2000, two-thirds of houses in the Mexican border region and slightly over half the houses nationally had bathrooms with running water. This is one reason why it is not surprising that women's LFPR did not begin to rise until after 1970 and why rates in Mexico are still lower than those in the United States. However, the LFPR of Mexican women is still rising, while in the United States it appears to have leveled off.

Trends for male LFPR are shown in Figure 6.3. In the United States, the rate decreased from 78 percent to 69 percent between 1950 and 1970 as U.S. men retired earlier, depended more on their wives for the family income, stayed in school longer, and entered the labor force later. Since 1970, both U.S. and Mexican male LFPRs have hovered around 70 percent. With respect to the border regions on the Mexican side, the male LFPR is higher than the Mexican national rate, while in the U.S. border region the male LFPR is lower than the national rate. In addition, U.S. men in the border region participate in the labor force at a lower rate than either their Mexican border counterparts or Mexican men nationally. In 2000, the U.S. border region male LFPR was 63 percent, eleven percentage points lower than the Mexican male LFPR. There are probably a number of explanations for the relatively low LFPR for men living in the U.S. border region, but two causes stand out: high unemployment rates and the informal economy. We look at these two issues in the next two sections.

UNEMPLOYMENT

Unemployment is defined as the percentage of the labor force that is currently without work. (See Box 6.1 for a detailed discussion of measuring unemployment.) National definitions vary, however, because definitions of the labor force and employment vary. In the United States, the labor force is considered to be the noninstitutionalized population, age sixteen years or older, that is either working or actively looking for work. Mexico's definition considers persons age twelve and older because it is recognized that young teens are often valuable contributors to family income. Both countries classify persons who have stopped looking for work (so-called discouraged workers) as out of the labor force, and therefore neither employed nor unemployed. Both countries also define one hour of work for pay during the reference week as employment. In the United States, however, family workers who receive no pay are considered unemployed as long as they work less than fifteen hours per week and are actively seeking other work. In Mexico, such workers are considered employed. Another minor difference concerns laid-off workers who are waiting to return to work within the next four weeks, or who expect to start a job within a month. These workers are considered employed in Mexico and unemployed in the United States. Table 6.2 summarizes the conceptual differences in the measurements.

It is possible to obtain a rough idea of how much the differences in definitions matter by adjusting Mexico's unemployment rate to take into account measurement differences. Martin does that for the 1990s and finds that reported Mexican unemployment would be 1.1 percentage points higher, on average, between 1991 and 1998 if Mexico used the same definitions as the U.S.[2] In Table 6.3, a comparison is made of five Mexican urban areas on the border with the U.S. counties across from them. Several U.S. counties appear to have very high rates of unemployment and the Mexican

TABLE 6.2 *A Comparison of Employment and Unemployment Concepts*

Condition	Mexico	United States
Work 1 hour for pay	Employed	Employed
Work without pay less than 15 hours in a family business	Employed	Unemployed
Laid off, expecting recall within 4 weeks	Employed	Unemployed
Waiting to start a job within 4 weeks	Employed	Unemployed
Part-time worker, seeking full-time work	Employed	Employed
No job, not looking for work	Out of the labor force, neither employed nor unemployed	Out of the labor force, neither employed nor unemployed

SOURCES: Fleck and Sorrentino (1994); Martin (2000).

TABLE 6.3 *A Sample of Border Unemployment Rates, 2000*

	Mexico		United States		
Urban Area	Unempl. Rate	Adj. Unempl. Rate*	County (Major City)	BLS	Census
Ciudad Juárez	0.8	1.9	El Paso	6.8	9.1
Matamoros	2.2	3.3	Cameron (Brownsville)	7.0	11.4
Mexicali	1.3	2.4	Imperial	17.5	12.5
Nuevo Laredo	1.1	2.2	Webb (Laredo)	6.2	9.3
Tijuana	1.1	2.2	San Diego	3.9	5.6
Mexico	2.2	3.3	U.S.	4.0	3.7

*Comparable to U.S.

SOURCES: U.S. Census Bureau (2000); U.S. Bureau of Labor Statistics (n.d.), *Local Area Unemployment Statistics*; INEGI (2005); Martin (2000).

rates are low, even after adjustment. In addition, the gap between U.S. border counties and their Mexican counterparts is much larger than the gap between the United States and Mexico overall.

The high rates of unemployment on the U.S. side are not unique to the year or to the sample of counties in Table 6.3. The simple average unemployment rate for the entire sample of border counties in 2000 was 8.4 percent, compared to the U.S average of 4.0 percent. In 1990, the U.S. border average was 12.3 percent (the U.S. national average was 5.6 percent), and more recently, in 2004, the border county average was 10.1 percent (the U.S. average was 5.5 percent).[3] In other words, the unemployment rate in border counties was about twice the national average unemployment rate. Schmaedick suggests that in at least a few cases, abnormally high averages in the border region are statistical artifacts, as the method for calculating local area (state and county) unemployment rates may be thrown off by a large foreign labor force that migrated daily or weekly.[4] This would apply, for example, to the two agricultural counties that are next to Mexicali: Imperial County, California, and Yuma County, Arizona. Imperial's 2004 rate of unemployment was 22.1 percent and Yuma's was 23.4 percent. Both counties have a large agricultural labor force that lives in Mexico and migrates, often on a daily basis, to the U.S. side.

When one looks at the U.S.-Mexico comparisons in Table 6.3, it is probably surprising to see such low unemployment rates in Mexico. Conventional wisdom often discounts the Mexican rate as either not comparable to U.S. rates or as politically manipulated to make the economic policies of the incumbent president look better. Given a persistent shortage of jobs at the national level and the tremendous out-migration from Mexico, how can unemployment rates be so low? Both the United States and Mexico use methods and concepts that are recommended by the International Labor Office, with the result that differences in who is counted as employed and unemployed are very minor. Hence the low Mexican rates are not due to conceptual differences or measurement methods. In addition, every nation's statistical office may feel political pressure, but contrary to the idea of widespread corruption or political manipulation, the Mexican data collection agency is professional and nonpartisan. It is hard to believe that the U.S. Census Bureau or the U.S. Bureau of Labor Statistics does any better.

An alternative explanation for the low unemployment rates in Mexico is that they are accurately measured, but that the socioeconomic context of unemployment is very different from that in the United States. Many poor people in Mexico have no savings to fall back on when they lose a job, and there is nothing equivalent to unemployment insurance or other income maintenance programs for the unemployed. Hence, a bout of unemployment puts extreme pressure on people to find work as quickly as possible. In addition, Mexico has a very large informal economy that can absorb workers. The work may not pay well, and the hours may be irregular, but for most people, informal jobs are better than no jobs and may mean the difference between eating and not eating. Informality is such an important concept that it is worth looking at in more detail.

THE INFORMAL ECONOMY

The informal economy includes a wide variety of activities, ranging from unlicensed street vendors and repair shops in the poorest Mexican colonias (neighborhoods) of cities to nannies, elder care, and restaurant workers in the most upscale neighborhoods of relatively well-off urban areas on both sides of the border. Debates over the meaning of informality have been going on for decades. In the early 1980s, the International Labor Office's Regional Employment Program (known as PREALC, from the Spanish name) explained the informal economy as a survival strategy used by rural migrants who arrived in urban centers only to find that employment opportunities were limited and they needed to create their own jobs.[5] It was described as a labor-intensive sector with the advantages of ease of entry and the possibility of flexible hours but the disadvantages of low wages, lack of security, lack of government or property rights protection, and lack of opportunity to create human and physical capital. Since this sector was associated with poverty, low productivity, and underemployment, a decrease in its size (a decrease in "underemployment") was seen by the ILO and others as a goal of economic development and a measure of economic progress.

While we know that participation in the informal economy cuts across all income classes and all types of firms, the unknown elements of this part of our economy are far greater than what is known. Researchers are divided over a number of basic questions, such as the value of goods and services produced, the level of employment, its links to formal sector production, and whether it is a dynamic, entrepreneurial economy or a dead-end, subsistence economy. Even the name is in dispute: informal, subterranean, underground, submerged, hidden, invisible, shadow, parallel, irregular, and unrecorded. Regardless of the preferred adjective, most analysts refer to a set of unreported activities that may or may not be legal but are largely outside official record keeping and usually do not appear in the statistics of national income and product. The term informal economy is used in this chapter as a way to refer to activities that are not licensed or registered with the proper authorities but are not purely illegal in themselves. In other words, these activities may be illegal as a result of failure to comply with regulatory and tax laws but would be permitted if properly registered. This definition rules out the drug trade, illegal gambling, and prostitution (where it is illegal), among other things.[6]

The informal economy is present on both sides of the border, but its characteristics and relative importance vary inversely with the degree of affluence. Its role is undoubtedly greater on the Mexican side, but it has been less intensively studied in the United States. This difference in our knowledge about the informal economy reflects the fact that in developing nations in general, and in Mexico in particular, the informal economy takes on several key roles in the economic and social life of cities and towns. It serves as a crucial survival strategy for the poor, as a significant provider of jobs to the unemployed, as a training ground for entrepreneurs, as a source of new businesses, and as part of a cost-reducing strategy for modern businesses. Within industrialized economies, the informal economy is generally viewed as a nuisance and as representing a marginal set of activities that are less essential to the overall economic performance of a region or a city. While this may or may not be true in the U.S. border region, we can be certain that the large concentration of immigrants and the importance of the tourism sector in many areas along the U.S. border ensure that the informal economy is more important in the U.S. border region than in many other parts of the United States. The characteristics most commonly associated with the informal economy are given in Table 6.4.

When there is no unemployment compensation, or where government-sponsored income maintenance programs do not exist or are very weak,

TABLE 6.4 *Characteristics of the Informal Economy*

Mexico	United States
Small, family-owned firms (1–5 employees)	Small firms
Labor-intensive production	Labor-intensive production
Spread through the economy, but most important in retail trade, repair services, domestic services, hotels, restaurants	Concentrated in a few sectors, especially in restaurants, bars, hotels, agriculture, construction, auto repair, apparel, domestic services, furniture manufacturing
Low barriers to entry	Low barriers to entry
Lack of capital	Lack of capital
Unregulated and competitive markets	Large immigrant workforce
Unrecorded, unreported, and untaxed	Unrecorded, unreported, and untaxed

the informal sector provides a way to survive. This is one of the reasons why Mexico's measured unemployment rate is so low: it has an informal economy, estimated to employ more than half the labor force, where workers can find jobs selling oranges on street corners, firing bricks in a backyard kiln, or working at some other low-paying, low-skilled, unregulated task. The U.S. border region has an informal economy as well, for example in construction, tourism, and domestic services such as cleaning, gardening, and handiwork, but the necessity that drives many workers into informality is not as great.

The view of the informal sector as an employer of last resort has continued into the present, but with a greater appreciation of the effort and cleverness of informal sector agents, who create their own businesses and opportunities. For example, Hernando de Soto argues that the informal sector is a creative, entrepreneurial response by migrants who are excluded from formal sector jobs in the cities. He agrees with the ILO that the informal sector developed from rural migration that encountered excessive regulation that prevented the formal recognition of new businesses and limited the creation of new, formal sector jobs.[7] For example, the World Bank estimates that it takes fifty-eight days on average to open a new business in Mexico. Permits and forms require eight steps, and in the end, new business owners spend the equivalent of 16.7 percent of an average

Informal sector worker, Ciudad Juárez.

Mexican income just complying with the procedures. In addition, new businesses must deposit in a bank an amount equivalent to 15.5 percent of an average income.[8] By comparison, the United States requires five steps on average, which take five days and cost 0.6 percent of an average income. New businesses are not required to deposit any amount in a bank. Given the time and money it takes to create a formal sector business in Mexico, it is not surprising that migrants to the border or other regions usually do not obtain formal recognition for their small businesses, and as a consequence, many, like Gabriel, the shoeshine man introduced at the beginning of the chapter, remain in undercapitalized, low-skilled activities. In effect, the informal sector may actually be a two-tiered sector where the upper tier of resourceful entrepreneurial activity is a creative response to bureaucratic overregulation. The much larger lower tier is a low-wage sector that is providing low-capital, low-productivity, last-resort jobs.[9] A large informal sector has a number of direct and indirect costs to an economy, including the loss of potential human capital and lower output.[10] Most analysts continue to agree that "formalization" of the informal sector is an important component of economic development.

It is difficult to precisely measure the size of the informal sector. Definitions of informality vary, participants usually do not want to be observed or examined, and the large number of measurement methods result in different estimates of its size. One definition is that it includes all nonprofessional workers who have no benefits. By this definition, 63.9 percent of Mexico's workforce was in the informal sector in 1999, up from 43.2 percent in 1990.[11] Schneider (2002) measured informality in 110 economies around 2000 with a model that took into account multiple indicators. He estimates that the informal economy is equivalent to 30.1 percent of Mexico's gross national product (GNP) and 8.8 percent of the United States'. Although no single number can accurately capture the size of the informal economy, the labor force numbers in Table 6.5 are more or less consistent with Schneider's estimate that the informal sector output is equal to 30.1 percent of Mexico's GNP. Given that informal sector firms generally have lower levels of productivity than the formal sector, it would take more than 30.1 percent of the labor force in informal employment to produce that share of income.

Table 6.5 provides two indicators of informality in Mexican border cities. The sample includes all workers, professional and nonprofessional, but is limited to the major urban areas included in the monthly labor market survey, *Encuesta Nacional de Empleo Urbano*. The two indicators are the percentage of the labor force that works in microsized enterprises of one

TABLE 6.5 *Indicators of the Informal Economy, Mexican Border Cities, 2000*

	Condition of Work (Percent of Labor Force)	
Municipio	Work in Microenterprises of 1–5 Workers	Work Without Benefits
Ciudad Juárez	27.5	32.1
Matamoros	32.4	37.7
Mexicali	27.8	35.8
Nuevo Laredo	40.5	46.0
Tijuana	33.2	39.0
Mexico*	40.9	46.1

*Based on forty-eight major urban areas.

SOURCE: INEGI (2005).

to five workers and the percentage of the labor force that receives no benefits through their place of work. Formal, private sector workers in Mexico are required to be registered with the Instituto Mexicano de Seguro Social (IMSS), through which they receive health care and other work-related benefits.[12] Hence, when workers receive no benefits, it indicates that they are not formally registered and most likely are in the informal economy. The micro-enterprise indicator is useful, as many studies have shown that the majority of informal sector workers are in these types of enterprises, mostly no doubt because of lack of capital and the inability of informal businesses to enter credit markets. Table 6.5 indicates that 40.9 to 46.1 percent of the total labor force is in the informal economy. More important, Table 6.5 indicates that the informal economy on the Mexican border is important, but less important than it is nationally. This goes hand in hand with the facts that the Mexican border region provides more opportunities for formal sector jobs and that the overall unemployment rate tends to be low.

WOMEN IN THE BORDER LABOR FORCE

In the Mexican border region, the maquiladora industries increased the demand for formal sector female labor and more than any other single factor may be responsible for higher female LFPRs after 1970. There are variations in the relationships between and among gender, work, and family,

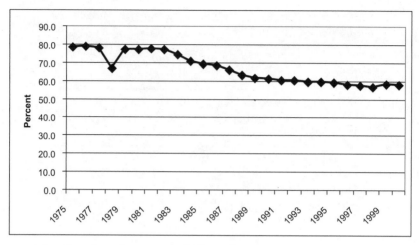

FIGURE 6.4. Percentage of women maquiladora workers, 1975–1999.

however. For example, Anderson and Dimon analyzed the effects of women's choices between work in the home, formal sector employment, and informal sector employment, in a Mexican border municipio (Tijuana). They found that the existence of formal sector maquiladora jobs increased the probability of single women's participation in the formal labor sector, making it more likely for a single woman to work in the formal economy rather than in the home or the informal sector in comparison with single women in a nonborder municipio (Torreón). On the other hand, the increase in formal sector jobs appeared to have very little impact on married women's decision to work outside the home.[13]

Mexico established its Border Industrialization Program in 1965 to provide jobs for male farm workers who were not allowed reentry into the United States after the ending of the guest worker program in 1964. Ironically, however, the majority of jobs in the maquiladora plants went to women: in 1975, 79 percent of the maquiladora workforce was female. After 1983, the proportion of female workers started a gradual decline, eventually falling to below 58 percent in 2000 (Figure 6.4). Women were preferred by Mexican managers, who argued that the nature of assembly work, especially electronic assembly, required patience and dexterity, traits they attributed to women. They also viewed women as more passive, more willing to follow directions, and less likely to organize into unions. By 2000, Ciudad Juárez had the highest percentage of working-aged women who participated in the labor force, 40 percent. Not coincidentally, this city also had the highest concentration of maquiladoras.

The opening of formal sector job opportunities for women has some important implications, since the wages earned by women working in the maquiladoras provide some economic and social independence. When women, especially married women, enter the labor market, they undermine gender expectations; consequently, they often enter the job market only out of dire economic need. A wife or daughter working in the formal sector, and especially in a leadership role, may be threatening to husbands and fathers.[14] In the workplace, conflicts are likely to take shape over working conditions for women (unequal pay, sexual harassment, occupational discrimination), changing gender roles, and the challenge to patriarchal social structures. No social change is without conflict, however, and greater equality and more options for women are an essential component of development.

SHIFTING WORK PATTERNS

Economic growth and development in both the United States and Mexico has caused major changes in the level and kinds of economic activity that are important along the border. In 1950, agriculture was extremely impor-

Women working in a Tijuana maquiladora.

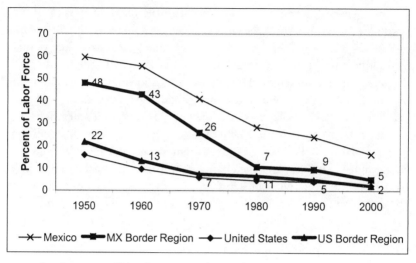

FIGURE 6.5. Percentage of labor force in agriculture and mining, 1950–2000.

tant, even as both sides of the border were becoming urbanized, and as late as 1980, the border region was described as a rural economy.[15] As shown in Figure 6.5, the Mexican border region has a much higher proportion of the labor force in agriculture than the U.S. border region, but the figure is considerably lower than the proportion for Mexico as a whole. Further, the relative decline in agriculture along the border has been dramatic on both sides. For example, between 1950 and 2000, the share of the labor force in agriculture (and mining) fell from 48 percent to 5 percent in the Mexican border region, and from 22 percent to 2 percent in the U.S. border region.[16]

At the same time that agriculture's role was shrinking, on the Mexican side of the border, the role of manufacturing was growing (Figure 6.6). Because of its relationship to job availability, economic growth, migration, and foreign exchange earnings, the growth of manufacturing has been one of the most important changes along the border over the past fifty years. It has also helped to insulate the Mexican border from the Mexican business cycle, and has served as one of the primary conduits for U.S.-Mexico integration. Before the mid-1970s, manufacturing on the Mexican border reflected the national pattern. After the mid-1970s, however, and particularly after the debt crisis of the early 1980s and its accompanying major currency devaluations, the maquiladora industry began its climb to

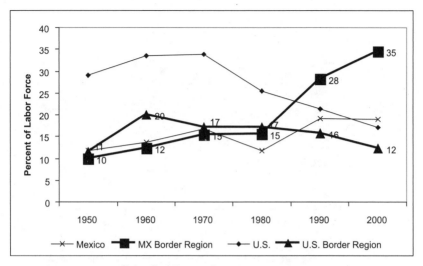

FIGURE 6.6. Percentage of labor force in manufacturing, 1950–2000.

prominence. By 2000, 35 percent of the Mexican border labor force was in manufacturing, with about 80 percent of the maquiladoras located directly on the border. The Mexican border region has a higher share of labor in manufacturing than the Mexican average. In the Chihuahua border region, the 2000 census reports that an amazing 45 percent of the workforce was in the manufacturing sector.

For both the United States and Mexico, the service industry is becoming an increasingly important source of employment, with slightly less than half of employment in Mexico (49 percent) and slightly more than half in the United States (52 percent) occurring in the service sector. The service sector category covers a large variety of labor, from highly paid professionals such as doctors, lawyers and accountants to very low-wage, low-skilled workers, including sales clerks and domestic workers. To differentiate in a very broad-brush manner, the service sector is split into two divisions: the proportion of the labor force in sales, entertainment, hotels, and restaurants, which tends to include lower-skilled, lower-paid workers (Figure 6.7), and the proportion of the labor force in financial and social services, which tends to include more of the professional and higher-skilled workers (Figure 6.8). The U.S. border region has maintained an almost constant 30 percent of the labor force in the category of sales, entertainment, hotels, and restaurants, always above the national average. Usually large retail and tourist sectors, both influenced by the border location, account for the higher than average proportion of workers in sales, hotels, and restaurants. In the Mexican border region the proportion in this category

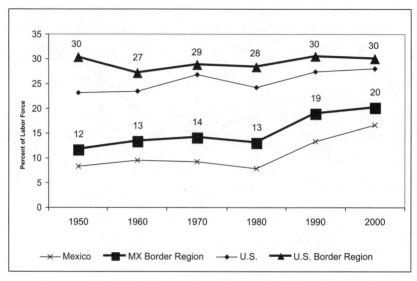

FIGURE 6.7. Percentage of labor force in sales, entertainment, hotels, and restaurants, 1950–2000.

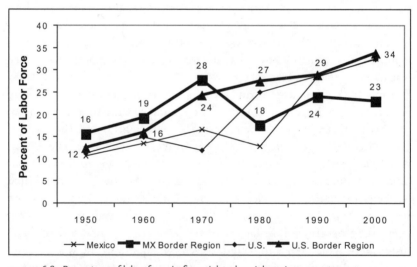

FIGURE 6.8. Percentage of labor force in financial and social services, 1950–2000.

has increased from 12 percent in 1950 to 20 percent in 2000, with most of the increase happening after the onset of the Mexican debt crisis in 1982 and the opening of the economy to foreign goods beginning in 1986.

The proportion of the higher-paid service sector in financial and social services, including health and education, increased from 12 percent to 34 percent between 1950 and 2000 in the U.S. border region (Figure 6.8).

Except for the 1970 census year, the national rate and the border rate have been very close. In the Mexican border region, however, this rate reached a high in 1970 of 28 percent, falling to 23 percent by 2000, well below the national level.

TWO MAJOR CONSEQUENCES OF THE WORKFORCE PATTERNS

In sum, there are two main characteristics of workforce patterns in the border region. First, on the Mexican side, manufacturing has grown to become the predominant sector, particularly after the national crisis of the early 1980s. Second, on the U.S. side, low-wage service sector jobs make up a larger share of the labor force than they do in the United States as a whole. In both cases, manufacturing in Mexico and low-skilled services in the United States, the distribution of activities is uneven across the counties and municipios, but the general pattern prevails in most places, and particularly in most population centers. Both of these characteristics are related to the border, and both have profound consequences for border residents and workers.

In the case of Mexican border manufacturing, Chapter 4 explained how a shift in the late 1980s in Mexican national economic policy toward a more open economy, together with the financial crisis that began in the early 1980s, created more non-oil exports, a devalued peso, and rapid growth in the maquiladora sector. Encouraged by a break on import taxes, foreign investment was drawn to the major urban areas of the Mexican border region, where access to the U.S. market was greatest and where a labor force could be found. A major consequence was the uncoupling of Mexican border municipios and border states from national cycles and trends in Mexico, and increasing integration with U.S. economic cycles and trends. When the U.S. economy expanded rapidly, the demand for goods and services produced by maquiladoras expanded, and when the United States entered a recession, its effects were felt along the Mexican border. Gruben's work, along with that of Gerber and Balsdons, shows strong linkages between overall U.S. industrial production and maquiladora employment, in both cyclical expansions and contractions.[17] For example, when the Mexican peso collapsed in late 1994, the Mexican economy went into a recession and GDP fell by more than 6 percent in 1995. At the same time, however, the maquiladora industry added 12 percent more workers.[18] By contrast, when the U.S. economy fell into recession in 2000, employment in the maquiladoras fell. In effect, the border maquiladoras have integrated a share of the Mexican economy with the United States.

On the U.S. side, manufacturing is much less significant, and is even less important than it is in the U.S. as a whole. Service sector jobs, however, and in particular retail trade jobs, are more important than in the rest of the United States. One hypothesis to explain this result is that the U.S. cities and towns on the border serve as a market center for residents of Mexico. Hence, the population base of the market area served by U.S. border communities is often much larger than their own U.S. population. In the largest border city, San Diego, the impact of purchases by Mexican citizens is significant, accounting for approximately 7.1 percent of retail sales in San Diego County.[19] Elsewhere along the U.S. border, purchases by Mexican residents are even more noticeable; for example, Patrick and Renforth estimated that between 20 and 50 percent of retail sales were to residents of Mexico in the four largest Texas border cities.[20] The significance of cross-border retail sales is that U.S. retail sectors are larger than is strictly needed to service the U.S. population base, and more important, sudden changes in Mexico can profoundly affect the economies of U.S. border communities.

Over the last few decades, one of the primary mechanisms for passing negative economic shocks from Mexico to U.S. border communities has been a change in the value of the peso. Prock noted that taxable retail sales in Laredo fell by 45.5 percent in the wake of the 1982–1983 devaluation of the peso, while Patrick and Renforth estimated an average 42 percent decline in retail sales in the four border cities they studied after the 1994–1995 devaluation.[21] The effects of a 40 or 50 percent decline in retail sales are devastating to local economies: businesses collapse, workers are laid off, real estate values plummet, and the local area goes into a deep recession.

In sum, the structure of economic activities along the border has increased the integration of Mexican municipios with the U.S. economy while at the same time increasing the vulnerability of U.S. border cities to the effects of steep devaluations in the Mexican peso. Since the 1994 devaluation, Mexico has used a flexible exchange rate system, which helps insulate the currency against sudden, deep declines in its value. Nevertheless, for two decades, from the mid-1970s to the mid-1990s, the peso experienced a number of steep declines, with destructive effects that were by no means limited to the Mexican side of the border. Though impacts on living standards and the quality of life were dramatic, fortunately they were not so long-lived as to undermine long-run progress in living standards. Trends in income, poverty, and the standard of living are taken up in the next chapters.

▓ ▓

CHAPTER 7

INCOME, EQUITY, AND POVERTY

One notable feature of the U.S.-Mexico border is that it is the point of contact between two large nations with very different income levels. The income gap between the two sides of the border is so large that it is difficult to identify any other countries in the world sharing a common border that have income differences as large as those between the United States and Mexico. In 2005, the World Bank estimated Mexico's per capita income to be $7,449 in current U.S. dollars and that of the United States to be $42,006—approximately six times greater.[1] This large an income gap intensifies the cultural and institutional differences between the two countries and generates significant differences in policy priorities. Inevitably, these differences create barriers and misunderstandings that complicate relations between the United States and Mexico.

Another notable feature is that the income levels of the communities on the U.S. side are below the U.S. national average, whereas income levels of communities on the Mexican side are above the Mexican national average. The situation is mirrored in the poverty rates, which tend to be higher than the national average on the U.S. side and lower than the national average on the Mexican side. In other words, the income gap and poverty rate differences in the border region are smaller than the differences between those same measures for the two countries as a whole; the border thus reflects a blend of Mexican and U.S. realities. In this chapter we examine these relationships and provide direct estimates of income per person for borderlanders.

INCOME AND LIVING STANDARDS

Income is the single most important indicator of living standards since it is directly linked to material well-being and economic development. Income can be used to obtain goods and services, including health care, education, cultural goods, and even a cleaner, healthier environment. Increases in income almost always lead to increased opportunities, whether those income increases occur at the individual, household, or national level; when we compare two or more regions, the residents of the higher-income region usually have a greater variety of choices and more opportunities than residents of lower-income regions. Income, then, is an essential component of well-being and living standards. It is not the only component, however.

Although income is central to our concept of people's well-being, it is important to recognize its limitations as a metric. In part, these limitations stem from the fact that no single number can convey all the factors contributing to complex, multidimensional variables such as living standards or well-being. Income does not tell us much about the importance of non-market, nonmaterial, relations and opportunities, such as the availability of leisure time, the opportunity to enjoy family and friends, or a feeling of personal well-being and safety, to name just a few. A high-income individual may spend hours commuting to work on crowded freeways, work long stretches without vacations or breaks, live in a polluted environment, and experience a lower quality of life than someone with less income. Most of these limitations of income as a measure of well-being are spelled out in introductory economic texts, and a few are addressed later in this chapter. We point out these limitations because we wish to avoid overstating what can legitimately be inferred from our estimates of comparative income data in the border region. Income colors the picture we paint, but it is not the only important element in our discussion.

CONCEPTUAL AND PRACTICAL ISSUES IN THE ESTIMATION OF BORDER INCOMES

Conceptually, the importance of income as a measure of standard of living lies in its purchasing power. Therefore, to examine trends in income over time and compare them across regions, a measure of income must represent constant purchasing power. To make these comparisons using U.S. and Mexican data, three adjustments have to be made. First, income over time needs to be adjusted for changes in the price level. Second, U.S. and Mexican incomes have to be translated into a common currency. Third, the income data have to be adjusted to make the definition of income the same on both sides of the border.

Adjusting for price-level changes is a standard procedure. The income data are divided by the consumer price index, which in this case has a base year of 1996. Then the data are cited in constant 1996 dollars. This adjustment increases the numerical values of incomes for earlier years, when overall prices were lower than in 1996, and decreases incomes in later years, when overall prices were higher than in 1996. Although there are a lot of imperfections in the consumer price index itself, this is still a reasonable approximation for constant purchasing power over time.

The issue of a common currency arises because incomes in Mexico are denominated in pesos and U.S. incomes are denominated in dollars. This difference may seem trivial, but conversion of Mexican pesos to U.S. dollars at market exchange rates overlooks another important conceptual problem, namely, that prices in the two countries are not the same. For many goods, particularly those with a high labor content, the cost in Mexico, measured in Mexican pesos, is significantly lower than the dollar value of the pesos. For example, in 2005, Mexico's per capita income was estimated to be $7,449. This dollar amount is the value of an average Mexican income (derived as the gross domestic product divided by total population) when it is converted to dollars at the average exchange rate in 2005. The problem with using this figure to represent average income in Mexico is that differences in prices in Mexico make the peso equivalent of $7,449 an inaccurate reflection of what the pesos could purchase. In 2005, Mexico's average income per person could actually buy goods and services worth $10,209 in the United States, even though the pesos could only "buy" 7,449 U.S. dollars. In other words, the market exchange rate of pesos for dollars was less than the U.S. dollar value of the goods and services the pesos could buy in Mexico. Since we want to know something about living standards, we must take into account price differences, or else we will overestimate the difference between U.S. and Mexican living standards.

The standard method for comparing incomes is to replace market exchange rates with purchasing power parity (PPP) exchange rates for converting pesos to dollars. PPP rates are artificially constructed exchange rates that are based on the costs of standardized baskets of goods and services in each country. They are provided by the World Bank and the Center for International Comparisons at the University of Pennsylvania.[2] Since Mexican income per capita was $7,449 in 2005 at market rates but $10,209 at PPP exchange rates, the real purchasing power of Mexican incomes was 37 percent higher than indicated by the market exchange rate

(10,209/7,449). In other words, when border incomes are estimated in pesos, they must be converted to dollars at the PPP exchange rate, or alternatively, converted to dollars at the market exchange rate and then increased by 37 percent in dollar terms.[3]

The third adjustment needed to compare border incomes arises from the incompatibility of U.S. and Mexican data. At the county level, the U.S. Department of Commerce provides estimates of personal income, while Mexico's national statistical agency, Instituto Nacional de Estadística, Geografía e Informática (INEGI), provides estimates of gross state product and has no income estimates at the level of the municipio. In other words, the geographic units (counties versus states) are different, as are the concepts of income (personal income versus total gross regional product). Hence, Mexican state values must be divided and allocated to each municipio, and U.S. county data must be adjusted to make them conceptually equivalent to total income rather than personal income.

Comparable income figures for the border counties and municipios are obtained in several steps. In the first step, as described in the technical appendix to this chapter, we estimate total income for each county in dollars and for each municipio in pesos. Mexican state income is allocated to the municipios in accordance with employment levels by sector. In step two, we convert the totals to per capita values by dividing them by population in each county or municipio. In step three, the peso estimates for the municipios are converted to dollar values using market exchange rates, and in step four, those values are adjusted to take into consideration the differences between market rates and PPP rates of exchange. The data appendix, accessible on the Web site associated with this book (http://latinamericanstudies.sdsu.edu/BorderData.html), provides the per capita income estimates for each of the counties and municipios for the census years 1970 to 2000 in constant 1996 U.S. dollars.

INCOME TRENDS IN THE BORDER REGION

Figure 7.1 shows the trends in real per capita income, measured in constant dollars (1996 = 100), in the two border regions and nationally. Both sides of the border saw increases in their per capita income over the period 1970 to 2000, although income growth on the Mexican side was nearly zero between 1980 and 1990, and the difference of almost $7,000 between the U.S. and Mexican border regions in 1970 grew to more than $12,000 in 2000. Nevertheless, the general observation made earlier, that income differences are less on the border than between the two nations overall, is

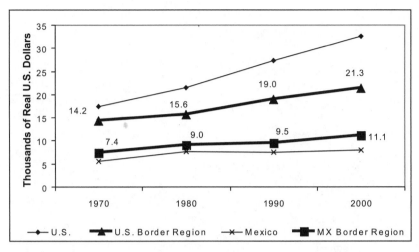

FIGURE 7.1. Per capita GRP for Mexico and the United States nationally and for the border regions, 1970–2000.

easily seen in the data. In 1970, the U.S. border income was less than twice Mexican border income (PPP definition), while the U.S. per capita income was almost three times the Mexican per capita income.

As the most heavily populated county on the U.S. border, relatively prosperous San Diego explains a large share of the U.S. border income. Outside of San Diego, however, conditions are different, and most counties on the U.S. side have incomes below the national average. Table 7.1 gives our estimates of gross regional product (GRP) per person for U.S. counties and Mexican municipios on the border by state. As shown in the table, California's border income (driven mainly by San Diego) is 2.7 times the level of the Baja California municipios' income. In the Texas border region, incomes are only 1.4 times the level of the corresponding Mexican border municipios. Note that the income gap between Texas and California border regions is larger than the gap between the Texas border and its Mexican counterparts. On the U.S. side, the greater variation in income shows a clear east-west gradient, as it consistently falls across the states moving from west to east.

On the Mexican side, GRP per capita peaks in the heavy manufacturing states of Coahuila and Chihuahua and then falls in the desert stretches of the less populated Sonora border. Income rises again in Baja California, but not to the levels of Coahuila or Chihuahua. The transborder area with the least difference is Coahuila and Texas, where the gap is only about 22 percent.

TABLE 7.1 *Gross Regional Product per Capita for Border Counties and Municipios*

Border Municipios and Counties	GRP per Person, 1999
U.S. border counties	23,628
California	29,618
Arizona	23,187
New Mexico	17,558
Texas	15,533
Mexican border municipios	11,029
Baja California	11,575
Sonora	10,047
Chihuahua	12,202
Coahuila	12,688
Nuevo Leon	10,306
Tamaulipas	9,357

SOURCE: Authors' calculations based on data from INEGI and U.S. Bureau of Economic Analysis.

Figures 7.2 and 7.3 show per capita income for census years 1970 to 2000 for the border regions of each border state. As can be seen, the income gaps between U.S. counties (grouped by state) are much larger than the gaps between Mexican municipios. In addition, Figure 7.3 highlights the "Lost Decade" of the 1980s, when income growth in Mexico was stagnant and in some areas even fell slightly. In all likelihood the turnaround in growth happened on the border in the late 1980s, as it did for Mexico as a whole, but because we are only able to estimate data points for 1985 and 1993, the restarting of growth cannot be timed with precision. Much of the growth from the late 1980s to 1993 probably represented a recovery from previous losses, except along the Chihuahuan border, where there were large increases in GRP per capita between 1985 and 1993. After 1993, most of the Mexican border experienced significant increases.

WHAT THE DATA DO NOT SHOW

Gross regional product per capita, the variable we are using to measure income, is suggestive, but by itself it gives a very incomplete picture of living conditions or the development status of the border region. There are a number of inherent limitations to using the data, and we must be clear about some of the major ones. First, we have estimated GRP, not disposable income. Comparable measures of the latter would require data that

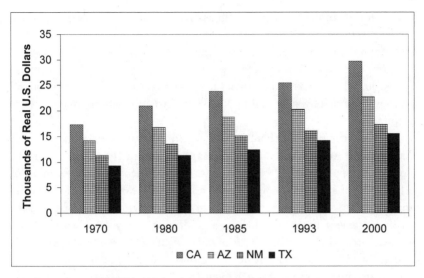

FIGURE 7.2. Per capita GRP in U.S. border regions by state, 1970–2000.

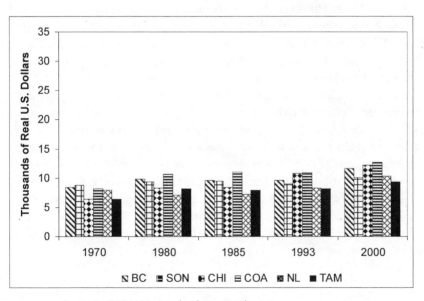

FIGURE 7.3. Per capita GRP in Mexican border regions by state, 1970–2000.

are not available, and we settled on GRP as a compromise. Per capita GRP provides a general idea of the consumption bundle available to individuals, but it is not a precise measurement. For example, it includes incomes generated in the region but paid to factors outside the region. Rental payments to a Texas firm for machinery used to produce auto parts in Ciudad

Juárez, for example, would show up as GRP in Juárez. Furthermore, GRP includes indirect taxes remitted to D.F, in the case of Mexico, or D.C. and state capitals, in the U.S. counties. Some of this revenue will flow back in the form of road construction, hospital services, schools, and other public goods, but where there is a disparity between taxes paid out of a region and services provided by state and national governments, our estimates do not account for this.

A second issue is that there is not a one-to-one correspondence between development and income. In particular, development is a multidimensional concept that must be defined to include income and a number of other additional factors. For example, a long and healthy life or the skills and education that permit individuals to tackle a wider range of activities are at least as valuable as income, and although they may be correlated with income, there is not a perfect relationship between them. Societies that allow individuals a healthier set of living conditions, more education, and greater opportunities for achievement and the realization of their potential may or may not have higher incomes than societies that offer less of these things. However, they surely must be viewed as more developed, if that word is to be seen as meaningful. In the next two chapters we address some of the issues raised by this observation and provide estimates for a border human development index similar to the one used by the United Nations Development Program.[4]

Finally, it should be kept in mind that all per capita estimates of income are averages for the geographic unit over which the measurement occurs. Per capita GRP or income per capita are abstractions that tell nothing about the actual incomes received by different groups in the area of measurement. That is, such estimates provide no information about income distribution, inequality, or the incidence of poverty. Since poverty and inequality, along with income, are important indicators of prosperity and the overall welfare of people within a region, the remainder of this chapter looks at some additional variables related to income inequality and poverty.

INCOME AND INEQUALITY

Growth in per capita GRP can occur even if most or all of the growth is only for the richest segment of society. Consequently, if we want to know something about living standards for different income groups in the border region, we need to consider variables beyond income per capita. Real median income per household is very similar to the mean income per capita,

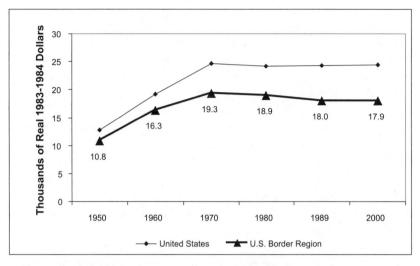

FIGURE 7.4. Real median family income, 1950–2000 (1983–1984 = 100).

but its characteristics make it a better reflection of income trends for the majority of the population. The median is defined as the midpoint of the income distribution, where 50 percent of the population earns more and 50 percent earns less. It is also measured for households rather than individuals. Because households typically pool their income, median household income is a better measure of trends in material conditions. Unfortunately, median incomes are available only for the U.S. side of the border.

Figure 7.4 shows a somewhat different trend than that for per capita average income. Real median family income, measured in constant 1983–1984 dollars, increased between 1950 and 2000, both nationally and in every border state and county. However, both nationally and in the majority of border counties, most of that growth happened between 1950 and 1970.[5] At the national level, real median income since 1970 has been relatively level, although by 2000 it was about $300 less than in 1970. In the U.S. border region, median household income was $1,300 lower in 2000 than in 1970, and the gap between the nation and the border increased from about $2,000 in 1950 to almost $6,500 in constant 1983–1984 dollars. In every U.S. border state and county, real median incomes were lower in 2000 than in their peak census year, usually 1970. In a few counties the peak occurred in 1980, and in a few more, including San Diego, the peak occurred in 1990.

The rank order of U.S. border county median household income closely parallels the rankings for per capita income, with San Diego number one

---

BOX 7.1   MEASURING INCOME INEQUALITY

One way to measure income inequality is to split the population into equal parts, in quintiles or deciles, arrange the population from poorest to richest, and then look at the proportion of income that goes to the poorest portion of the population, the proportion of income to the second poorest part, and so on. For example, in 2000 the poorest one-fifth of the U.S. population accounted for 5.4 percent of U.S. income and the richest one-fifth accounted for 45.8 percent of income. For Mexico in 2000, the World Bank database puts those same two percentages at 3.1 percent and 59.1 percent.

It is possible to plot this distribution by plotting the cumulative percentage of population on the x-axis of a diagram and the cumulative percentage of income on the y-axis. The curve that is plotted is called the Lorenz curve, as shown in the diagram. The 45-degree line in the diagram represents a perfectly equal distribution of income, since 10 percent of the population (horizontal value) must have 10 percent of total income (vertical value) if there is complete equality. Given that population is arranged from poorest to richest and complete equality does not exist anywhere, the Lorenz curve always lies below the 45-degree line, and the more below the 45-degree line it lies, the more unequal is the distribution.

The Gini ratio is the ratio of the area between the 45-degree line and the Lorenz curve divided by the whole area under the 45-degree line (A/(A + B)). The Gini ratio must vary between zero (complete equality) and one (complete inequality). If income were distributed perfectly equally, the area between the 45-degree

---

and the only county above the national median household income. Pima County in Arizona, home to the city of Tucson and the University of Arizona, had the second highest median income. At the other extreme, the two counties with the lowest median incomes were Presidio and Starr Counties in Texas. The geographic pattern for median household income also parallels that for per capita income, with the highest median family incomes in the west and the lowest along the eastern border in South Texas.

There are two explanations for the conflicting trends in the U.S. border region of a rising real per capita income and a slightly falling real median family income. One is that family size is decreasing. In 1970, the average household size in the U.S. border region was 3.4 people, declining to 2.9 in 2000. A decline in family size reduces the number of workers in each family and, all else equal, causes a decline in median household income. Hence, if the economy is growing but the number of single-income households in increasing, per capita income can rise while median household income falls or remains constant.

line and the Lorenz curve would be zero. On the other hand, if 99.9 percent had zero income and 0.01 had 100 percent, the Lorenz curve would approach one. In other words, the closer to one the Gini ratio is, the greater is the inequality in income distribution.

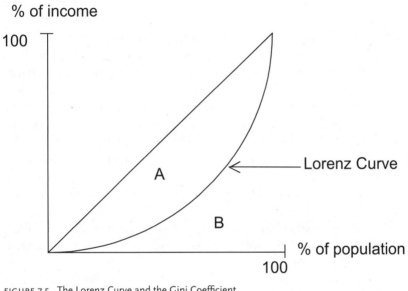

FIGURE 7.5. The Lorenz Curve and the Gini Coefficient.

This explanation does not directly tackle the issue of income distribution, however. Income distribution grew more unequal in the United States and in its border region, particularly after 1970 or 1973, when the United States (and many other parts of the world) experienced a significant fall in its rate of growth of income and a significant rise in inequality. Peach has calculated Gini coefficients for U.S. border counties, border states, and the United States for the census years 1970, 1980, 1990, and 2000 (Box 7.1).[6] As income inequality increased nationally, a similar trend occurred in every border state and border county, with the lone exception of Kinney County, Texas. Furthermore, all border states had more income inequality (higher Gini coefficient) than the United States as a whole. The difference between the border counties and the United States nationally appears fairly constant over time. Peach's estimates show that the Gini coefficients for the border counties and the United States as a whole were 0.37 and 0.35, respectively, in 1969. By 1999 they had risen to 0.45 and 0.42, but the national versus border differential had changed little.

Most border counties also had slightly greater income inequality than their respective states. Growing inequality helps explain how average incomes can rise while median incomes are constant nationally and falling in the border region: since 1970, all the gains from economic growth have gone to the upper half of the distribution. Families in the bottom half have merely maintained their 1970 living standard or have experienced a decline.

Increasing income inequality in the United States has been attributed in part to the growth of the knowledge-based economy, which requires more skill and education and increases the disparity in wages between professional and skilled workers, on the one hand, and unskilled workers on the other. Educational attainment is a good proxy for skill levels, and it is consistently lower in the border region. In 2000, for example, educational attainment in the U.S. border region compared unfavorably to the national level, with nearly 7 percent more adults in the border region without a high school education. Consequently, as the national wage gap between skilled and unskilled widens, the border becomes relatively worse off.

The characteristic of lower educational attainment in the U.S. border region points toward the second possible explanation for more inequality in the distribution of border incomes. The U.S. border has absorbed large numbers of workers from central Mexico, who arrive in the United States with much less schooling, on average, than the resident population. Between 1970 and 2000, the share of the U.S. border population that was foreign born more than doubled, rising from 8.8 percent to 19.8 percent (see Chapter 2). The increase in the foreign-born share of the population, mostly due to migration from Mexico, lowered average educational attainment and, together with national and international trends toward increasing wage premiums for skilled workers, resulted in rising inequality.

In addition to the rising wage premium for skilled workers, other factors help explain the patterns of inequality for the U.S. border. Lower labor force participation rates, higher unemployment rates, and higher (but falling) youth dependency ratios are all potentially important.[7] Each of these factors contributes to having a larger share of the population not working, which lowers total income and potentially causes greater inequality. Case studies of Imperial County in California confirm this for a single county and support Peach's generalizations for the border as a whole, while analysis of income losses to Texas border counties stemming from lower than average high school graduation rates pegs the loss of personal income at $3.6 billion in 1990.[8]

El Cenizo (outskirts of El Paso), Webb County, Texas.

Vacation home on a lake near Nueva Ciudad Guerrero, Tamaulipas.

INCOME AND INEQUALITY ON THE MEXICAN BORDER

An equivalent measure of median family income is not available for Mexican municipios. In many Mexican contexts, however, the minimum wage is used as a standard measurement for income, and salaries are often quoted as multiples of the minimum wage. For example, the income data in the Mexican census are stated in terms of the number of people earning less than one minimum wage, less than two minimum wages, less than three, and so forth. Families usually have more than one wage earner, so this is not the same as family income. Nonetheless, because most salaries are quoted in terms of the minimum wage in Mexico, the trend in the real value of the minimum wage is important from an accounting perspective, even if the value of the minimum wage is not a good indicator of actual income. Furthermore, since the debt crisis of 1982, Mexico has tried to encourage job growth by disconnecting the minimum wage from the real cost of living. That is, upward adjustments in the minimum wage have been well below changes in the costs of goods and services, and as a result, the purchasing power of the minimum wage has declined substantially, especially during the 1980s.

Figure 7.6 plots the path of the real Mexican minimum wage in the border region in 1994 pesos.[9] As shown, the real minimum wage grew steadily from 1960 to a peak in 1976. During this period of a rising real value for the minimum wage, the Mexican peso became increasingly overvalued, and in 1976 the first of several peso devaluations took place. After the onset of the debt crisis in 1982, the real minimum wage began a dramatic decline that continued throughout the 1980s. The peso crisis of 1994–1995 caused another decline in its value, and since then it has been roughly constant, without signs of increasing. It is currently well below its 1960 value.

Although the minimum wage is administratively determined and is not considered a price floor in any meaningful sense, trends in the real value of the minimum wage have been associated with trends in income inequality and poverty. In general, when the real (adjusted for price changes) minimum wage rises, income inequality falls and poverty declines, whereas a fall in the minimum wage over a prolonged period is associated with the opposite effects. For example, as the real value of the minimum wage rose, the Gini coefficient for Mexico as a whole fell (signifying greater equality), from 0.54 in 1968 to 0.42 in 1977, where it remained until the debt crisis in 1982. Thereafter, as the real minimum wage fell, the Gini coefficient for Mexico rose from 0.43 in 1984 to 0.47 in 1992 and 0.51 in 1996, and by 2000 the Gini coefficient had reached 0.53, close to its 1968 level.[10] Over the same period

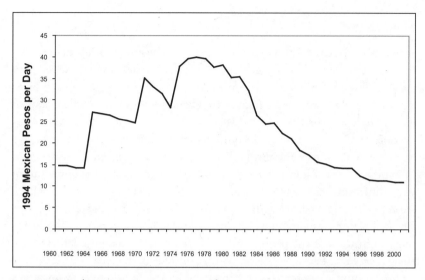

FIGURE 7.6. Real Mexican minimum wage per day, 1960–2000 (in 1994 pesos).

(1984–1996), the share of national income received by the bottom 40 percent of the population fell from 14.4 to 12.7 percent, and the share received by the richest 10 percent rose from 32.4 to 38.2 percent of total income.[11]

Using data from the National Household Survey of Income and Expenditures (*Encuesta Nacional de Ingresos y Gastos de los Hogares*, or ENIGH), Peach and Molina have calculated Gini coefficients for the six Mexican border states during the 1990s.[12] The ENIGH survey is composed of samples drawn from across the nation; the number of observations in any given state is too small to permit an accurate estimate of state-specific Gini coefficients. Nevertheless, for the Mexican border states, Peach and Molina estimate that by 2000, income distribution at the state level was slightly more equal than for the nation as a whole. Border states had a Gini coefficient of 0.53 in 1992 (compared to the national figure of 0.55) and 0.45 in 2000 (compared to 0.53 nationally). Though Gini ratios are not available at the municipio level for all the municipios, there is an estimate for Mexicali in 2004 of 0.42, close to the state-level estimate.[13] Mexicali is one of the better-off municipios, with many government jobs, since it is the state capital, and it also has a large maquiladora sector, making it likely to have a slightly more equal distribution than the Mexican border region as a whole. In fact, increasing salaries in the border region maquiladoras may be an important factor contributing to the improvement in income distribution in the border states during the 1990s.

POVERTY

Along both sides of the border, patterns of poverty parallel income and income distribution patterns. That is, low incomes and more inequality translate into higher rates of poverty, while higher incomes and more equality imply lower rates of poverty. Several studies have noted that poverty rates tend to be lower in the Mexican border region than for Mexico as a whole and higher in the U.S. border region than for the U.S. as a whole.[14]

In a general sense, the term *absolute poverty* is defined as insufficient income to cover a family's basic needs. As in the case of the minimum wage, however, official poverty lines are administratively set and may have little bearing on what a family actually needs to survive and stay together. The definitions adopted for the United States follow the official government definition of the poverty rate. For Mexico, we adopt a definition of the poverty rate based on the percentage of wage earners earning less than one minimum wage in 1970 and 1980 and less than two minimum wages in 1990 and 2000.[15] Although this is a somewhat arbitrary definition, it has some basis in real conditions. For example, Article 123 of the Mexican Constitution of 1917 states that minimum wages are to be set at a level sufficient to satisfy the basic needs of a family; this may have been the case up until the 1982 debt crisis, but a study by the Centro de Estudios de Trabajo reported that a family with income below one minimum wage would have insufficient income to meet basic needs and hence would be in poverty. By 1985, 2.5 minimum wages were required to meet the basic minimal necessities.[16] Since the purchasing power of minimum wages in Mexico in 1990 was about half what it was in 1980, by 1990 two minimum wages was a better measure of the poverty line for Mexico.

The trends in poverty for Mexico, according to the definition given above, are shown in Figure 7.7.[17] As shown, the level of poverty declined in the 1970s, rose in the 1980s, and fell again in the 1990s. Border trends and trends for Mexico overall are similar, with national poverty levels appearing to be consistently higher than along the Mexican border. Of course, individual wage data rather than family income give only a rough approximation of the trends in poverty, since there can be more than one wage earner per family. Two studies of poor Mexican families' survival strategies, one in Guadalajara and the other in Tijuana, indicate that as real wages fall, more members of a family tend to join the labor force in order to survive. This pattern is common throughout Latin America and suggests that family income will not fall as much as individual wage income.[18] Furthermore, families tend to "smooth out" their consumption

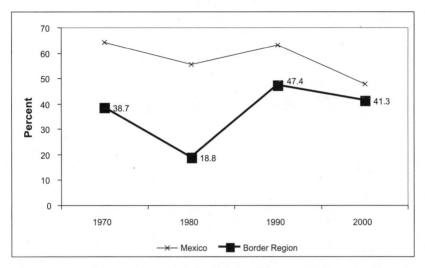

FIGURE 7.7. Proportion of workers earning less than minimum wage in Mexico, 1970–2000. For 1970 and 1980 the line shows the proportion earning less than one minimum wage, and for 1980 and 2000, the proportion earning less than two minimum wages.

over time through borrowing and drawing down savings, if any, so that actual consumption nearly always is less variable than income or wages. Even the poor, without access to credit, may be able to borrow from family and friends. Nevertheless, the data give a rough estimate of trends.

Given the trends in real wages and the failure of the minimum wage to keep up with inflation (especially during the high-inflation, low-growth period of the 1980s), the data suggest that there was a significant increase in poverty on the Mexican side of the border during the 1980s. At the same time, labor force participation rates increased (Chapter 6), a fact consistent with the hypothesis that families sent more family members into the workforce. The increased labor force participation rate would have prevented overall family income from falling as far below the poverty level as the reported trend in individual wages might suggest.

In contrast to the Mexican border region, U.S. border counties, and especially South Texas, have poverty rates that are much higher than the U.S. national average. The U.S. government defines a family poverty line as income equal to the minimum number of dollars needed to provide for basic needs. It is calculated as the minimum cost of an adequate diet multiplied by approximately three. The assumption is that families spend one-third of their income on food, with the rest going to pay for housing, clothing, transportation, medical care, education, and other basic needs. The exact

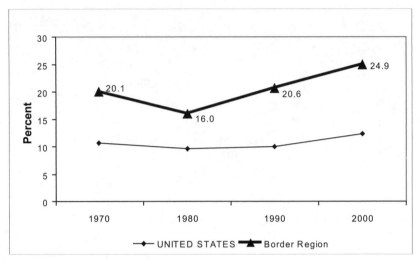

FIGURE 7.8. Proportion of families below U.S. poverty line, 1970–2000.

dollar amount varies with family size and, over time, with inflation. The poverty rate of a region is the percentage of families whose incomes fall below the poverty line. The census measurements of this proportion for 1970 through 2000 are plotted in Figure 7.8 for the U.S. national and border regions. Figure 7.8 shows that U.S. national and border poverty rates tend to move together but that the border region suffers from a much higher level of poverty. Although the proportion of families in poverty nationally varied from just below 10 percent (1980) to over 12 percent (2000), variation on the border ranged between 16 percent (1980) and 25 percent (2000). That is, in the year 2000, poverty rates in the U.S. border region were more than two times the national average. Figure 7.8 is consistent with the hypothesis that economic growth in the 1950s and 1960s, along with the war on poverty launched by President Lyndon B. Johnson in the 1960s, lowered absolute poverty rates, both nationally and on the border. Throughout the 1970s, national poverty rates did not change much except for temporary increases during recessions. However, poverty rates rose substantially during the 1980s and 1990s.

Not surprisingly, the lowest poverty rates in U.S. border counties occurred in the two most urban counties at the western end of the border, San Diego, California, and Pima (Tucson), Arizona, while the highest rates were seen in Maverick and Starr counties in Texas. As of 2000, no border county had a poverty rate less than the national rate, and only three border counties had poverty rates below 20 percent (San Diego County,

California; Pima County (Tucson), Arizona; and Jeff Davis County, Texas). Jeff Davis County is a sparsely populated county (2,200 people living on 2,258 square miles) of mountains and cattle ranches, while San Diego and Pima counties have large, prosperous cities. In general, however, poverty is not correlated with either rural or urban counties, as some of the most impoverished are rural counties (Hudspeth and Culberson in Texas), whereas others are urban (Hidalgo and Cameron in Texas).

PROSPECTS FOR POVERTY ALLEVIATION

Trends in poverty depend in part on general economic trends, and it is no surprise that estimates for poverty in Figures 7.7 and 7.8 follow changes in the level of economic growth of both countries. The 1970s were years of growth and falling poverty rates. The United States in the 1980s experienced growth rates below the long-run average, whereas in Mexico, the Lost Decade brought high rates of inflation and no economic growth. Consequently, although poverty rates in the United States increased somewhat during the 1980s, in Mexico they increased dramatically. The 1990s were not much better for Mexico, even though growth returned. The 1994–1995 peso crisis once again caused a sharp drop in real wages, maintaining the high rate of poverty. In the United States during the first half of the 1990s, poverty rates, which had started to decline toward the end of the 1980s, increased again. However, with the high growth rates of the last half of the decade, the poverty rates declined down to where they had been at the end of the 1970s.

Growth and poverty alleviation are not perfectly correlated. All else equal, rising or high levels of inequality make it more difficult for economic growth to pull people out of poverty.[19] That is, given two countries or regions with similar growth rates, a reduction in the poverty rate resulting from economic growth will be less in the country or region with higher levels of inequality. This situation occurs because a larger share of income goes to high-income groups in less equal countries, with poor people receiving a smaller share of the income generated by economic growth. In the border region, inequality is higher on the U.S. side than it is in the United States nationally, and it is lower on the Mexican side than in Mexico overall but still high by world standards. Consequently, poverty reduction is not likely to happen very quickly or significantly on either side through the cumulative effects of economic growth alone.

Since economic growth alone cannot "cure" poverty, poverty alleviation requires a focused set of policies designed to provide poor people the assets they need to improve their lives.[20] These policies are beyond the scope of this book, but broadly defined, the assets needed by poor people include human capital (education and experience), physical and financial capital, adequate health care, jobs, and economic opportunity. Some of these assets may be purchased privately when incomes are sufficient, but in general, education, health care, entrepreneurship, and small business development are not equitably allocated by market mechanisms. Hence, these assets need either to be provided publicly or to receive some form of public support to fill the gaps in their market provision. Resources for public schools, nutrition and reproductive health, small business development, and numerous other forms of public and private investment are essential to overcoming the challenges of poverty. When viewed as an investment in human capital, well-allocated public funds that succeed in reducing poverty rates have very high returns.

Increasing inequality and persistent poverty limit the possibilities for future economic development since development requires an expansion of human capabilities, which in turn necessitates improvements in health care, housing, and education, as well as income and economic opportunity, among other factors. For this reason, we turn to a consideration of the overall quality of life and measures of human development in the next two chapters.

TECHNICAL APPENDIX

Methodology for Calculating Income

The U.S. Department of Commerce's Regional Economic Information System (REIS) provides estimates of U.S. personal income at the state, county, and metropolitan statistical area (MSA) level.[21] Since Mexican data are presented on a GDP basis, U.S. data must be adjusted to make them comparable in economic accounting terms.[22] Personal income at the county level is therefore adjusted upward by a factor that compensates for the difference between the personal income concept and the gross product concept. The assumption we make is that county personal income is the same proportion of county regional product as state personal income is of state product:

(1)   County PI/Total County Product = State PI/Total State Product

This is a widely used method in the regional science literature for converting local personal income estimates into a regional product equivalent.[23]

After conversion to regional product, the U.S. CPI is used to obtain 1996 dollars, and as a final step, the data are converted to per capita terms.

The income or output of Mexican municipios is less straightforward to estimate, for several reasons. First, Mexico's national statistical agency, INEGI (Instituto Nacional de Estadística, Geografía e Informática), does not calculate income levels below the state level. Second, the state-level data are available only for selected years (1970, 1980, 1985, and annually 1993–2000). And third, all income measures are in pesos, which must be converted to an equivalent dollar measure.

Our method for estimating gross product involves a disaggregation of gross state product (GSP) for the six Mexican border states into municipio shares based on each economic sector's share of GSP and each municipio's share of state employment in each sector. Let Y_m equal municipio m's total income, Y_s equal state s's total income, e_{im} be sector i's employment in municipio m, and e_{is} be total state employment in sector i and state s. Then

(2) $Y_m = \lambda Y_s$, where $0 < \lambda < 1$, and

(3) $\lambda = \Sigma_i (Y_{is}/Y_s)(e_{im}/e_{is})$.

Equation (2) states that any municipio's total income is a fraction of the state's total income, and equation (3) shows how to estimate the fraction, λ, as an employment share. Specifically, it states that municipio m's share of state income is equal to the sum of the products of state-level sectoral income shares times municipio-level employment shares. There are nine sectors.

Equation (3) assumes the same productivity within a given sector and across the municipios of a given state. For example, agriculture in each border municipio in the state of Chihuahua is assumed to have a share of total state agricultural output that is the same as its share of total state agricultural employment. This may bias upward rural incomes and bias downward urban ones, since productivity within a sector is likely to be greater in urban areas than in rural, particularly in manufacturing. However, given the concentration of manufacturing within the border municipios, this is not likely to create a significant bias. Furthermore, we feel that the use of sector- and municipio-specific employment data is the best way to divide state-level output into its municipio-level shares since this method covers 100 percent of municipio economic activity, and it relies only on the relatively mild assumption of equal labor productivity within a given sector and across the municipios of a given state.

Conversion from current pesos to constant 1996 dollars at purchasing power parity (PPP) exchange rates is accomplished using the series RG-DPCH (chained real international dollars) from the Penn World Table, version 6.1.[24] Use of the RGDPCH is necessary for this exercise since we are not interested in the value of border incomes if spent "on the other side" (converted from pesos to dollars or vice versa at market exchange rates). Rather, we are estimating the value of production in real terms, taking into account the price differences between the United States and Mexico. In at least one test, border prices for identical goods in Ciudad Juárez and El Paso were shown to differ significantly if converted at market exchange rates.[25] Hence, the use of PPP exchange rates is necessary to make the conversion from pesos into dollars of equivalent purchasing power.[26] State products given by INEGI are converted to PPP dollars using the RGDPCH series, and municipio incomes are then calculated as λ times the state income. As a final step, per capita estimates are obtained by dividing by population.

▪ ▪

CHAPTER 8

LIVING STANDARDS

María is in her mid-fifties and has seven children, ranging in age from twenty-eight to six. Originally from Guadalajara, she married and had her first three children while living in Culiacán, Sinaloa. Around 1980, she moved from Culiacán to Tijuana, where she and her husband bought land in a marginal area without services. The city grew up around them, how-ever, and they slowly became part of the urban center with a full range of amenities, including electricity, water, and sewage. Other parts of her life did not go quite as well, and about five years after they arrived in Tijuana, María's husband abandoned the family, leaving her to support and raise her seven children.

At first María worked during the day as an undocumented domestic in San Diego and at night doing take-out sewing for an apparel firm. All of her children except the two youngest entered the workforce by the time they were ten years old and began contributing to the family income. After some years, María was fortunate enough to get a job as a cook in one of Tijuana's best restaurants, one catering to both local upper-class Tijuana families and U.S. visitors. Cooking at the restaurant enabled her to find jobs that paid better than average wages for three of her sons, who worked as waiters at night and on weekends so that they could continue in school.

María always emphasized education for her children, even when her life situation did not allow them to attend school easily. She finished pri-mary school in an era when the median education in Mexico was around four years of schooling, and she also took a course in nursing to qualify as a nurse's aid. She understood clearly that education is a way to rise above poverty and insisted that her children remain in school despite having to work. Her three oldest sons all completed college at Tijuana's branch of the Universidad Autónoma de Baja California and are now working as an orthodontist, an architect, and an accountant. Two of them are married to women they met in university and who also have professional careers. The fourth grown son dropped out of school after secondary school and is working as a manager of a liquor store; his mother complains that he is not doing well.[1] María's oldest daughter dropped out of high school one semester before finishing, though she plans to go back and finish. Her two other daughters are still in high school and primary school.

After cooking for the restaurant for eleven years, María calls herself retired and considers herself "lazy." She now runs a day-care center in her living room for her eleven grandchildren while her older children and their spouses work. Her children do not pay her for these services but instead buy her groceries and other items, and have been maintaining and expanding her house while giving her appliances and nice furniture. What was once a small two-room house now has five rooms with concrete floors. With the help of education, María and the next generation of her family have moved from poverty to the middle class, where all of their lives are much more comfortable.[2]

María's story illustrates the changes in living standards addressed in this chapter. Living standards as a concept encompasses many elements, including housing, public amenities such as running water and electricity, education, health care, and, of course, income. All of these elements reflect, to one degree or another, something that might be called economic development, but no single element can paint a complete picture of the material quality of life. Economists and other social scientists have long used gross domestic product (GDP), usually in real per capita terms, as a crude indicator of the level of well-being in society and as a means to compare the same place at different points in time, and different places at the same time. Within its limitations, real GDP per capita provides a crude indicator of development, but GDP omits or hides a number of important features of any economy, such as environmental conditions, political and civil liberties, inequality in income distribution, nonmarket transactions, leisure, and the negative effects of many goods and services (tobacco, pornography, fast food).

More than just economic growth in output, in this book we consider economic development in a broad sense, as encompassing a variety of changes that improve the overall material quality of life of a society. For economic development to take place, infrastructure must be expanded

---

BOX 8.1 ECONOMIC GROWTH AND DEVELOPMENT

It is possible to have economic growth without economic development, but economic development usually requires some expansion in output. Growth without development occurs under many potential scenarios, but a common one throughout Latin America is extreme income inequality that concentrates the benefits of overall economic growth in the hands of a select few. Conversely, development requires some growth, since there are almost always strong barriers to redistribution when an economy is stagnant.

Economic development involves structural, institutional, and qualitative changes that expand the possibilities for improving the quality of life. This seemingly innocuous statement is controversial for a variety of reasons, but no currently rich society has achieved its status as a developed economy without undergoing profound transformations. Agriculture declines in importance, transportation and communication networks expand, formerly isolated areas are knit into the fabric of the national economy, large-scale migration from countryside to city occurs, and cities expand as centers of opportunity and national economic life. These changes are monumental and involve a fundamental rearrangement of social and community networks. They also create new environmental pressures. Urban congestion, the loss of traditions, and a new relationship between men and women are just some of the challenges confronting a developing economy.

In Chapter 9 we shift our discussion from economic development to human development, but many of the issues remain the same regardless of the framework one uses to clarify them. At a minimum, the objectives of economic development include expanding and distributing output to meet the basic needs of citizens for food, water, shelter, health, education, and security; increasing the levels of living in a way that benefits the majority; and expanding the range of economic, social, and personal choices available to both men and women.

---

and the fruits of economic growth must be distributed in a way that benefits the majority of a society rather than just a small elite group (Box 8.1.) Although per capita income will increase whenever there is economic growth, if the gains from that increase are concentrated in the upper income brackets, indicators such as infant mortality, illiteracy, and the proportion of housing without amenities such as plumbing (already low for the upper classes) will not be reduced for less advantaged groups, and the role of economic growth in bringing opportunities and increased choices to more people will be limited. For this reason, quality-of-life indicators are considered important for acquiring an understanding of the level of economic development.

INDICATORS OF IMPROVED STANDARDS OF LIVING

There is a significant gap between the U.S. and Mexican levels of economic development. In fact, the U.S.-Mexico border divides one of the greatest economic disparities in the world. The interactions between the regions that lie on the border, however, help lessen the level of economic disparity and may lessen the effects of poverty on both sides. For example, the proximity of the United States provides Mexican border dwellers with discards: clothing, building materials, furnishings, appliances, used cars and car parts, and old tires, which are used for everything from retaining walls to stairways to planter boxes. Six old wooden garage doors that sell for $25 apiece are all that is needed for a house, including the roof. The Mexican side provides U.S. border dwellers with access to cheaper housing, lower-cost doctors and pharmaceuticals, and lower-cost labor, among other things. The quality-of-life indicators for the U.S. counties that border Mexico tend to be lower than the U.S. national average, while for the Mexican municipios on the border these indicators tend to be higher than the Mexican national average.

Differences in economic development are reflected in the type of data gathered by the census bureaus of the respective countries, and as economic development has occurred over the approximately fifty-year period considered here, changes in data gathering have also occurred. Therefore it is not always possible to get data on both sides that are exactly parallel or comparable over time. As examples, the United States stopped collecting data on literacy after 1970, and counts houses that "lack some plumbing," while Mexico maintains detailed statistics on lack of running water, lack of sewage disposal, types of sewer hookups, lack of electricity, and so forth.

To gain a better understanding of the progress of economic development, changes in living standards, and a comparative view of the two sides, the rest of this chapter examines comparative trends in housing, education, and health. It presents a picture of steady progress, but it also shows a development gap that can be measured in years and in the degree of disparity.

TRENDS IN THE QUALITY OF HOUSING

Adequate housing is critical for a decent quality of life, and economic development in the U.S. and Mexican border regions has improved housing conditions in most communities. Nevertheless, the wide disparity between rich and poor is clearly visible in the wide range of variation in housing:

Del Rio, Texas.

Ojinaga, Chihuahua.

on both sides of the border one can find both mansions and shacks, as well as housing in between those extremes.

Housing is substandard if it lacks basic services: electricity, sewage disposal, or water, or if there are too many people crowded into too small a space. For example, Carmen in San Diego shares her nice two-bedroom apartment with her husband, her four children, and her mother. Although substandard housing was not eliminated over the last half of the twentieth century, the proportion of substandard housing declined substantially. We examine trends in the proportion of housing lacking services, size of housing, and the number of people per house. The indicators for housing lacking services collected by the U.S. Bureau of the Census differ substantially from those collected by the Mexican census bureau, INEGI, owing to differences in levels of economic development on the two sides. Only data on the number of occupants per house are the same and comparable. However, there are parallel relationships in the indicators that allow us to develop a picture of the basic trends.

Housing without Basic Services

The housing services of most interest are electricity, water, and sewage disposal. Electricity is the cheapest to provide and is usually the first service provided, whereas a sewer system is the most expensive and usually provided last, and safe drinking water is in between these two. Mexican border cities have substantial numbers of houses without running water, although the proportion has fallen over time. Frequently, water trucks are the main source of water, but water from a truck is about three times as expensive as piped water, meaning that the poor pay substantially more than the rich for water. In general, people without piped water use barrels for their cleaning and bathing water supply and store-bought bottled water for drinking. One rough estimate of budgets of poor people in Tijuana in the mid-1980s indicated that people in poor areas could be spending as much as 5 percent of their income on water.[3]

Figure 8.1 shows the trends in the proportion of housing lacking running water and the proportion lacking sewerage for the Mexican border region and for Mexico as a whole. These trends show a substantial improvement over time, with 37 percent of border housing lacking running water in 1950, compared to 7 percent in 2000. A similar improvement occurred with respect to sewer access, as the proportion of housing in the Mexican border region lacking a sewer connection dropped from 59 percent to 14 percent between 1960 and 2000.[4] Throughout the period the border region has had a substantially smaller proportion of housing lacking these

Tijuana house. Note the water barrels in the yard and the creative use of tires.

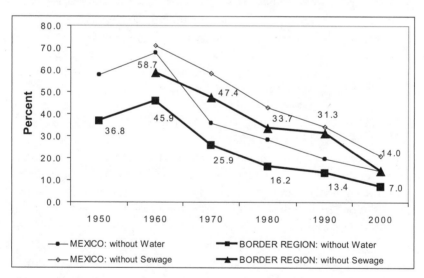

FIGURE 8.1. Percentage of Mexican private housing without water and/or sewage disposal, 1950–2000.

basic services. In 2000, 7 percent of Mexican border region housing lacked running water, compared to 14 percent nationally.

Substantial improvement is also seen on the U.S. side, although data collection does not permit a direct comparison. As shown in Figure 8.2, 35 percent of housing in border counties lacked some plumbing in 1950.

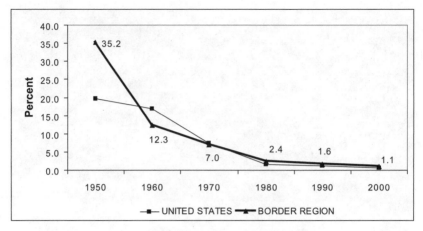

FIGURE 8.2. Percentage of U.S. dwellings lacking some plumbing, 1950–2000.

By 2000 this figure had fallen to 1.1 percent. However, where the Mexican border region has a substantially lower proportion of houses lacking services than Mexico as a whole, the U.S. border region has more than twice the proportion of houses without some plumbing compared to the U.S. as a whole. Another fact worth mentioning is that the proportion of Mexican border municipio housing lacking plumbing in 2000 was very close to the proportion of housing lacking some plumbing in the U.S. border region in 1960, a crude indicator of the development gap.

House Size

The data used to examine house size for Mexico and the Mexican border region are the proportion of one-room houses and the proportion of houses with three or fewer rooms. These trends are shown in Figure 8.3. The proportion of one-room houses in the border municipios fell from 45 percent in 1960 (the first year that the Mexican census collected this type of data) to a low of 9.4 percent in 1990, but then rose to 12.4 percent in 2000. One possible explanation for the recent negative trend is the increase in migration from the interior of Mexico to the border region during the 1990s. Following Mexico's unilateral reduction of trade barriers beginning in 1985 and the initiation of NAFTA in 1994, U.S.-Mexico trade increased rapidly, as did employment in the maquiladora manufacturing plants (see Chapter 4), offering plentiful jobs on the border at a time when the rest of Mexico was in a recession. The rapid migration from the Mexican interior put pressure on the supply of border housing, resulting in an increase in

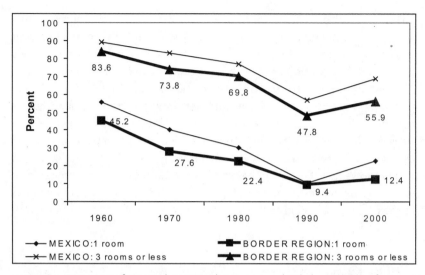

FIGURE 8.3. Percentage of Mexican housing with one room and with three rooms or fewer, nationally and for the border region, 1960–2000.

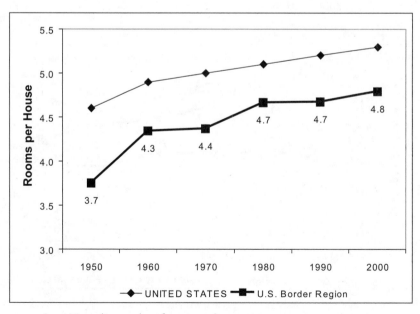

FIGURE 8.4. U.S. median number of rooms per house, 1950–2000.

one-room dwellings. The pattern for houses with three or fewer rooms was similar, with the proportion falling from 84 percent in 1960 to 48 percent in 1990, but then climbing to 56 percent by 2000. The border municipios have a lower proportion of small houses than Mexico as a whole.

The U.S. Census Bureau reports on the median house size, meaning that half the houses are smaller and half larger. In the Mexican border region, with 56 percent of dwellings having three rooms or less, one can surmise that the median was slightly under three rooms. The U.S and U.S. border region trends in median house size are presented in Figure 8.4, which shows that the median has increased steadily, from 3.7 rooms in 1950 to 4.8 rooms per dwelling in 2000.[5] Median house size remains smaller in the U.S. border region than nationally, where it was 5.3 rooms per dwelling in 2000.

Housing Occupancy Rates

In addition to the increase in house size, the average number of occupants per dwelling has declined in both the U.S. and Mexico border regions, but particularly on the Mexican side. Average occupancy in the border municipios fell from five persons to slightly under four persons between 1960 and 2000, while over the same period average occupancy in the U.S border region fell at about half that rate, from 3.4 to 2.9 persons (Figure 8.5). Much

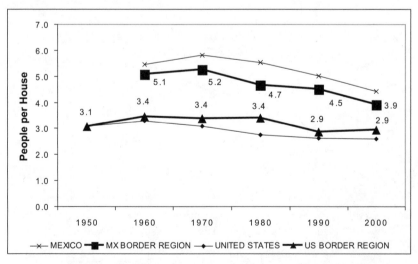

FIGURE 8.5. Average occupants per dwelling in the United States and Mexico, nationally and in the border regions, 1950–2000.

of this decrease in the number of people per house can be explained by the decrease in family size resulting from a falling fertility rate (discussed in Chapter 2). As we have seen in the other housing indicators, average occupancy is higher in Mexico as a whole than in the Mexican border region but lower in the United States as a whole than in the U.S. border region.

Strategies to Find Affordable Housing

Rapid population growth in both border regions has increased the demand for housing, which has outstripped supply in many areas. The consequence has been an increase in housing prices to sometimes astronomical levels. In San Diego, for example, an area with limited land for housing and rapid population growth, the median house price rose from $179,000 in January 1990 to $259,000 in December 2000. By the end of 2005, the median house price had climbed to over half a million dollars, affordable only to families in the top 10 percent income bracket. Rents have also climbed to much higher levels, and because the minimum wage in California is $6.75 per hour, housing shortages and unique coping strategies have become common. One strategy has been to crowd more people, sometimes multiple families, into an apartment or house. Another is to accept longer commuting times as families migrate into neighboring counties where land is cheaper or move across the border into Mexico. Among the lowest paid and the worst off are an increasing number of homeless families. The San Diego urban homeless population in 2004 was estimated to exceed 7,000 people, of which 32 percent were families with children; those families are not earning enough to afford both food and rent.[6] San Diego may be more difficult than many other places on the border, however. That is, while poor people struggle to get by no matter where they live, the struggle in San Diego is probably harder, since the gap between the incomes of the poor and the cost of housing is larger than in the rest of the U.S. border region.

In the Mexican border region, affordable housing for the poor is available through locations on the edge of the city where services are not yet available but there is land that can be bought cheaply or squatted on. Frequently, on the edges of large cities, an invasion of squatters occurs, in which a group of organized people take over a plot of land and put up shacks overnight. Through time, these irregular areas become regularized with property titles, urban services, and more permanent construction, such as bricks, cinder blocks, and cement.

An example is the story of a colonia in Mexicali. This colonia was started by an invasion of squatters, but the invasion was not done all at once by a large group, as is often the case. Instead, this invasion took place by family groups arriving one at a time. The woman of the first family to move there described the scene as follows: Her family couldn't join other invasions, so they decided to settle on a piece of land. This plot of land (south of Mexicali, but within a half-hour drive to the city center) was all bushes and had been used as a dump. At first, her house had three walls and a sheet for the fourth wall. Her husband was gone part of the time, so she was frequently alone with the children. One by one, families began to arrive and claim space around her, and an extended family would claim several lots and erect several houses for the various parts of the family. In spite of the irregular settlement of the colonia, it is laid out with fairly regular-looking lots and straight dirt streets, evidence of planning and coordination on the part of the squatters.

It took three years for the city to provide electricity to the colonia, but by 1987 electricity had arrived. Elena, elected president of the colonia, organized petitions and demonstrations, and everyone who could afford the bus fare went down to city hall to demand services. Two years after Elena became president, electricity arrived, but running water took about ten years, and sewer hookups arrived when the colonia was about eighteen years old. Educational services also take a while, and lower grades usually arrive first. There is a kindergarten and a primary school in the colonia, and a secondary school is in an adjoining colonia, about half a mile away. In 2003, they were talking about paving the roads, but people still do not have legal title to the land. Elena worries about it a little but continues to invest in her house. She can't afford to miss work to lobby for land titles and doesn't want to use her two-week vacation for that purpose. She started out with a small house, made out of heavy industrial cardboard, that was partly surrounded by a curtain for walls. She now has a block house of five rooms, including a living room, dining room, and kitchen. The floor is all tile, the furnishings are nice, and there is a fireplace in the living room. She says she is working at it little by little.

Texas land laws allow a similar process of community development since Texas landholders can subdivide land and sell it without making any improvements. Lots are sold with very little down and low monthly payments, so they are very affordable, even to low-income families. Developers can sell land using a system of contracts for deeds (CFDs) instead of mortgage loans in which no title or equity is provided until the lot is completely paid for. Interest rates on the loans tend to be high, and it takes a long time under this arrangement to pay for the land. In 1995, Texas passed the Colonias Fair Land Sales Act to curb abuses of CFD financing. The law

Cheap land, few amenities (near El Paso, Texas).

requires developers to record contracts in county registers and to provide annual summaries of the status of the CFD to buyers. Developers must also document the availability of services such as water, sewage systems, and electricity, and they must inform buyers if the lot is on a floodplain.[7]

People with a strong desire to own their own piece of land are willing to buy into this system. Purchasers can put a mobile home or small wooden structure on the lot and begin to plan and dream of enlarging and improving their home. Over time, the home and neighborhood improve, often at a rate that is related to the amount of effort devoted to community organizing by the residents. As in Mexico, electricity is the first to arrive. A sewer line is usually last, with paved roads, phone lines, and water arriving one by one in the meantime. Since 1989, the Texas Water Development Board has used the Economically Distressed Areas Program funds to finance water and sewage hookups in colonias.[8]

With the introduction of water, property values increase, and more people move into the neighborhood. The community may, in fact, become incorporated as a city, as was the case with El Cenizo, now an incorporated city outside of Laredo (Webb County), Texas. Over a ten-year period, with outside community organizers to help, they lobbied for and obtained electricity, water, and pavement on some streets, and a nice-looking school was built. Still, it is a long way into Laredo, where most of them work, with commuting times in excess of an hour and bus transportation that runs once per hour. Long work days coupled with long commuting times mean that there are lots of latchkey children in the neighborhood, with all the problems that can arise from this situation, including gangs and drugs. El Cenizo was successful in lobbying the school to provide an after-school program for children. Its leaders are now writing grant proposals for money to build a library, and in the meantime they are collecting books. Long distances from an urban core also mean difficulties in obtaining adequate health care, as travel time to doctors and emergency rooms, along with wait time for ambulances to respond, limit access to quality care. El Cenizo received national recognition when it passed a law that all city business was to be conducted in Spanish. This law turned out to be unconstitutional in the state of Texas.

The stories of the colonia in Mexicali and El Cenizo serve to illustrate the process of improving living conditions over time. With new invasions of squatters or sales of subdivided raw land, each of which occurs farther away from the urban core and centers of employment, the slow process of gaining services and building community begins again. But housing in the colonias is affordable, making home ownership possible, even if at great sacrifice of conveniences. With the arrival of services, especially water, property values appreciate and living there becomes more comfortable. As one woman who lived in a Texas colonia for 16 years before it got water said, she likes living in the community now, but there were a lot of hard years leading up to "now."

TRENDS IN EDUCATIONAL ATTAINMENT

Education, or, as economists like to call it, the creation of human capital, has long been recognized as a key ingredient in economic development, growth, and prosperity (see Box 8.2). With the advent of the knowledge-based economy, the importance of education has increased even more.[9] Modern production techniques require more knowledge, so that higher-level skills and advanced schooling receive a premium in the workplace. In the global economy, having a well-educated workforce is an essential ingredient for attracting business into a region. Training workers, even if for only relatively low-skilled jobs, is easier and faster if the workers already have a good educational background. As labor becomes more educated and more productive, wages and salaries increase, reducing the poverty rate and improving the distribution of income. This not only improves living

BOX 8.2 THE LINK BETWEEN EDUCATION AND INCOME

Few question the existence of a linkage between educational attainment and income. Economic theory attempts to explain this linkage through the concept of human capital. As people become more educated, their abilities to understand situations, analyze and solve problems, and adapt to new situations increase. This increases their productivity and output in the workplace, which in turn increases their earnings capacity.

A large body of economics literature has attempted to measure the effects of additional years of education on income. For example, in his classic study, Jacob Mincer tested the relationship between earnings and years of education of white, nonfarm U.S. male workers while controlling for experience. Not surprisingly, he found a statistically significant increase in earnings associated with additional years of education.[1] Several studies have calculated rates of return on investment in education, especially at the high school and college levels, while others have calculated ratios of earnings of college graduates to earnings of high school graduates, finding a significant increase in the ratios during the 1980s.[2] Although these studies are all based on U.S. data, some researchers have estimated returns on education internationally and have found that the social returns on education are higher in developing countries than in developed countries and higher for basic and secondary education than for higher education, both of which findings are consistent with the hypothesis of diminishing marginal returns on increasing levels of education. For Mexico, based on 1992 data, these researchers estimated returns on secondary education to be 14.6 percent and returns on higher education to be 11.1 percent. They concluded that investment in education continues to be a very attractive investment opportunity. Fullerton calculated educational returns for the Texas border counties and estimated that raising border county college graduation rates to the same level as that for Texas as a whole would increase the gross regional income by nearly $1.5 billion (in 1990 dollars).[3]

Notes

1. Mincer (1974), *Schooling, Experience and Earnings.*

2. Hanoch (1967), "An economic analysis of earnings and schooling"; Raymond and Sesnowitz (1975), "The returns to investments in higher education: Some new evidence"; Murphy and Welch (1992), "The structure of wages"; Coleman (1993), "Movements in the earnings-schooling relationship, 1940–1988."

3. Psacharopoulos and Patrinos (2004), "Returns to investment in education: A further update"; Fullerton (2001), "Educational attainment and border income performance."

standards, it also adds to the size of the domestic market, which encourages investment and dynamic business development.

María's story at the beginning of the chapter shows the possibility of rising above poverty through access to education. But hers is a very unusual story. For this to happen with any regularity, free, high-quality public education must be available to all. Mexico's system of high-quality, private primary education and underfunded, low-quality public education tends to perpetuate the social and economic inequalities in the society. The United States has in general done better at providing public schools, and the gap in education between the two countries continues to be serious.

At the same time, educational attainment has increased significantly in the last half of the twentieth century in both the U.S. and Mexican border regions. In Mexico, starting at very low levels in 1950, the increase in primary (grades one through six) and secondary (grades seven through nine) educational attainment was especially great.[10] When longtime residents of Mexican border cities were asked about changes over this fifty-year period, many remarked on the increase in opportunities for education. For example, San Luis Rio del Colorado, Sonora, had only one elementary school in 1950 and no secondary school, high school, or institution of higher education institution. By 2000, San Luis had grown into a large town with a good school system, including two universities.

Basic Literacy

In the 1970s, Mexican educational policy shifted its focus from developing world-class universities to more emphasis on universal coverage of basic education and literacy. Between 1970 and 2000, enrollment in basic education more than doubled, with most of the increase occurring between 1975 and 1985.[11] Literacy improved dramatically, especially in the border region. In 1950, the literacy rate in the Mexican border region was below the national level (41.2 percent versus 44.2 percent nationally). Thereafter the proportion of the population illiterate fell more rapidly in the border region, as shown in Figure 8.6. By 2000, only 3.5 percent were illiterate in the border region, compared to the national rate of 9.5 percent. By comparison, the illiteracy rate of the U.S. population in 1950 was 3.3 percent, falling to 1.2 percent in 1970; after 1970, the U.S. Census ceased to collect data on illiteracy.[12] The Mexican border municipio with the highest illiteracy rate in 1950 was Ojinaga, Chihuahua, with 74 percent illiterate. By 2000, the only border municipio with an illiteracy rate higher than the national rate of 9.5 percent was Hidalgo, Coahuila, with 10.3 percent.

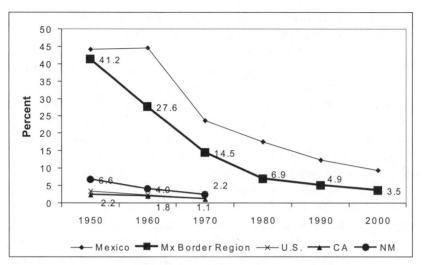

FIGURE 8.6. Percentage of the population without basic literacy, 1950–2000.

Primary school in Tijuana.

Emphasis on universal access to primary education in Mexico led to a major expansion of public primary education. Individual communities were responsible for building and maintaining the school buildings, while the state provided the teachers and textbooks. In the border states between 1950 and 1990, average student-teacher ratios fell from 65:1 to 31:1 in Baja California, from 40:1 to 30:1 in Sonora, from 44:1 to 29:1 in Chihuahua, from 45:1 to 28:1 in Couhuila, and from 43:1 to 28:1 in both Nuevo Leon and Tamaulipas.[13] Beginning in the 1990s, a national initiative to improve the quality of primary education led to the creation of PRONALEES (Programa Nacional para Leer y Escribir), which resulted in revised primary education textbooks, teacher guides, and teacher training in using the new materials. The aim was to shift teaching styles away from traditional "stand and deliver" methods toward more interactive learning. Though still underfunded and of poorer quality than in the United States, coverage of primary schooling has become nearly universal, but only in 1992 did Mexico expand compulsory education to include secondary school (grades seven, eight, and nine). Consequently, in comparison to the United States, the border region in Mexico (and the nation as a whole) continues to have a substantial education deficit.

Post-Primary Schooling

With respect to post-primary schooling, the Mexican census reports the proportion of population age fifteen years and older that have completed more than primary school, while the U.S. census gives the proportion of population aged twenty-five years and older who have completed less than the ninth grade. Although these categories are not identical, they allow for a certain amount of comparison.

Despite its higher rates of illiteracy, the Mexican border region in 1950 did better than the nation as a whole in producing people with more than a primary education, although both the border and the nation produced very few students with secondary school and beyond. In 1950, only 5.3 percent of the Mexican national population and 7.7 percent of the Mexican border population aged fifteen years and older had more than primary school (sixth grade) education. By 2000, the shares had grown to 52.6 and 60 percent nationally and in the border region, respectively. Figure 8.7 shows the sizable gains between 1950 and 2000. In 2000, the border states of Baja California and Nuevo Leon had the highest proportion of population with more than primary school (67 percent each), and were both 15 percent above the national level. Some localities did better; for example, in Mier,[14]

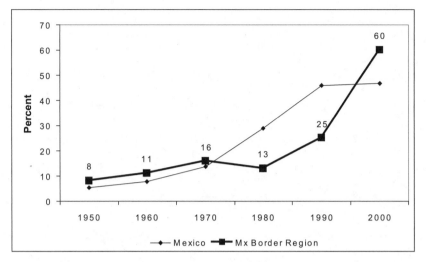

FIGURE 8.7. Percentage of Mexican population aged fifteen and older with more than primary schooling, 1950–2000.

Tamaulipas, 73.1 percent of the population aged fifteen and over completed more than primary school. The lowest percentage in the Mexican border can be found in Janos, Chihuahua, where only 21.7 percent had more than a primary school education. The Chihuahua border region has only one municipio that does better than the national average, Ciudad Juárez.[15] In 1992, Mexico expanded compulsory education from six to ten years, requiring schooling from kindergarten through the ninth grade. Since then there have been significant gains along the Mexican border in the share of the population with more than a primary school education.

In the United States, where twelve years of education have long been compulsory in all states, completion of primary school is taken for granted, but the U.S. census does report the proportion of population aged twenty-five years and older who have completed less than the ninth grade.[16] Figure 8.8 shows that this proportion was falling both nationally and in the U.S. border region until 1980, when it was 8 percent nationally and 5.3 percent in the border region. However, between 1980 and 1990 this proportion rose in the United States as a whole, from 8 percent to 10.4 percent, and even more so in the border region, from 5.3 percent to 13 percent. Between 1990 and 2000 the national proportion fell back to 7.5 percent, slightly below the 1980 proportion, while in the border region it continued to rise during the 1990s, increasing to 14.5 percent in 2000, almost twice the national proportion. The increase in the percentage of the twenty-five-and-over

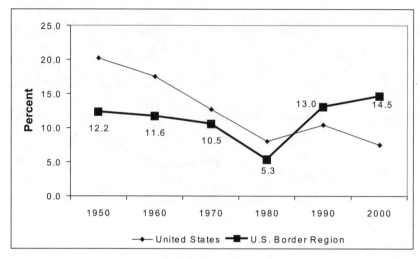

FIGURE 8.8. Percentage of U.S. population aged twenty-five and older with less than a ninth-grade education, 1950–2000.

population with less than a ninth grade education was especially dramatic in the Texas border region, where it went from 6.2 percent in 1980 (below the national level) to 32.9 percent in 1990. Border regions in the other three border states also show increases in the percentage of adults with less than a ninth grade education, although not as dramatically as in the Texas border region.

One possible explanation for this negative trend in educational attainment is the increase in foreign migration into the border region. Statistical analysis shows a significant positive relationship between an increase in the foreign-born population and the proportion of the population with less than a ninth grade education for 1990 and 2000 census data, indicating that this wave of migrants is associated with relatively low levels of education. When the same equation is estimated for data from 1950 through 1980, however, the coefficient is significantly negative, meaning that prior to around 1980, migrant inflows were associated with a decline in the proportion of population with low levels of education. The results indicate that the wave of migrants after 1980 had lower education levels than those of earlier years. (See the technical appendix to this chapter for the estimated equations.)

High School Education

Though both nations and their respective border regions have shown substantial gains in the proportion of the population with high school education or more over the fifty-year period from 1950 to 2000, the gaps between Mexico and the United States are still huge. The education gaps are a direct measure of the development differences on the border, as well as a harbinger of differences in the potential for increased development. In 1950, only one-third of the U.S. population aged twenty-five and older had at least a high school diploma, a figure that reached four-fifths of the population by 2000. In contrast, at the beginning of Mexico's "development decades" in 1950, only 2.6 percent of the population aged fifteen and older had high school or more, and by 2000 the percentage had increased to just above one-fifth. Figure 8.9 shows that in 1950, Mexican border municipios had slightly better rates than the nation as a whole (3 percent versus 2.6 percent) for high school education or more but were far behind the U.S. border counties (39 percent). By 2000, the Mexican border region stood at 20 percent, while the U.S. border region was at 74 percent. What the numbers clearly show is that Mexico and its border region have a substantially greater deficit in high school graduates and many fewer opportunities for families of modest means to send their children to high school.

Comparisons of the Mexican border to Mexico as a whole show that there was not much difference in the proportions of the population with high school or more. On the U.S. side, comparisons of the U.S. border to the United States as a whole are favorable to the border from 1950 (34 percent for the nation versus 39 percent for the border region) through 1980,

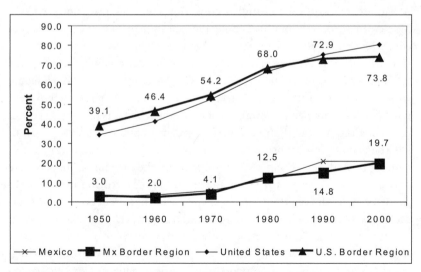

FIGURE 8.9. Percentage of the population with high school or higher education. For Mexico, the figures are for the population aged fifteen years and older, while for the United States, they are for the population aged twenty-five years and older.

but by 1990 the border had 2.3 percent fewer high school graduates than the national proportion of 75.2 percent. In 2000, the border had 73.8 percent with a high school education, compared to 80 percent nationally. The U.S. border region appears to have a growing gap in high school graduates relative to the nation as a whole.

Higher Education

During the 1950s and 1960s, Mexican development policy emphasized rapid economic growth; as a means to that end, it focused on expanding higher education, to include the establishment of ten public universities, of which four were located in the border states: Tamaulipas in 1950, Chihuahua in 1954, and Baja California and Coahuila in 1957. Of these, the Universidad Autónoma de Baja California (UABC), located in Mexicali, later with branches in Tijuana and Tecate, was the only one located in a municipio touching the border.[17] Later, the Universidad Autónoma de Ciudad Juárez, in 1973, and in 1982, the Colegio de la Frontera Norte (COLEF, located in Tijuana, with research offices along the border) were added. In addition to these institutions, a variety of private universities and technological institutes also came into existence and provided much greater access to higher education for young people who could not afford to leave town. The result has been a supply of local skilled and professional people that is contributing to the economic development of the region.[18]

Trends in attainment of higher education are shown in Figure 8.10. In Mexico in 1950, only one in 100 people had four or more years of higher education, and it was not until 1970 that the proportion began to rise. Nationally the increase was greater than in the border region, primarily due to major urban centers such as Mexico City, Monterrey, and Guadalajara, which pulled up the national average. The Mexican border population with four or more years of higher education reached a peak of 4.5 percent in 1990, although the figure fell to 3.4 percent in 2000. The decline parallels the decline in post-primary schooling in the U.S. border region and is perhaps related. For example, as migrants from the interior of Mexico were drawn to the border to fill the maquiladora manufacturing jobs that expanded rapidly during the 1990s, it could easily have reduced the percentage (but not the number) of people with college education. Nationally in Mexico, however, the proportion with four or more years of higher education continued to rise during the 1990s, reaching 7 percent in 2000, which is a little higher than the proportion of college educated in the United States in 1950.

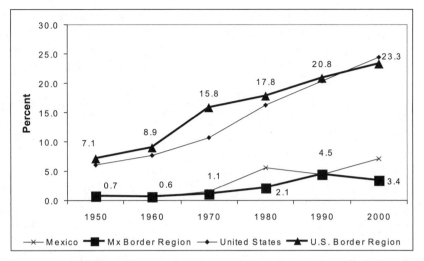

FIGURE 8.10. Percentage of the population with four or more years of higher education, 1950–2000.

In the United States, only 6 percent of the population had received a bachelor's degree or higher by 1950, but with national investments in higher education such as the G.I. bill, this proportion increased to 24.4 percent in 2000. While the U.S. border region closely followed the national trend, Figure 8.10 shows that it was below the national average in 2000. California was at the upper end of attainment in higher education and Texas at the lower end.

Education and Inequality in Mexico

Mexico has made good progress in reducing illiteracy and in increasing secondary school attainment. However, the ubiquitous problems of poverty and inequality hide some of the unpleasant facts behind aggregate statistics, as poorly funded public primary schools for lower-income groups and good private primary schools for upper-income groups unequally divide the benefits of public spending on education. Higher-income families can use their wealth to send their kids to higher-quality private schools and then take advantage of publicly funded university education. Lower-income families must rely on public elementary and secondary schools, where teachers are poorly paid, facilities are meager, and grade repetition rates are high, as are dropout rates. These schools tend to leave students unprepared for high school, let alone university. In addition, poverty forces some children to drop out before completing primary or secondary school-ing, even were the public schools of high quality. In 1996, 71 percent of the poorest quintile of population had less than a complete primary education (six years) and only 2.2 percent had high school and above. Meanwhile, in the richest quintile, 18.2 percent had less than a complete primary educa-tion and 54.5 percent had high school and above. Furthermore, 8 percent of children in the lowest quintile were not attending school, while 0.3 per-cent of the richest quintile were not in school. In the highest quintile, 34 percent had a university education.[19]

TRENDS IN LIFE EXPECTANCY AND INFANT MORTALITY

Indicators of health are important in their own right and can also serve as partial indicators of development, since economists and other social sci-entists view a long and healthy life as one of the basic characteristics of a developed economy. Systems to provide for health needs require not only economic resources but also a social commitment and the political will to view access to health services as a basic human right. As with educa-tion, the process of providing health care is self-reinforcing: the level of economic development determines the resources available for health care, while at the same time a healthier population is more productive and gen-erates more resources. In effect, health care and education are investments in human capital, and both contribute not only to people's enjoyment of life but also to an increase in society's productive capacity.

We present two health indicators for the border regions: life expectancy at birth and the infant mortality rate. Data for life expectancy are not available for individual counties and municipios, but they are available for both countries and all the border states. Table 8.1 shows a dramatic increase in life expectancy in both countries. Mexican life expectancy in-creased from fifty to seventy-six years between 1950 and 2000, while in the United States life expectancy rose from sixty-eight to seventy-seven years. The U.S. border states have had life expectancy rates that are slightly lower than the national rate, whereas by 2000, all Mexican border states had a longer life expectancy than the national average. The gap between the United States and Mexico also closed significantly over this period, dropping from eighteen years longer in the United States in 1950 to only one year longer in 2000. On the border, people in Mexican border states ac-tually had slightly longer life expectancies than those in U.S. border states in 2000.

Another useful indicator is infant mortality, measured as the number

TABLE 8.1 *Life Expectancies by Place and Date of Birth*

Place	Year					
	1950	1960	1970	1980	1990	2000
United States	68.2	69.7	70.8	73.7	75.4	77.0
California			69.2	71.7	74.6	75.9
Arizona			67.2	70.6	74.3	73.6
New Mexico			66.6	70.3	74.0	75.7
Texas			68.7	70.9	73.6	75.1
Mexico	49.7	58.9	63	68	71	75.7
Baja California				69.1	70.8	76.6
Sonora				68.4	70.1	76.4
Chihuahua				67.8	69.7	76.1
Coahuila				69.4	71	76.5
Nuevo Leon				72.3	74	77
Tamaulipas				69.6	71.3	75.8

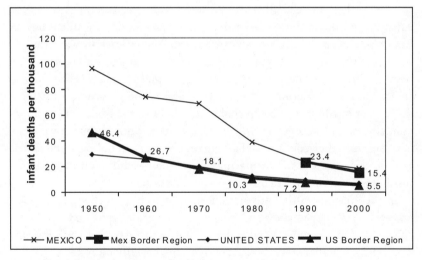

FIGURE 8.11. Infant deaths per 1,000 live births.

of infant deaths per 1,000 live births. The trends are shown in Figure 8.11. Infant mortality is sensitive to the level of health services, but also to the level of sanitation, safe water, and adequate shelter. Mexican municipio data are available only for 1990 and 2000, while U.S. county data are available for the whole period. Border region rates closely mirror the national rates and, like life expectancy, have improved substantially on both sides of the border, closing the U.S.-Mexico gap very substantially. Mexican national rates fell from 96.2 infant deaths per 1,000 live births in 1950 to 18.2 in 2000, while the Mexican border rate was 15.4 in 2000. Infant mortality rates in the United States declined from 29.3 to 6.9 between 1950 and 2000, and stood at 5.5 in the border region in 2000.

SUMMING UP TRENDS IN THE QUALITY OF LIFE

All of the indicators of the quality of life presented in this chapter—housing, health, and education—suggest significant progress in the border regions of both nations over the fifty-year period under examination. Furthermore, the gains in the Mexican border region are generally greater than in Mexico as a whole, but the gains in the U.S. border region are lower than for the United States as a whole.

With respect to housing, the average number of people per house has declined in both border regions, and the proportion of housing without water and sewerage has declined substantially.

Mexico has reduced illiteracy to low levels and federal government expenditures on education as a percentage of the total government budget have risen, even if unevenly across time and sometimes in ways that do not benefit all income segments equally.[20] Mexico and its border region have made substantial gains in achieving primary education, but less so in advancing completion of high school and higher education. By 2000, 20 percent of adults had completed high school in the Mexican border region compared to 80 percent in the U.S. border region, a substantial gap. The gap in higher education also remains high. A troubling trend in the U.S. border region is the increasing proportion of adults with less than a ninth grade education since 1980.

In the area of health, both sides of the border have seen significant increases in life expectancy and reductions in infant mortality, two variables that tend to move hand in hand, and health gaps between the U.S. and Mexican border states had decreased substantially by 2000

Despite gains in several areas, there is still some distance to go in housing, health, and especially education outcomes before the gaps with the richest areas of the world are closed. Inequality in Mexican society remains a major issue and is reflected in all areas of life, including housing, health care, and education. Public universities tend to benefit mainly the children of middle- and upper-class families but rarely children of working-class and poor families, María's children being rare exceptions. Aggregate statistics obscure rather than illuminate the condition of society's poorest, and access to the basic resources of quality education, health care, and adequate shelter remains elusive for those at the bottom, regardless of which side of the border they are on.

TECHNICAL APPENDIX

Immigration and Educational Attainment

To test the hypothesis that the increasing proportion of adults with less than a ninth grade education after 1980 in the U.S. border region is related to immigration, the proportion of the population aged twenty-five and over with less than a ninth grade education is regressed on the proportion of the population that is foreign born. The estimated equation is:

$$\text{LT9} = \alpha + \beta(\text{FB}) + \epsilon,$$

where LT9 is the percent of the over-25 population with less than nine years of schooling, FB is the percent of the population foreign born, and ϵ is a random error term. The estimation uses pooled data with a cross-section of the twenty-five U.S. counties that touch the border and a time dimension of the six census years, 1950 through 2000. The total sample has 150 observations (6 x 25), and cross-section weights are used to minimize heteroskedasticity.

The sample is first estimated for the entire period 1950–2000, and then reestimated for two subperiods 1950–1980 and 1990–2000 (see Table 8.2).

TABLE 8.2 *Regression Results for Immigration and Educational Attainment*

Dependent variable: Over-25 population with less than 9 years of schooling

	1950–2000	*1950–1980*	*1990–2000*
Constant	0.071	0.097	0.084
	(7.60)	(16.91)	(10.93)
Foreign born	0.435	−0.153	0.816
	(6.24)	(−5.11)	(13.45)
R^2	0.395	0.277	0.817
N	150	100	50

NOTE: All coefficients are statistically significant at the 1 percent level; *t* statistics are in parentheses.

The estimated coefficients for the whole sample are positive and statistically significant. The coefficient on FB indicates that a one percentage point increase in the foreign-born population is associated with slightly more than a four-tenths of a percentage point increase in the adult population with less than a ninth grade education.

A more informative approach splits the period in two, up to 1980 and 1990 to 2000. The estimated equation for 1950–1980 has a significant but negative relationship between foreign born (FB) and the population with less than nine years of schooling (LT9), while the coefficient of FB in the 1990–2000 sample is significantly positive and implies a much larger effect. These estimates suggest that from 1950 to 1980, foreign-born migrants to the U.S. border region raised the level of schooling. The impact is quantitatively small (0.15 percent) but significant nonetheless. This suggests that during the earlier period, many permanent migrants had greater than a ninth grade education, or at a minimum those with nine or more years arrived in higher proportion than the resident population. After 1980, however, the profile of migrants appears to have changed, and more migrants with less than a ninth grade education seem to have arrived at the border. In this later period, a one percent increase in the foreign-born population increased the proportion of population with less than a ninth grade education by slightly more than eight-tenths of a percent.

■ ■

CHAPTER 9

HUMAN DEVELOPMENT IN THE BORDER REGION

Nearly everyone would agree that quality-of-life improvements and human development depend on more than just material wealth or income. As economists and social scientists, we would like to affirm this point while at the same time maintaining standards for measuring human development and welfare that are comparable across countries and through time. This is a tall order, since, as the United Nations Development Program has noted, "The basic purpose of development is to enlarge people's choices," and no simple numerical measurement can possibly portray the level of development in all of its dimensions and complexity. Nevertheless, simple, comparable measures are very useful both to policy makers and to researchers trying to understand the effects of economic changes on quality of life.[1]

For many decades after World War II, development economics focused on national output and income aggregates such as real per capita gross domestic product (per capita GDP) as indicators of social well-being and variables that could be compared across countries and across time. Real per capita GDP is simple to interpret and relatively easy to obtain using modern data collection standards. Because income can be used to purchase health care, education, cultural goods, and a better environment, its connection to development is pervasive and robust. Residents of San Diego, for example, have more opportunities and choices than residents of Reynosa or Matamoros in part because they have higher incomes and can afford more of the things that enrich their lives, such as travel, safe drinking water, education, and so on. Nevertheless, real per capita income by itself omits many important aspects of human development.

The recognition that no single number can adequately capture and express all the dimensions of human development led to the search for alternatives to per capita GDP. Development economists have discussed various quality-of-life measures for countries, some of which were covered in the previous chapter. These measures have included health indicators such as life expectancy, infant mortality, and number of physicians per capita, along with education indicators such as literacy and school attendance and a variety of other environmental and social factors, such as access to safe drinking water, caloric intake, and quality of housing. One problem with a long list of indicators, often not varying in the same direction, is that it is hard to compare and rank the development levels of different countries, because variable definitions and data collection standards vary by country. For example, the Mexican national statistics office, INEGI, produces a composite index of sixty-eight variables that it uses to rank states, municipios, and AGEBS (*areas geográficas estatísticas basicas*, or basic geographic statistical areas, a sub-municipal unit of analysis).[2] This is a useful series for within-Mexico comparisons of socioeconomic conditions, but it cannot be used to compare Mexico or regions of Mexico to areas outside the country because the same variables are not universally available.

To provide a summary statistic for improvements in quality of life and human development that is broader than per capita income, we used the ideas set forth by the United Nations Development Program (UNDP) to construct a modified version of their Human Development Index (HDI). The HDI is a summary indicator of the level of human development that combines material living standards (per capita income), education (enrollment and attainment), and longevity/health (life expectancy). Equally weighted averages of income, education, and health produce an indicator that is still somewhat crude but goes beyond the traditional focus on income to incorporate the human capital variables of education and health. All three—income, education, and health—are important determinants of development since they measure basic features of individual and social capacity for making choices and exercising freedom. The education and health indicators also have the advantage of indirectly reflecting income distribution. The developers of the index readily acknowledge that the concept of human development is more complex and richer than this simple index might suggest, but the index represents a step forward in the search for an internationally comparable measure that would allow us to monitor progress in at least three key dimensions of human development.[3]

The UNDP has produced a worldwide HDI since 1992 and has extended its measurements back to 1975 for a large number of countries. The index is scaled from zero to one and is arbitrarily divided into high human development countries (those with scores above 0.8), medium human development countries (those with scores of 0.5 to 0.79), and low human development countries (countries with scores below 0.5). One important aspect of this measure is that its ranking can differ substantially from rankings based exclusively on per capita GDP, especially where incomes are distributed unequally.[4]

In recognition of the usefulness of the HDI, this chapter constructs an HDI for the U.S.-Mexico border region, using the county and the municipio as the unit of analysis. This index enables a symmetrical comparison of all communities on both sides of the border along its entire extent, from the Gulf of Mexico to the Pacific Ocean.

CALCULATION OF THE BORDER HUMAN DEVELOPMENT INDEX

The Border HDI (BHDI) is constructed using the same three equally weighted components as are used by the UNDP to construct national HDIs: per capita income, education, and health. However, within the broad education and health categories, it was necessary to modify the specific indicators used so as to derive variables that are available for both counties and municipios and are comparable on each side of the border. Specifically, we substituted infant mortality data in the BHDI for the life expectancy variables used by the UNDP, and we substituted the proportion of the adult population with a high school education or more for the UNDP's literacy variable. Otherwise the variables are the same, as is the method for weighting the variables.

The general formula for calculating each sub-index is:

(1) $\text{BHDI}_{i,j} = (\text{Observed}_{i,j} - \text{Minimum}_{i,j}) / (\text{Maximum}_{i,j} - \text{Minimum}_{i,j})$

where i represents the ith county or municipio and j is the jth indicator (income, education, health). The numerator in each case represents the gap between the observed value and the minimum possible value, and the denominator is the difference between the maximum and the minimum. Consequently, the ratio represents progress made relative to the total progress possible. If the observed value is equal to the maximum value, the index will equal one, and if the observed value equals the minimum value, the numerator will equal zero. Hence, the BHDI must vary between zero and one. A detailed description of the estimation follows.

The Income Sub-Index

Income is a proxy for a decent material standard of living. Income is necessary to be able to enter the market and purchase the things people want and the things that make their lives more comfortable and enjoyable. Per capita GDP is used to measure income, but it must first be converted to U.S. dollars using the concept of purchasing power parity exchange rates. The per capita GDP figure used in the BHDI is in constant 1996 dollars.[5] One assumption of the UNDP that we follow is that increases in income at the higher levels contribute less and less to additional human development. Accordingly, the income index is calculated using the logarithm of income instead of absolute income; this reduces the weight of income increases when income is already high.[6] In calculating the income index, we follow the assumptions of the UNDP, including the somewhat arbitrary setting of the minimum income at $100 and the maximum at $40,000.

Figure 9.1 shows the summary border region and national values of the income sub-index. The gap in income between the two border regions has remained fairly constant, varying from a low of 0.10 in 1980 to a high of 0.12 in 1993. The gap was 0.11 index points in both 1970 and 1999. In respect to individual counties and municipios, Table 9.1 shows that the income sub-index, based on gross regional product, or GRP, per capita, for individual

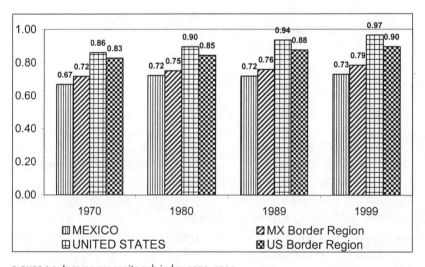

FIGURE 9.1. Income per capita sub-index, 1970–1999.

TABLE 9.1 *Income Sub-Index: Gross Regional Product*

	1970		1980		1989		1999
MEXICO	0.670	MEXICO	0.724	MEXICO	0.720	MEXICO	0.731
BorderReg	0.719	BorderReg	0.752	BorderReg	0.761	BorderReg	0.786
UNITED ST	0.861	UNITED ST	0.896	UNITED ST	0.936	UNITED ST	0.966
BorderReg	0.828	BorderReg	0.845	BorderReg	0.877	BorderReg	0.896
SD	0.862	SD	0.894	SD	0.926	SD	0.953
Terrell	0.833	JeffDavis	0.875	Pima	0.896	Pima	0.920
Pima	0.833	Imperial	0.866	Terrell	0.886	Terrell	0.907
Imperial	0.831	Pima	0.863	Hidalgo, NM	0.874	Brewster	0.893
Cochise	0.820	Brewster	0.855	Imperial	0.871	Cochise	0.879
Yuma	0.814	Cananea	0.850	Cochise	0.870	Yuma	0.876
Grant	0.808	Grant	0.849	Yuma	0.870	Grant	0.869
Culberson	0.801	Nava	0.849	Brewster	0.859	El Paso	0.867
Cananea	0.797	Yuma	0.844	Grant	0.855	Imperial	0.867
Doña Ana	0.791	Hidalgo, NM	0.844	Doña Ana	0.852	Hidalgo, NM	0.865
El Paso	0.786	Santa Cruz	0.838	El Paso	0.849	Doña Ana	0.865
Santa Cruz	0.783	Terrell	0.834	Jeff Davis	0.844	Santa Cruz	0.858
Hidalgo, NM	0.783	Cochise	0.834	Santa Cruz	0.838	Val Verde	0.854
Jeff Davis	0.782	Culberson	0.834	Val Verde	0.836	Culberson	0.842
Luna	0.780	Doña Ana	0.819	Luna	0.836	Jeff Davis	0.839
Valverde	0.774	Presidio	0.815	Kinney	0.824	Kinney	0.836
Brewster	0.772	El Paso	0.806	Cameron	0.822	Cameron	0.836
Tijuana	0.754	Luna	0.801	Webb	0.819	Luna	0.834
Hudspeth	0.752	Val Verde	0.801	Hidalgo, TX	0.806	Webb	0.834
Presidio	0.751	Hudspeth	0.790	Acuña	0.799	Hudspeth	0.830
Nogales	0.751	Cameron	0.784	Culberson	0.795	Hidalgo, TX	0.824
Acuña	0.747	Kinney	0.777	Presidio	0.794	Acuña	0.824
Webb	0.740	Webb	0.776	Hudspeth	0.789	Zapata	0.813
Agua Prieta	0.740	Piedras Negr	0.773	Juárez	0.786	Juárez	0.805
Caborca	0.739	Hidalgo, TX	0.772	Zapata	0.785	Tijuana	0.798
Kinney	0.735	Naco	0.771	Nava	0.782	Nava	0.798
SLR Colora	0.735	Acuña	0.771	Nogales	0.777	Nogales	0.790
Cameron	0.734	Tijuana	0.770	Piedras Neg	0.772	Piedras Neg	0.790
Puerto Peña	0.732	Zapata	0.767	Tijuana	0.768	Maverick	0.789
Piedras Negr	0.732	Nogales	0.767	Maverick	0.761	Presidio	0.788
Anáhuac	0.730	Mexicali	0.765	Ascensión	0.759	Mexicali	0.787
Santa Cruz	0.729	Agua Prieta	0.763	Cananea	0.757	Cananea	0.780
Mexicali	0.727	Guerrero, Ta	0.758	Mexicali	0.756	Anáhuac	0.774
Sáric	0.727	Tecate	0.755	Nuevo Lare	0.747	Tecate	0.771
Naco	0.725	Nuevo Lared	0.750	Caborca	0.745	Ojinaga	0.770
Tecate	0.722	Juárez	0.747	Puerto Peña	0.744	Nuevo Lared	0.768
Nuevo Lared	0.716	SLR Colora	0.743	Tecate	0.743	Reynosa	0.765
Hidalgo, TX	0.715	Matamoros	0.742	Matamoros	0.743	Agua Prieta	0.765

(continued)

TABLE 9.1 *(continued)*

	1970		1980		1989		1999
Altar	0.709	**Ocampo**	0.740	**Agua Prieta**	0.741	**Jiménez**	0.761
Mier	0.708	**Reynosa**	0.735	**SLR Colora**	0.739	**Puerto Peña**	0.759
Juárez	0.704	**Puerto Peña**	0.732	**Anáhuac**	0.738	**SLR Colora**	0.758
Matamoros	0.703	Maverick	0.732	**Reynosa**	0.738	**Caborca**	0.757
Miguel Alem	0.698	**Miguel Alem**	0.728	**Ojinaga**	0.737	**Guadalupe**	0.757
Guerrero, Ta	0.697	**Caborca**	0.724	Starr	0.736	**Matamoros**	0.756
Gustavo Día	0.687	**Saric**	0.719	**Naco**	0.730	Starr	0.751
Reynosa	0.687	**Santa Cruz**	0.718	**Jiménez**	0.729	**Miguel Alem**	0.748
Zapata	0.684	**Valle Hermos**	0.713	**Miguel Alem**	0.725	**Guerrero**	0.744
Maverick	0.679	**Rio Bravo**	0.713	**Guadalupe**	0.716	**Ascensión**	0.743
Nava	0.673	**Mier**	0.712	**Camargo**	0.712	**Praxedis G. G.**	0.742
Valle Hermos	0.671	**Anáhuac**	0.711	**Santa Cruz**	0.712	**Ocampo**	0.737
Camargo	0.665	**Altar**	0.703	**Ocampo**	0.712	**Naco**	0.734
Rio Bravo	0.665	**Camargo**	0.701	**Praxedis G.**	0.711	**Camargo**	0.730
Hidalgo, Co	0.662	Starr	0.688	**Rio Bravo**	0.710	**Mier**	0.728
Ocampo	0.654	**Guerrero, Co**	0.685	**Gustavo Día**	0.709	**Hidalgo, Co**	0.728
Starr	0.651	**Gustavo Día**	0.679	**Altar**	0.708	**Rio Bravo**	0.728
Ojinaga	0.646	**Ojinaga**	0.660	**Mier**	0.700	**Gustavo Día**	0.727
Manuel Ben	0.643	**Hidalgo, Co**	0.656	**Valle Hermo**	0.699	**Valle Hermo**	0.725
Ascensión	0.640	**Ascensión**	0.648	**Hidalgo, Co**	0.695	**Manuel Ben**	0.725
Janos	0.616	**Guadalupe**	0.641	**Guerrero, Co**	0.693	**Janos**	0.724
Guadalupe	0.614	**Jiménez**	0.631	**Manel Ben**	0.693	**Altar**	0.721
Jiménez	0.609	**Janos**	0.608	**Guerrero, Ta**	0.690	**Guerrero, Ta**	0.720
Guerrero, Co	0.599	**Praxedis G.G.**	0.600	**Sáric**	0.690	**Sáric**	0.695
Praxedis G.G.	0.594	**Manuel Ben**	0.598	**Janos**	0.689	**Santa Cruz**	0.695

NOTE: Mexican municipios are in boldface.

communities had a range of 0.59 to 0.86 in 1970 and a range of 0.70 to 0.95 in 2000, with a slow upward trend in incomes and a slight decrease in the numerical value of the range (indicating a trend toward greater equality across communities). The three communities with the highest income index in 1970, 1990, and 2000 were San Diego, California, Pima, Arizona, and Terrell, Texas. Terrell is a sparsely populated rural county with a population of only 1,081 in 2000, mainly affluent ranchers, and with much of its labor supplied by undercounted, undocumented workers. The communities with the lowest per capita income in 2000 were Saric and Santa Cruz, both in Sonora. Santa Cruz saw its average income wane in the 1990s as it became a major staging area for Mexican workers trying to cross into the United States. Although migrants to the United States are far from the poorest of the poor, it appears that becoming a staging area for migration can have negative consequences on average income levels.

In general, and as expected, incomes in the U.S. counties were above those in the Mexican municipios, but there are a few exceptions. In 2000, Ciudad Acuña in Coahuila had the highest average income for a municipio, higher than that of four Texas counties, Zapata, Maverick, Presidio, and Starr. Five more municipios were above the last three of these counties, and twenty municipios, including all the Baja California municipios, had average incomes above the average income of Starr County, Texas, the poorest county in the U.S. border region.

The Education Sub-Index

The educational component of the BHDI is composed of two data series: the percentage of school-aged children who are enrolled in school and educational attainment. Both series are assumed to have maximum possible values of 100 and minimums of zero. The enrollment component is the same as that used by the UNDP and is calculated by dividing the number of people enrolled in kindergarten through twelfth grade by the population aged five to nineteen years for the United States and six to nineteen years for Mexico.[7] The educational attainment segment of the education index as calculated by the UNDP is the literacy rate. However, the U.S. Census Bureau stopped collecting state and local literacy data after 1970.[8] Furthermore, as the UNDP itself admits, there are problems with the definition of literacy. Their definition is "the ability to read and write, with understanding, a simple statement related to one's daily life," but this definition is problematic in two ways.[9] First, it lacks an exact meaning, and second, data are gathered in different ways in different countries, raising concerns about reliability. Some countries equate illiteracy with never having attended school and some equate literacy with having attended and completed four years of primary school. In view of the lack of U.S. data on literacy, the BHDI substitutes the proportion of the population aged twenty-five years and older who have at least a high school education (twelve years or more of schooling) as the measure of educational attainment. This is arguably a better measure for a developed country than for a developing country, but it has the advantage of producing comparable data for the United States and Mexico. Enrollments are weighted one-third and educational attainment two-thirds in the construction of the final index.

Both countries have increased the percentage of the population less than nineteen years old who are enrolled in school, but the increase is most dramatic on the Mexican side of the border. In 1950 the Mexican border region (the combined border municipios) had 39 percent of its six- to nineteen-year-old population in school, compared to 27 percent nationally. This proportion increased to 69 percent in 1990 and to 75 percent in 2000. Nationally, the proportions in those census years are slightly higher, at 71 percent and 76 percent, respectively. For the United States, the border region proportions are also slightly lower than the national figures. Of the population aged five to nineteen years, 83 percent were enrolled in school in the U.S. border region in 1990 and 90 percent in 2000. Nationally, the corresponding proportions are 87 percent and 93 percent.

For educational attainment, we used the proportion of the population aged twenty-five and older who have graduated from high school (that is, they have completed twelve years of schooling). In 1950, only 34 percent of adults in the U.S. border region had twelve or more years of education. This figure increased to 74 percent in 2000 but always remained below the national rate. In the Mexican border region in 1950, only 2.6 percent had twelve or more years of education, increasing to 30 percent by 2000, almost up to the 1950 U.S. level. The Mexican border region, though higher in per capita income than Mexico as a whole, is lower in educational attainment.

As shown in Figure 9.2, there is a substantial gap in educational attainment between the United States and Mexico, both nationally and in the

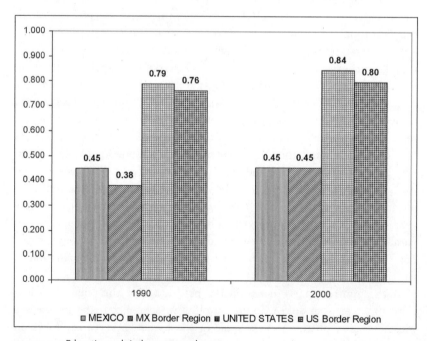

FIGURE 9.2. Education sub-index, 1990 and 2000.

TABLE 9.2 *Education Sub-Index*

	1990		2000
MEXICO	0.448	**MEXICO**	0.453
MX Border Region	0.381	**MX Border Region**	0.453
UNITED STATES	0.791	**UNITED STATES**	0.845
US Border Region	0.763	**US Border Region**	0.800
SD	0.812	Pima	0.860
Cochise	0.798	SD	0.858
Pima	0.796	Brewster	0.843
Jeff Davis	0.768	Grant	0.836
Grant	0.758	Cochise	0.835
Hidalgo, NM	0.752	Jeff Davis	0.816
Terrell	0.749	Terrell	0.814
Doña Ana	0.736	Hidalgo, NM	0.768
Brewster	0.728	Kinney	0.764
El Paso	0.716	El Paso	0.750
Yuma	0.711	Yuma	0.743
Luna	0.690	Doña Ana	0.733
Kinney	0.681	Santa Cruz, AZ	0.720
Santa Cruz, AZ	0.658	Imperial	0.705
ValVerde	0.657	Val Verde	0.698
Imperial	0.650	Culberson	0.680
Culberson	0.642	Cameron	0.680
Zapata	0.636	Webb	0.664
Cameron	0.632	Zapata	0.660
Webb	0.623	Hidalgo, TX	0.644
Hudspeth	0.611	Luna	0.623
Hidalgo, TX	0.609	Hudspeth	0.618
Presidio	0.586	Presidio	0.612
Maverick	0.528	Maverick	0.589
Starr	0.520	Starr	0.539
Mexicali	0.420	**Cananea**	0.504
Tijuana	0.403	**Mexicali**	0.502
Nogales	0.400	**Nogales**	0.492
Naco	0.397	**Reynosa**	0.483
Gustavo Díaz Ordaz	0.396	**Matamoros**	0.466
Nuevo Laredo	0.392	**Nuevo Laredo**	0.457
Reynosa	0.385	**Tijuana**	0.449
Matamoros	0.383	**Tecate**	0.445
Piedras Negras	0.382	**Caborca**	0.439
Juárez	0.377	**Juárez**	0.439
SLR Colorado	0.376	**SLR Colorado**	0.433
Agua Prieta	0.369	**Miguel Alemán**	0.422
Tecate	0.361	**Agua Prieta**	0.421
Caborca	0.347	**Valle Hermoso**	0.416
Miguel Alemán	0.347	**Mier**	0.416

(*continued*)

TABLE 9.2 *(continued)*

	1990		2000
Cananea	0.332	**Rio Bravo**	0.407
Rio Bravo	0.328	**Puerto Peñasco**	0.402
Acuña	0.323	**Gustavo Díaz Ordaz**	0.402
Mier	0.320	**Piedras Negras**	0.401
Valle Hermoso	0.314	**Acuña**	0.390
Guerrero, Tam	0.312	**Ojinaga**	0.389
Nava	0.299	**Altar**	0.367
Altar	0.295	**Nava**	0.367
Ocampo	0.293	**Anáhuac**	0.363
Camargo	0.287	**Camargo**	0.352
Anáhuac	0.283	**Guerrero, Tam**	0.348
Puerto Peñasco	0.250	**Ocampo**	0.336
Ojinaga	0.248	**Naco**	0.325
Santa Cruz, Son	0.247	**Ascensión**	0.321
Hidalgo, Coa	0.243	**Santa Cruz, Son**	0.308
Sáric	0.232	**Praxedis G. Guerrero**	0.288
Guerrero, Coa	0.223	**Guadalupe**	0.285
Guadalupe	0.221	**Sáric**	0.283
Praxedis G. Guerrero	0.206	**Jiménez**	0.257
Janos	0.206	**Guerrero, Coa**	0.254
Manuel Benavides	0.199	**Janos**	0.246
Jiménez	0.195	**Hidalgo, Coa**	0.246
Ascensión	0.159	**Manuel Benavides**	0.217

NOTE: Mexican municipios are in boldface.

border regions. The U.S. index numbers are almost twice as large as the Mexican numbers. The education index rankings of all the border communities are listed in descending order in Table 9.2. In 1990, the education index ranged from 0.81 in San Diego county to 0.16 in the municipio of Ascension, Sonora. In 2000, the range was from 0.86 (Pima, Arizona) to 0.22 (Manuel Benavides, Chihuahua). On the U.S. side of the border, only two counties were above the national index of 0.845: San Diego, California, and Pima, Arizona. On the Mexican side, six municipios had indices above the national level, with Cananea, Sonora, and Mexicali, Baja California, the top two. There is no overlap between U.S. and Mexican border communities for this sub-index. The education sub-index as measured for Starr, Texas, the lowest-scoring U.S. county in 2000, was 0.54, above that of Cananea, Sonora, at 0.504.

In light of the border location of these communities, Mexican enrollment data might be biased downward and U.S. data biased upward to the extent that some Mexican students cross the border and attend U.S. schools. These children would be counted in the Mexican census, while their enrollment would be counted on the U.S. side. Although shifting the enrollment to the Mexican side could reduce the gap a little, it would not eliminate the substantial gap, since the major source of the gap is from differences in educational attainment, which has twice the weight of enrollment in the construction of the index.

The Health Sub-Index

The UNDP uses life expectancy at birth, a measure of longevity, for the indicator of health. Life expectancy data are available at the national and state levels for both the United States and Mexico but are not available at the county or municipio level for either country. Therefore, we have substituted the infant mortality rate in calculating the BHDI. The infant mortality rate is one of the components of the Physical Quality of Life Index, which preceded the creation of the HDI. Development economists have long viewed infant mortality as a key indicator of quality of life, not only because it is an indicator of the level of medical care available but also because it is closely correlated with housing conditions, sanitation levels, and access to safe water, as well as longevity. The infant mortality rate is the number of infant deaths per 1,000 live births, and a higher infant mortality rate indicates worse conditions in health care, housing, sanitation, and water. Since the other indicators in the HDI imply improvement with higher values, the infant mortality rate must be converted into an infant survivability rate, equal to 1,000 minus the infant mortality rate. The converted rate is the number of infants who survive out of 1,000 live births, with a maximum of 1,000 and minimum of zero. For example, in 2000 the Mexican border region had an infant mortality rate of 15.4 infant deaths per 1,000 live births. This translates into 984.6 infants who survived per each 1,000 live births. Mexico did not start publishing numbers of births and infant deaths at the local level until the late 1980s, limiting the calculation of this sub-index of the BHDI to the 1990 and 2000 census years.

Figure 9.3 shows the health sub-index for the national and border regions for both countries, and Table 9.3 gives the municipio- and county-level health indices and rankings. The U.S. and Mexican indices increased nationally and in their respective border regions, but the Mexican indices increased much faster than the U.S. indices, so that by 2000, the gap between the two countries in infant survivability rates was very small. At the county/municipio level some of the indices are 1, meaning that no

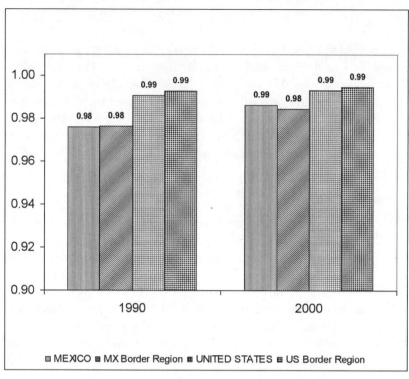

FIGURE 9.3. Health sub-index, 1990 and 2000.

TABLE 9.3 *Health Sub-Index: Infant Survival Rate*

	1990		2000
MEXICO	0.976	**MEXICO**	0.986
MX Border Region	0.977	**MX Border Region**	0.985
UNITED STATES	0.991	**UNITED STATES**	0.993
US Border Region	0.993	**US Border Region**	0.995
Santa Cruz, Son		**Sáric**	1
Hudspeth	1	**Praxedis G. Guerrero**	1
Culberson	1	**Manuel Benavides**	1
Jeff Davis	1	**Hidalgo, Coa**	1
Terrell	1	**Guerrero, Tam**	1
Kinney	1	Culberson	1
Guadalupe	0.999195	Jeff Davis	1
Praxedis G. Guerrero	0.997899	Presidio	1
Starr	0.995641	Terrell	1
Hidalgo, TX	0.994439	Zapata	1
Valle Hermoso	0.993837	Cameron	0.996392
Camargo	0.99375	Santa Cruz, AZ	0.996241
Imperial	0.993715	**Valle Hermoso**	0.996034
Luna	0.993651	El Paso	0.99559

Val Verde	0.993562	Val Verde	0.995501
Maverick	0.993485	Imperial	0.995334
Cameron	0.99315	Doña Ana	0.995041
Grant	0.993007	Hidalgo, TX	0.994987
El Paso	0.992879	Yuma	0.994679
Webb	0.992572	SD	0.994059
SD	0.992552	Maverick	0.993976
Anáhuac	0.992233	Webb	0.993941
Yuma	0.992147	Pima	0.993926
Doña Ana	0.992053	**Mier**	0.993865
Pima	0.991959	Starr	0.993831
Cochise	0.99176	Cochise	0.993667
Presidio	0.991525	**Miguel Alemán**	0.993432
Santa Cruz, AZ	0.990679	**Nava**	0.992982
Rio Bravo	0.990044	**Rio Bravo**	0.992751
Guerrero, Tam	0.989899	Brewster	0.991304
Zapata	0.989848	**Janos**	0.991124
Hidalgo, NM	0.989583	**Anáhuac**	0.991091
Miguel Alemán	0.989432	Grant	0.990476
Gustavo Díaz Ordaz	0.987203	**Nuevo Laredo**	0.990176
Ascensión	0.987013	**Gustavo Díaz Ordaz**	0.990123
Janos	0.985915	**Guadalupe**	0.989418
Naco	0.985612	**Matamoros**	0.988328
Matamoros	0.984986	**Ascensión**	0.98797
Manuel Benavides	0.983051	**Ocampo**	0.987952
Nuevo Laredo	0.982843	**Piedras Negras**	0.987607
Brewster	0.981982	**Naco**	0.9875
Reynosa	0.981449	**Camargo**	0.987406
Nava	0.980723	**Acuña**	0.987165
Puerto Peñasco	0.98041	Hidalgo, NM	0.987013
Piedras Negras	0.977754	**Caborca**	0.986577
Acuña	0.977586	**Reynosa**	0.986232
Mexicali	0.977376	**Tecate**	0.985159
Ojinaga	0.97686	**SLR Colorado**	0.984058
Caborca	0.975439	**Cananea**	0.983689
Guerrero, Coa	0.975	**Santa Cruz, Son**	0.983607
Ocampo	0.974684	**Altar**	0.983402
Tecate	0.974328	**Mexicali**	0.981839
Jiménez	0.972868	**Tijuana**	0.981574
SLR Colorado	0.97134	**Jiménez**	0.9801
Altar	0.970588	**Ojinaga**	0.979927
Nogales	0.970495	**Juárez**	0.979649
Tijuana	0.969573	**Puerto Peñasco**	0.979144
Sáric	0.96875	Luna	0.979003
Cananea	0.968254	**Nogales**	0.978592
Juárez	0.959424	**Guerrero, Coa**	0.977778
Agua Prieta	0.956853	**Agua Prieta**	0.973333
Mier	0.954545	Kinney	0.972973
Hidalgo, Coa	0.931034	Hudspeth	0.967742

NOTE: Mexican municipios are in boldface.

infant deaths occurred in that year, an occurrence that is far more likely in relatively low-population communities and may also reflect the availability of hospital services. In 2000, there were ten communities with no infant deaths, five on the Mexican side and five in Texas. Comparisons of the index range in 1990 with 2000 show that this range was the smallest for the three sub-indices. The health index ranged from 0.931 to 1 in 1990 and from 0.968 to 1 in 2000. The gap between the U.S. and Mexican border regions decreased during the 1990s from 0.016 to 0.010.

In the health sub-index more than in the other sub-indices, there is a great deal of overlap between U.S. counties and Mexican municipios, unlike the education sub-index, for example, where the upper portion is all U.S. and the lower portion all Mexican. This overlap in U.S. counties' rankings and Mexican municipios' rankings on the health sub-index is an indication that Mexico has made major gains in health and narrowed the health gap with the United States. Nevertheless, health issues continue to be a serious problem in some locations, irrespective of which side of the border one is on. The two communities with the lowest infant survivability index are two Texas counties, Kinney and Hudspeth, with 0.973 and 0.968, respectively.

THE BORDER HUMAN DEVELOPMENT INDEX

The income, education, and health sub-indices are combined into the Human Development Index, with each component weighted equally. As such, the BHDI presents a much broader view of the level of economic development than a view based solely on income. Use of the logarithm of income further reduces its importance, as increases contribute less to the value of the index at high incomes than at low incomes. Furthermore, income is not independent of the health and education indicators, since higher education and better health lead to higher productivity, which in turn leads to higher per capita income, and a higher income allows the purchase of more education and health.

In the aggregate, as shown in Figure 9.4, there is a significant gap between the United States and Mexico and their respective border regions. The U.S. BHDI is below that of the equivalent U.S. HDI (using the same variables as the BHDI) and with a slightly larger gap in 2000 than in 1990. The Mexican BHDI is slightly below its equivalent national HDI in 1990 but above it in 2000. Mexico's border region also made larger gains than the U.S. side, increasing by 0.04 from 1990 to 2000, while the U.S. BHDI increased by 0.02.

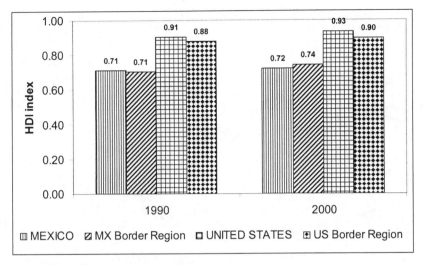

FIGURE 9.4. Border Human Development Index, 1990 and 2000.

The rankings of the border communities ranged from 0.623 to 0.910 in 1990 and from 0.647 to 0.935 in 2000 (Table 9.4). San Diego, California, had the highest BHDI in the entire sample, followed by Grant County, New Mexico, in both 1990 and 2000. Pima County, Arizona (Tucson), dropped from third place in 1990 to fourth in 2000. With a big increase in its BHDI, Brewster County, Texas, moved from ninth place in 1990 to third place in 2000. At the bottom of the ranking are three Mexican municipios, Janos and Manuel Benavides, Chihuahua, and Hidalgo, Coahuila. These three communities changed rankings between 1990 and 2000, but in both years they were the bottom three.

In the BHDI rankings, no U.S. county ranks lower than the highest-ranking Mexican municipio. This is true even though there is a considerable amount of intermingling of counties and municipios in the infant survivability sub-index and some overlap in the per capita income sub-index. However, the gap in educational attainment between the lowest-ranking U.S. counties and the highest-ranking Mexican municipios is large, and is the biggest factor in the BHDI gap across the border. Nevertheless, the

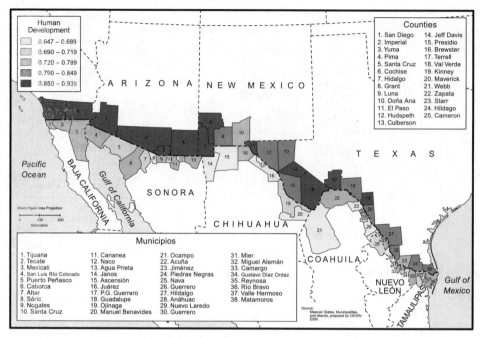

MAP 9.1. The Border Human Development Indices by region.

TABLE 9.4 *Border Human Development Index*

	1990		2000
MEXICO	0.715	**MEXICO**	0.724
MX Border Region	0.706	**MX Border Region**	0.741
UNITED STATES	0.906	**UNITED STATES**	0.934
US Border Region	0.878	**US Border Region**	0.897
SD	0.910	SD	0.935
Pima	0.895	Pima	0.924
Cochise	0.887	Brewster	0.909
Terrell	0.878	Terrell	0.907
Hidalgo, NM	0.872	Cochise	0.903
Jeff Davis	0.871	Grant	0.899
Grant	0.869	Jeff Davis	0.885
Doña Ana	0.860	Hidalgo, NM	0.874
Yuma	0.858	Yuma	0.871
Brewster	0.856	El Paso	0.871
El Paso	0.853	Santa Cruz, AZ	0.858
Luna	0.840	Kinney	0.858
Imperial	0.838	Imperial	0.855
Kinney	0.835	Val Verde	0.849
Santa Cruz, AZ	0.829	Culberson	0.840

Val Verde	0.829	Cameron	0.837
Cameron	0.816	Webb	0.830
Culberson	0.812	Zapata	0.825
Webb	0.812	Hidalgo, TX	0.821
Zapata	0.804	Luna	0.812
Hidalgo, TX	0.803	Hudspeth	0.805
Hudspeth	0.800	Presidio	0.800
Presidio	0.790	Maverick	0.791
Maverick	0.761	Doña Ana	0.789
Starr	0.751	Starr	0.761
Mexicali	0.718	**Mexicali**	0.757
Nogales	0.716	**Cananea**	0.756
Tijuana	0.714	**Nogales**	0.753
Piedras Negras	0.711	**Reynosa**	0.745
Juárez	0.707	**Tijuana**	0.743
Nuevo Laredo	0.707	**Juárez**	0.741
Naco	0.704	**Nuevo Laredo**	0.738
Matamoros	0.704	**Matamoros**	0.737
Reynosa	0.701	**Tecate**	0.734
Acuña	0.700	**Acuña**	0.734
Gustavo Díaz Ordaz	0.697	**Caborca**	0.728
SLR Colorado	0.695	**Piedras Negras**	0.726
Tecate	0.693	**SLR Colorado**	0.725
Caborca	0.689	**Miguel Alemán**	0.721
Agua Prieta	0.689	**Agua Prieta**	0.720
Miguel Alemán	0.689	**Nava**	0.719
Nava	0.687	**Puerto Peñasco**	0.713
Cananea	0.686	**Ojinaga**	0.713
Rio Bravo	0.676	**Mier**	0.713
Anáhuac	0.671	**Valle Hermoso**	0.713
Valle Hermoso	0.669	**Anáhuac**	0.709
Camargo	0.664	**Rio Bravo**	0.709
Guerrero, Tam	0.664	**Gustavo Díaz Ordaz**	0.706
Ocampo	0.660	**Altar**	0.690
Mier	0.658	**Camargo**	0.690
Puerto Peñasco	0.658	**Guerrero, Tam**	0.689
Altar	0.658	**Ocampo**	0.687
Ojinaga	0.654	**Ascensión**	0.684
Santa Cruz, Son	0.653	**Naco**	0.682
Guadalupe	0.645	**Guadalupe**	0.677
Praxedis G. Guerrero	0.638	**Praxedis G. Guerrero**	0.677
Ascensión	0.635	**Jiménez**	0.666
Jiménez	0.633	**Santa Cruz, Son**	0.662
Sáric	0.630	**Sáric**	0.659
Guerrero, Coa	0.630	**Guerrero, Coa**	0.658
Janos	0.627	**Hidalgo, Coa**	0.658
Manuel Benavides	0.625	**Janos**	0.654
Hidalgo, Coa	0.623	**Manuel Benavides**	0.647

NOTE: Mexican municipios are in boldface.

differences between the lowest-ranking counties and the highest-ranking municipios in both the education sub-index and the overall BHDI declined between 1990 and 2000. With respect to the overall index, in both 1990 and 2000 the lowest-ranking county was Starr, Texas, and the highest-ranking municipio was Mexicali, Baja California. In 1990, Starr's BHDI was 0.751 and Mexicali's was 0.718, a difference of 0.036; by 2000 Starr's BHDI was 0.761 and Mexicali's was 0.757, only 0.004 lower. This exercise of examining the sub-indices of the BHDI points to education as the biggest source of the gap in economic development and suggests that closing the education gap may be the most important step in eliminating the development gap along the border.

CLOSING THE HUMAN DEVELOPMENT GAP

Although the BHDI is a relatively simple index, its construction is a useful exercise. In his discussion of the UN's HDI, Nobel laureate Amartya Sen recognizes the "inescapably crude" nature of the HDI, but also points out that it can "broaden substantially the empirical attention that the assessment of development processes receive," in part because it is "not exclusively focused on economic opulence."[10] In this regard, we think that the BHDI provides a useful if rough comparison of the counties and municipios along the U.S.-Mexico border.

The BHDI shows a modest convergence during the 1990s, which is a small improvement that did not come about through a decline in U.S. values but through faster improvement on the Mexican side. Nevertheless, the convergence is very slight, and at the rate of the 1990s, it would take about twelve more decades to completely close the gap. Not surprising to development specialists is the fact that the sub-index of health (infant survivability) shows the smallest gap, both in 1990 and 2000. Sanitation improvements and modern medicines are in some ways much cheaper and easier to obtain than higher incomes or higher levels of education, and health indicators often lead other developmental improvements. In this respect, the border region is not an exception. By 1990, the gap in the health sub-index was only 0.015, and by 2000 it had fallen to only 0.010. Further, a number of Mexican municipios ranked among the top ten in health in both years, and quite a few municipios ranked higher than some U.S. counties.

In contrast to health, the differences in education are the largest for the three indices and the main determinant of the broader difference in the overall BHDI. Although there was definite improvement between 1990 and 2000, no Mexican municipio ranked above the lowest-ranking U.S.

Autonomous University of Baja California, Tijuana.

county. An important outcome of this exercise of developing an HDI for border regions is the recognition of the size of the education gap relative to the health and income factors. This has significant implications for an approach to closing the human development gap in the border region, and more generally between the United States and Mexico.

Since World War II, Mexico and the Mexican border region have made great strides in providing public education to a larger share of the population. In this regard, its experience is similar to that of many other Latin American countries, but at the same time, the pattern of educational expansion differs significantly from that seen in other developing areas such as Asia. In particular, the border shows the general educational trend in Mexico and Latin America of significant declines in illiteracy and simultaneous expansions of higher education. Far less progress has been made in raising the completion rates for secondary education (the equivalent of high school in the United States or preparatory school in Mexico). Morley notes that

> Asia put a lot of its education dollars into eliminating the bottom tail of its educational distribution and universalizing secondary education. Latin America let most of its young cohorts leave school after the primary level, using the money instead to expand university coverage.[11]

In 2000, Mexico and the Mexican border were considerably below where the United States was in 1950 with regard to educational attainment, as measured by high school completion rates. Between 1880 and 1930, the states of the United States raised the school-leaving standard from eighth grade to twelfth grade, and although some states were in the lead and others lagged, a national consensus slowly emerged during a half-century of educational expansion. In most of Latin America, including Mexico and its border region, the same expansion has yet to occur. It was only in 1992 that Mexico increased compulsory education from six years (primary school) to ten years.

This is important, for two reasons: first, education must be a key component in anyone's definition of human development, and second, education is directly related to income, both as a cause and as a result. Increased education leads to increased productivity, which in turn leads to increased per capita income. At the same time, a higher income provides the resources for an expansion of schooling and the demand for higher skills and more training to keep up with economic advances. In the border region in particular, limits on the growth of high school education are likely to negatively impact the growth of border manufacturing, since its potential to create higher wages and well-paying jobs is dependent on the skills and ability of the labor force. Completion of high school or its equivalent signals that a worker can be easily trained for many of the jobs of modern manufacturing, while completion of less than high school signals uncertainty and risk with regard to finding an adequate labor force for higher-skilled, better-paying manufacturing work. In sum, it is difficult to imagine a feasible public policy that would be more effective at removing some of the development gap between the United States and Mexico in the border region than a broad expansion of the equivalent of high school on the Mexican side.

■ ■

CHAPTER 10

THE FUTURE OF UNITED STATES–MEXICO BORDER REGIONS

The economic dynamism of the U.S.-Mexico borderlands has attracted a steady stream of migrants, both national and international, who in turn have generated more economic growth while creating a rich multicultural stew of music, language, food, architecture, and other artifacts of daily life. People and customs from Mexico and the United States fit comfortably together along the border, often blending into a mix of Anglo, Latino, occasionally Asian, and sometimes indigenous cultures. This blend makes the border a unique part of North America, a place where the cultural and political identities of many residents are not accurately characterized as simply U.S. or Mexican but are the result of many complex interactions between two large and diverse nations. Given the shared history of the United States and Mexico, the blending of identities along the border has a larger significance than our simple understanding of ethnic diversity and is sometimes viewed by the interiors of both countries as threatening or challenging to the national culture and the dominant political assumptions.

The border has a number of different economic regions, from the Lower Rio Grande Valley to the Upper Valley, through the unpopulated desert and mountains of the interior, to the highly urbanized West Coast. The cultural and economic gaps between the U.S. and Mexican sides are narrowest in the eastern half, where Texas meets Tamaulipas, Coahuila, and Chihuahua, and more or less widen continuously as one moves west toward California and Baja California. The latter states are geographically distant from the industrial heartlands of their nations and to some extent constitute separate spheres of economic and cultural gravity. California's urbanized south coast is a settling ground for immigrants from around the world, and the state border with Baja California is relatively short, so that the development of California's economy has depended far more on trans-Pacific relations than on its networks with Mexico. Nevertheless, the opening of Mexico's economy in the 1980s began a shift in economic relations that is inevitably pulling California into a closer relationship with Baja California and the interior of Mexico.

The multidimensional integration of Mexico and the U.S. border communities is apparent in their relatively smaller (though still large) cross-border development gap. Mexico's border communities tend to be better off, in aggregate, than their counterparts in the rest of Mexico, while U.S. border communities tend to be poorer than the U.S. national average. The relative poverty of the U.S. side obscures the facts that job creation on both sides has been well above average over long periods of time and that the economic interactions that take place in the border regions serve as an engine of growth for Mexico and some parts of the United States. In turn, high job growth feeds and is fed by the rapid population growth occurring on both sides. Job growth by itself, however, has not been enough for U.S. border incomes to catch up to national levels, in part owing to the below-average accumulations of human capital but also owing to the inability of local communities to resolve national obstacles to cross-border mobility.

Over the past twenty years, and particularly after September 11, 2001, security issues have taken on a greater prominence in border relations. Calls for tighter border controls as the primary means to stop unauthorized crossers, interdict drugs, and thwart terrorists have dominated the national discourse on cross-border relations. In the heightened concern over security, the needs of the border regions for easy and flexible border crossings are often overlooked, as is the fact that many of the migration policy issues that obstruct a closer U.S.-Mexico relationship are issues that relate directly to the development gap between the two countries. Mexico's profound economic policy reforms and efforts to create a more democratic state, which have predictably and inevitably created an outflow of migrants, add to border tensions. Failure to recognize the importance of economic policy reforms and the role of the development gap in the generation of emigration from Mexico is apparent in the national debates of both countries, but particularly on the U.S. side, where a narrowly focused U.S. national security agenda pushes aside a broader understanding of the historical contexts of U.S.-Mexico relations and the contemporary social science of migration. The U.S. tendency to seek a quick solution through increasing militarization of the border imposes a disproportionate share of the burden on border communities while failing to stop undocumented migration. Migrants read clearly the mixed message of tougher enforcement only at the border and the availability of jobs once they arrive.[1]

Mobility and migration, security, and economic development are national as well as border issues. Nevertheless, most of the tensions and costs that make these issues difficult are located in the border regions. Local costs to borderlanders are greater because the weight of economic, cultural, and social interactions is most intense along the border, precisely where security controls and mobility checks are greatest. National policies intended to deter international terrorists and drug traffickers are usually designed without consideration of local business needs, families in cross-border living arrangements, local commuters and shoppers, and cities and counties that need to jointly solve transborder problems such as pollution, runaway children, stolen cars, and emergency response. Consequently, policies designed to satisfy national political objectives are often incongruent with the goals of borderlanders, which include higher incomes, a cleaner environment, and cross-border mobility. The remainder of this chapter discusses the interactions among the three interrelated issues of cross-border mobility, border security, and the economic development gap. We also suggest some policies that might help ease border tensions and bring greater prosperity.

MOBILITY AND MIGRATION

The issues of mobility and migration are not new. The United States is a nation constructed by immigrants, and Mexico is a state built by Europeans on the foundation of many Native American societies. More broadly, it appears to be a constant of economic development that rapid industrialization of national economies generates large emigrations. Neither Mexico nor the United States is an exception to this generalization, as Mexico currently sends people north, while the American experience was to move farther and farther west, encroaching on Mexican territory and filling in and occupying the lands of Native Americans. Nineteenth-century migrations such as the experiences of U.S. pioneers were necessarily different from twentieth-century migrations of Mexican "pioneers," given the historical differences in communication and transportation technologies and the differences in national policies with respect to the movement of people. Nation-states in the late twentieth and early twenty-first centuries are much more restrictive toward migration than their predecessors were in the nineteenth century. One consequence of the attempt to close borders is that contemporary frustrations over migration policy are exacerbated by the lack of recognition and acceptance of things that nineteenth-century societies more or less took for granted, namely, that industrial develop- ment and rapid economic change are disruptive and inevitably create out- migration. Blaming Mexico for its inability to tame its emigration makes no sense, since its emigration is an unavoidable side effect of the economic changes it must undergo on its way to economic development.

The contemporary flow of Mexicans northward is partly about wages, but its relationship to the development gap is far deeper than dollars per hour. Migration satisfies the needs of Mexicans who lack social safety nets such as life insurance and access to credit but who are intent on advancing their own economic well-being and that of their families and communi- ties. One of the benefits of economic development is that it reduces un- certainty about the future, in part by creating social safety nets and other organizational and fiscal elements of industrial economies such as credit and insurance markets. In the absence of those things, having one or two family members with jobs in the United States allows families—and, on a larger scale, communities—to diversify their assets and minimize the risks of job loss, crop failure, sickness, early death, and other devastating losses. Jobs in the United States also allow the possibility of remittances being sent home, sometimes filling gaps in credit by providing resources for building a house, creating a small business, or paying for an educa- tion. In these ways, migration is a response to the absence of insurance and credit markets in the sending country, and, as economic development moves forward, the missing markets are created and the advantages of migration diminish.

When viewed in a long-run historical framework, emigration from Mexico is not about the failure to create enough jobs or stagnant economic development. Rather, the fundamental issue for Mexico and its emigrants is the "creative destruction" of the process of economic development that is common to all capitalist systems.[2] The decline and eventual disappear- ance of some productive forms, such as subsistence farming and various small-scale artisans and service providers, causes the displacement of individuals, families, and even communities. The children of displaced workers may find jobs in the new economy, but the employment shift is generational and fraught with uncertainty, as a fifty-five-year-old subsis- tence farmer is unlikely to turn to factory work. The histories of Western Europe, the United States, and the high-income East Asian economies tell us that there is a period of many decades during which disruption and eco- nomic change generate a significant outflow of people.[3] In all likelihood, the United States and Mexico have another two to four decades of high migration, with the consequence that the impacts of migration on border communities have to be seen not as a problem in need of a fix but rather as a long-run condition that must be addressed in multiple ways over an extended period.

National policies can either ameliorate or exacerbate international tensions and local problems stemming from migration. Ironically, in the case of the United States, active national policy and anti-immigrant political rhetoric have often heightened tensions. For example, before 1968, there were no quantitative restrictions on the entry of Mexicans into the United States, and border crossing from Mexico did not require a visa.[4] In 1965 the U.S. passed laws that imposed visa requirements for entry (these laws took effect in 1968), and as a consequence, the period of illegal immigration began. Border control was stepped up somewhat but still remained relatively lax, as Mexican migrants could easily evade the understaffed Border Patrol at relatively little financial cost. Urban crossings were easy, and it was unnecessary to pay a coyote (migrant smuggler), so migrants quickly blended into the urban landscape, where work was plentiful. When they were occasionally caught trying to enter, undocumented immigrants were deported back to the Mexican side, where they could try again. Most migrants made it on their first try, and after a stint of working and sending money home, about 75 percent returned to their families in Mexico.[5]

Two decades after the immigration reforms of 1965, migration policy changed again with the Immigration Reform and Control Act (IRCA) of 1986. Funding for the Border Patrol (since 2003 called Customs and Border Protection, or CBP) increased from $268 million in 1986 (in constant 2002 dollars) to more than $1.6 billion by 2002, while staffing over the same period rose from 3,638 to 11,663.[6] Nor was this the entire extent of spending and staffing for border control, as the reorganization of customs, security, and immigration agencies under the umbrella of the newly created Department of Homeland Security meant that Immigration and Customs Enforcement (ICE) and U.S. Citizenship and Immigration Services (USCIS) added their human and financial resources to border enforcement. The result was not only a much larger border control force, longer and higher walls, and more surveillance equipment, but also a continued flow of undocumented border crossers who stayed longer in the United States. Apprehension rates and the proportion of Mexicans attempting to cross remained about the same as in the pre-1986 era, but the high walls and tight security in mainly urban areas served to divert undocumented border crossers to the deserts and mountains and increased the physical and financial costs of crossing. Migrants increasingly relied on relatively expensive and often unreliable coyotes to guide them, so that the risks of dying of exposure increased dramatically.[7] In response, many migrants choose to stay in the United States permanently and to move their families to join them rather than risk going back and forth. Before IRCA, the probability of a migrant returning to Mexico varied between 0.25 and 0.30 per year, with an average U.S. stay of 3.0 years, but after the reform the probability of returning fell to 0.10 and the average trip length increased to 8.9 years.[8] In short, immigration reform has increased the financial and human costs of immigration without decreasing the flow of Mexican immigrants into the United States. Instead, immigration reform began the transformation of a circular flow of temporary individual migrants into a one-way flow of long-term migrants who had major incentives to bring their families with them. This failed policy is wasting money and lives but is not decreasing the rate of undocumented immigration.

In the border region, the implementation of various federal operations designed to prevent border crossing in areas outside the official ports of entry has had a negative effect on border residents because these operations increased crossing times and created congestion. Border wait times are not something that policy makers in either national capital pay much attention to, as the view from afar is that they are a small price to pay for security. In the border regions, however, waiting times and increased congestion are not a small price to pay because they have large impacts on people whose lives are conducted on both sides of the border. The static economic costs are relatively straightforward to estimate, although a majority of border communities lack the technical expertise and resources to do so. In San Diego, however, an independent analysis commissioned by the San Diego Association of Governments (SANDAG) shows that the revenue, job, and total output effects of longer waiting times at the border are far from trivial. SANDAG estimates show that the San Diego–Tijuana border region loses between $2.1 and $2.7 billion in annual output from longer pedestrian and personal vehicle waits at the border, and $6 billion from longer waits for commercial truck crossings. A fifteen-minute increase in waiting time for pedestrians and personal vehicles, spread over a year, translates into a loss of $1 billion. Costs are borne disproportionately on the U.S. side, primarily because wages are higher there, but the costs to Mexican businesses are not trivial.[9] Furthermore, some costs remain inestimable, since it is impossible to know precisely what would have happened in the absence of a longer waiting time to cross the border. Increased pedestrian and personal vehicle waiting times in other large metropolitan border areas such as El Paso–Juárez, McAllen-Reynosa, and Brownsville-

Matamoros may not be quite as large, given that they are smaller populations than San Diego–Tijuana, but losses due to long waiting times for commercial truck crossings may be even greater in areas such as Laredo–Nuevo Laredo, the busiest freight crossing on the border.

In some rural areas, the costs are much greater when considered in relation to economic size. Even though none of the 9/11 terrorists entered from Mexico, and many of them had legal visas to enter the United States, in the rush to create security after the attack on the Twin Towers, several rural border crossings were permanently closed, including a river ford in Redford, Texas, that had been in more or less continuous use for more than 10,000 years. Another example is Boquillas, an isolated town on the Mexican side of the Rio Grande, directly across from Big Bend National Park. Until 9/11, its economy was based on the national park tourists, who were ferried across the river to enjoy a Mexican lunch and buy a few souvenirs. Tightened security after 9/11 ended the practice, and because the town is a long way from paved roads and the nearest border crossing, it is headed toward extinction. Similarly, the twin rural communities of Jacumba, California, and Jacume, Baja California, have been cut in two by new enforcement practices, so that a five-minute commute to work or a stroll across the border to the local store or to use the public phone has turned into a journey of more than an hour, often with long waits in line at the border.

BORDER SECURITY

Attempts to slow or stop undocumented migration and to increase security have added tensions to the border, significantly increased the costs of transporting goods and people across the border, and contributed directly to the inability of transborder communities to become cohesive, high-functioning economic regions. Although border security is an old problem, and although the urgency of doing something about undocumented migration waxes and wanes, pressures on border regions greatly increased after September 11, 2001. The tendency to see the border exclusively in terms of security and crime prevention is an ever-present danger to border communities but one that is often held in check by economic, social, and other forces. After September 11, however, the checks were removed and a green light was given to U.S. federal policy makers who see the border as little more than a security issue. Insofar as no significant investments were made in improving border crossing infrastructure, the priority on security was operationalized as a slowdown in border crossing, a closing of customary but unofficial crossing points, and a big jump in the opportunity costs of cross-border activities.

Because borders involve the international transport of goods and people, national agendas take precedence over local needs, particularly when border communities do not have a clear view of their own needs or are unable to express them in a coherent and unified voice to policy makers in distant capitals. In the U.S.-Mexico border, small communities such as Jacumba in the United States or Boquillas in Mexico are hardly able to express their needs to far-away capitals, while large communities, such as San Diego and Ciudad Juárez, with multiple levels of government and decision-making authority have a hard time organizing across the border to reach a consensus on issues as complex as cross-border relations.

Ironically, with increased openness in U.S.-Mexico trade relations, the border began to see large increases in the flow of people and goods simultaneously with the implementation of a more rigid set of U.S. border controls. Prior to 9/11, the United States began Operation Hold the Line in El Paso (1993), Operation Gatekeeper in San Diego (1994), Operation Rio Grande (1997), and Operation Safeguard in Arizona (1999). After 9/11, governmental customs and immigration services were reorganized as primarily security agencies, and a number of new programs were instituted that placed greater controls on entering and exiting the country, such as U.S.-VISIT and the Secure Border Initiative.[10] According to the director of the Office of Homeland Security, the latter is an attempt to "address all aspects of the border security problem across the board—deterrence, detection, response, apprehension, detention, and removal."[11] As is evident in this and other statements, national policy makers understand security as an issue of immigration and the border as a problem of unauthorized entry. Hence the application of new technologies is not to facilitate the mobility of legal crossers but to provide "the capacity to integrate multiple state of the art cameras and sensors into a single comprehensive detection system and expand infrastructure systems throughout the border where appropriate to strengthen our efforts to reduce illegal entry."[12] Unfortunately, the application of inspections and technologies that slow crossings hurts a substantial proportion of the exchange benefiting both sides of the border and severely limits the gains from U.S.-Mexico economic integration. In addition, it leads directly to the death of more than one immigrant per day, and it imposes huge costs on individuals, businesses, families, and communities in the border region.

THE DEVELOPMENT GAP

The issues of security and even more so of migration are intricately related to the gap in economic development between the two countries and the two border regions. In our analysis of human development in Chapter 9 we decomposed the development gap into gaps in income, education, and health. By 2000 the health gap had become very small, but the income gap remains large today, and the education gap is enormous. Though the cross-border differences in development are not as large as the average national differences, they are still very large, creating tensions in the border regions as well as nationally.[13] Finding and acting on policies that will narrow the twin gaps in income and education is the necessary next step in lowering tensions on the border.

The income gap between the U.S. and Mexican border regions is one of the largest cross-border income differentials in the world. Tension at the border is directly related to the size of the income gap between the two sides. As surely as the desert traps heat, wage differentials pull workers across the border, and during periods of high U.S. unemployment, flows of undocumented workers fuel antimigrant, anti-Mexican sentiments. In spite of NAFTA and the large amount of private direct investment in Mexico's border manufacturing, wage differentials have continued to grow over time. The boom in cross-border trade and export-processing production on the Mexican side has not stopped wage and income differentials from increasing. In real terms, adjusted for differences in purchasing power, the per capita regional product is more than twice as much on the U.S. side as on the Mexican side.[14] When measured at the more visible market exchange rates, the differential is even larger. In 2005, for instance, average per capita income measured at market exchange rates was six times higher in the U.S. border region than in the Mexican border region. In specific sectors it is even greater, for example in manufacturing, where the average annual wage in Arizona in 2001 was $47,990, or more than nine times the average wage earned by a maquiladora worker across the border in Sonora ($5,220). The visible market exchange rate differential may be even more important than differences measured in terms of purchasing power as a force pulling migration since a significant proportion of the money that migrants earn is sent back to their families in Mexico, where it is exchanged into pesos at the market rate of exchange.

Furthermore, these income differentials depend on aggregate figures, which hide much of the variation that occurs within Mexico. Mexico's high level of inequality and the poor quality of infrastructure and housing for many residents of the Mexican border region undermine the relevance of aggregate income as a single indicator of living conditions. To a degree, the same is true for the United States, as both border regions have seen persistently high and even increasing poverty rates in recent years despite substantial long-run economic growth. Along the U.S. border, real median income had a slight downward trend between 1970 and 2000 even though real per capita income increased, suggesting that all of the real economic growth that occurred during that thirty-year period was concentrated in the upper half of the income distribution. During that same period, the percentage of U.S. border region families that were below the poverty line increased from 20 percent in 1970 to 25 percent in 2000. The persistence of poverty and the concentration of growth in the upper half of the income distribution both indicate that economic growth by itself will not be an effective policy for poverty alleviation. Rather, poverty reduction requires focused antipoverty policies that concentrate on increasing human and physical capital available to the poor as well as the provision of basic services for the poor.[15]

The primary asset available to poor people is their labor. Consequently, the role of education and its creation of human capital is central to the development gap, regardless of whether the discussion is about the gap between U.S. border communities and the U.S. average or the gap between U.S. and Mexican border communities. Education is an essential component of economic well-being and has a major impact on economic growth and income levels because of its direct relationship to worker productivity. As shown in Chapter 9, the cross-border gap in educational attainment is the largest component of the Border Human Development Index gap between the Mexican and U.S. border regions. In 2000, 30 percent of Mexican border region adults older than twenty-four years had at least a high school education, compared with 74 percent in the U.S. border region (and 80.4 percent for the United States as a whole).[16] It was only in 1992 that Mexico revised its education law to raise the cutoff for compulsory education from sixth grade to ninth grade, and whereas the new requirement contributed to a strong increase in the percentage of the population with more than primary education, it still left Mexico decades behind the United States. As early as 1930, all U.S. states had established twelve years of schooling as the norm.

It is clear from this study and others that Mexico, including the border region, which attracts migrants from throughout the country, would benefit greatly from a stronger emphasis on public middle school (secondary) and high school education. A larger pool of high school graduates would increase the overall sophistication of Mexico's labor force and would help attract more sophisticated forms of investment, both in manufacturing and in services. Indeed, one of the keys to the economic success of several high-growth East Asian economies has been their public support for the wide dissemination of high school as the school-leaving standard. A similar movement in Mexico would address the issue of industrial upgrading in Mexican manufacturing and the need to move toward increasingly skill-intensive forms of manufacturing in order to raise wages while remaining competitive with China and other global competitors. In the longer run, this would push Mexico through its high-emigration development phase and work toward closing the development gap.

EASING TENSIONS

If mobility and migration, security, and development are related, then so is the way forward. The current positions of both Mexico and the United States on migration are incoherent, contradictory, and harmful to people in the border regions.[17] Until the issue of mobility is viewed within a framework that considers the historical context of the twin cities along the border, further legislation is not likely to be favorable to borderlanders or to ease tensions arising from migration and security issues in the border region. Ultimately, the debate about entering and exiting the United States and Mexico must be posed in terms of infrastructure, economic development, and local community needs, in addition to national security and crime prevention.

In the post-9/11 period, the United States has dramatically stepped up the financial resources it is willing to pour into border control and inspections, but far too little thought has been given to the needs of border residents and the ways in which new infrastructure might facilitate legal crossings. Cross-border pedestrian traffic, personal vehicle crossings, and commercial truck flows continue to grow at a rapid pace, but new ports of entry remain on the drawing board, staffing remains inadequate to the task of keeping more gates open, and national policies generate a sense that the priorities of national governments are antagonistic to local communities. One of the greatest ironies may be that the assumed trade-off between more rapid crossing and increased mobility, on the one hand, and security and crime prevention efforts on the other is a false dichotomy. Congested crossings and long border waits create so much background noise and chaos that it becomes harder to detect the presence of security threats or criminal elements. A smoother, more rapid flow of border crossers and increased use of electronic identification of regular border crossers would make crime prevention and detection of security threats easier, not harder.

In part, ineffective and harmful policies are the result of trying to solve all problems at once with only one set of policies. Border enforcement has been given at least three distinct roles: security (prevention of terrorist attacks), order (crime fighting), and control (stopping unauthorized entry). None of these can be done well if all are done simultaneously by the same agencies. For example, militarization of the border has increased the cost of crossing, measured in both money and lives, has discouraged migrants from making return trips to Mexico, and has resulted in a larger proportion of permanent migrants, who then need to find a way of bringing their families with them. The increasing cost of coyotes (hired guides for crossing the border illegally) has the additional unintended but predictable result of attracting organized crime into the business of supplying coyotes. In short, the results of the massive increase in expenditure are an increase in crime and violence at the border and increased deaths among people trying to cross, but no reduction in migration. It has, however, caused a shift away from temporary and revolving forms of migration toward permanent migration.[18]

Another set of short-sighted policies are those of some local communities and a couple of border states that have tried to refuse health care and education to undocumented immigrants. These policies are usually based on estimates of local costs and benefits, where costs are calculated in terms of health care, education, and criminal justice expenditures, while benefits usually include excise, property, income, and social security taxes paid, and some qualitative recognition of the impact of low wages on the prices of various goods and services. The implicit assumption of these calculations—beyond the mistaken notion that costs and benefits can be accurately quantified—is that no costs or benefits would accrue if all undocumented immigrants returned home. The calculation is mistaken on several counts, but perhaps most particularly with regard to the assumption that undocumented immigrants are not "home" in the United States. In fact, many of them will never return to Mexico or other countries of origin since their families, jobs, and social networks are now located in the United States.[19] This point has not entered the public discourse about the local school and health care costs imposed by undocumented immigrants and their children. Yet it is fundamentally important, since the alternative to providing schooling and health care to the children of undocumented immigrants is not a cost savings but rather an illiterate, unvaccinated, and uncared-for population located in the midst of border communities and other places where undocumented immigrants settle. Hence the true cost of withholding education and health care may be far greater over the long run than the cost of providing these services. In that sense, the vigorous and sometimes strident discussion in some border communities about the costs imposed on local social services by undocumented immigrants and their children is a fantasy debate since it is based on false assumptions about the likelihood of undocumented immigrants returning to Mexico.

What is needed is a policy approach that is based on an honest and more comprehensive analysis of the causes of migration and that works in a positive way to curb the tensions associated with it. The first step is to put political rhetoric aside and openly recognize the fact that the political economy of the United States favors the rights of businesses to hire labor at the lowest possible cost, including low-wage workers from abroad. As long as the demand for foreign workers continues, the supply will follow, and a policy that simply focuses on the supply side is doomed to fail. Once this need for unskilled, cheap labor is acknowledged at a policymaking level, the next logical step is to dramatically increase the number of work visas to a level that meets the demand for this labor. This would allow Mexicans who seek work to enter legally, giving those trying to enforce security at the border much better control. But for this policy to work, it must be coupled with strong enforcement of employers to hire only documented workers. Legalizing this workforce would help to restore a circular flow of migrants between their homes in Mexico and their work in the United States, and would give them the option of leaving their families in Mexico.

One way to help defray the costs of administering such a program (besides the savings on the number of Border Patrol agents needed) and to help local communities with the added social costs of migrants would be to charge a fee for these visas, perhaps in the neighborhood of several hundred dollars (still cheaper than the costs of coyotes). This fee could be used to cover the administrative costs of the program, to compensate migrant-receiving communities for the costs of added social services, including health and education, and to provide development funds for education and infrastructure investment in the sending Mexican communities. This last use of a portion of the fee represents one approach toward narrowing the development gap in the long run. On the Mexican side of the border, policies that increase the effectiveness and coverage of public education, especially at the high school level, would also work toward closing the development gap.

Many other effective programs have been suggested by others. The point here is not to specify a quick fix or a particular program but rather to emphasize that it is in the interest of both countries to speed up the passage of Mexico through its period of high emigration. Ultimately, this means that issues of mobility within North America must be addressed as fundamental historical and social trends, and not as problems of individual law breakers who enter the United States without authorization. The long-run view recognizes the unique relationship between the United States and Mexico and especially between their border regions, and is beneficial to border communities because it gives them the opportunity to express their needs for easier, faster flows of goods and people, as opposed to the current trend of more difficult and limited entry and exit.

Above all, border regions need more ports of entry, more lanes at existing ports, and the application of technology and human resources to speed up cross-border flows of people, services, and goods. In the same way that population growth at the border has overwhelmed environmental infrastructure, it has also overwhelmed border-crossing infrastructure. In parallel with the lack of resources for addressing environmental problems, the lack of resources for facilitating easy cross-border transactions and social relations is a major obstacle to development and prosperity.

TOWARD ECONOMIC DEVELOPMENT

The trends in demographic, economic, and quality-of-life indicators that we have presented here show considerable improvement over the last half of the twentieth century. At the same time, significant poverty remains and shows little sign of declining, and there is scant evidence of a decline in the development gap between the U.S. and Mexican border regions. The Universal Declaration of Human Rights asserts the right of all people to enjoy living standards adequate for their health and well-being. These standards must meet basic needs, including security in the event of unemployment, illness, disability, widowhood, and old age. The declaration confirms the right to education, free at fundamental stages, with technical and professional education generally available. Idealism alone, however, is not the only reason why more attention and resources should be focused on the borderlands. Increased prosperity and a reduction in cross-border inequality will also serve the material and security interests of both the United States and Mexico. Investments in human and physical capital on both sides of the border, including infrastructure for safe drinking water and sanitation, as well as paved roads and electricity, schools and health clinics, and increased infrastructure for border crossing, will help prepare the region for the future and assist in the realization of the economic benefits of the U.S.-Mexico relationship.

It may seem quixotic to suggest public investment in a time of such "private opulence and public squalor," particularly when current politics make it doubtful that the U.S. Congress is going to appropriate funds any time soon for border development.[20] Nor would the anti-U.S. rhetoric and political tactics of a portion of Mexico's political class allow them to accept U.S. funds. However, rather than waiting passively to be surprised by an unexpected turn of events, a number of analysts have begun to imagine creative solutions to funding border development programs. The Council on Foreign Relations, political scientist Robert Pastor, and others have begun to imagine the possibilities for an expanded North American community and the institutions needed for its realization. Among others, a North American investment fund, perhaps modeled after the idea of regional and cohesion funds in the European Union, could potentially serve as a means of funding projects with the greatest impact on the development gap. Free movement in the border region, together with an expanded visa program that imposes the equivalent of a social security tax on cross-border workers but puts the money into a fund for investment projects in Mexico, is a way around U.S. taxpayer objections and Mexican fears of U.S. meddling. In the immediate border region, the cross-border characteristic of many problems, such as air and water pollution, makes it worthwhile to argue for an expansion of cross-border negotiating authority for local and state governments. The point is that although every imaginable funding mechanism is likely to have political problems and limitations, creative thinking can overcome many of the barriers.

INTEGRATION IS NOT OVER

Unless the course of history over the last few hundred years is reversed, it is safe to assume that U.S.-Mexico integration—economic, cultural, linguistic, institutional, and other forms—is going to continue. Cross-border differences are significant and the challenges are great, but it is not something that individuals or even national governments have the power to choose. While Washington, D.C., and Mexico, D.F., engage in high-level diplomatic talks, with important people flying back and forth and issuing joint statements, a vast ocean of individuals, families and friends, service organizations, businesses, educational institutions, local government officials, nongovernmental organizations, and churches is strengthening cross-border ties. This behavior is about as natural as the passage of wildlife and weather across the border, and short of some unimaginable cataclysm, it will continue to unfold and develop throughout the next century as it did in the last one. Private firms like Toyota Motors may pay attention to spats between the presidents of Mexico and the United States, but after taking note, they still build their plants in Texas and Coahuila because the locational advantage is geographic and economic, and not exclusively political. Likewise, U.S. racists and xenophobes may grab headlines with rants about undocumented immigrants, but emergency responders still need to collaborate, social workers need to help children who cross the border, and grandchildren are still going to visit their grandparents on the other side.

Perhaps the greatest disadvantage for residents of border communities is that it is difficult to speak with one voice, and hence it is difficult to be heard in national capitals. Business people want to facilitate trade, families want to visit their relatives, and friends want to socialize. U.S. citizens are crossing into Mexican border regions to find more affordable housing, medical care, and pharmaceuticals, while Mexican citizens are crossing to find jobs with better wages, education, and high-tech medical care. Business managers and workers in larger numbers live on one side and work on the other, just-in-time inventory systems depend on the smooth flow of parts across the border, and agricultural and fishing interests need to get their products to market on the other side as quickly as possible. Local governments are officially prevented from engaging in direct negotiations with their counterparts across the border, yet the pressure of events requires them to do so since natural disasters, crime, sewage spills, and medical emergencies are often cross-border events and frequently require spontaneous cross-border assistance. Nongovernmental organizations such as churches, foundations, environmental groups, and service organizations have a multiplicity of needs for cross-border communication, movement, and financial engagement, while schools in the border region, including institutions of higher education, want to move students and teachers back and forth, to share library resources, and to learn about each other's systems. All of these needs are of practical concern, because they address the everyday functioning of the relations and institutions that fill the lives of many residents in the border region. It is the responsibility of border communities to express these needs in a coherent and collaborative way so that it maximizes the chances for federal policy makers to hear it. As long as border communities are unable to articulate their needs, they will not be included in public policy debates, and there is little chance that they will get what they need, let alone what they want.

In the final analysis, cross-border integration is a natural process driven by people who understand they are living in an increasingly binational, bicultural context. Integration in all forms will continue under almost any imaginable scenario, and with care it will provide benefits to be shared by all; ignoring it or trying to suppress it will be expensive, harmful, and ultimately unsuccessful, as the prosperity and crises of one side of the border are inevitably tied to the other side. Enlightened self-interest calls for a sharing of resources to build a solid economic system, including effective educational institutions capable of producing a productive workforce and joint actions to secure clean air and water and adequate and affordable housing. Policies that facilitate joint economic development are, in the end, the policies that have the best chance of easing the border migration and security tensions.

Mexico, D.F., and Washington, D.C., frequently have high-level talks about contentious issues such as migration, drug policy, and trade. National politicians must be sensitive to their constituencies, and inevitably they keep one eye on domestic politics while speaking across international borders. Hence, it is often the case that rhetoric at the national level is not helpful to U.S.-Mexico relations or to the border regions that are often the implicit focus of the rhetoric. Regardless of the tenor of the national debates, however, a long-run, profound integration is occurring between the United States and Mexico, and given the shared histories of many border communities, it is not surprising that it is much deeper in the border

Border crossing bridge from Ciudad Juárez to El Paso, Texas.

regions. This is a localized and grassroots form of integration that stands in contrast to lofty visions of national policies and the integration of nation-states. It often seems to exist outside the awareness of national politics, perhaps because the border is so far from both capitals and because its social and cultural differences have made it seem unimportant to national interests. The challenge for border communities is to change this misperception of integration and to express their needs clearly so that they can be communicated within the national public discourses of both countries. With population growth and increasing trade and investment flows, border communities are becoming increasingly important to national interests and must assume greater weight in national debates. As this happens, the goal for border communities should be to articulate their particular needs within the larger frameworks of national policy debates and to work collaboratively with partners from across the border to make those needs visible in their respective capitals. Regardless of their success or failure, however, the long-run integration of the U.S. and Mexico in the border regions is under way and will continue into the foreseeable future.

NOTES

1. Audits, warnings, and fines all decreased dramatically between 1986 and 2000, even though a key provision of IRCA legislation was employer inspections. In 2004, for example, nationwide, three employers were fined. See Brownell (2005), "Declining enforcement of employer sanctions." To date, the United States does not have the political will to deprive employers of their illegal immigrant labor force.

2. Alegría (2002), "Demand and supply of Mexican cross-border workers."

3. Peach (1997), "Income distribution along the United States border with Mexico: 1970–1990."

4. Peach and Molina (2002), "Income distribution in Mexico's northern border states."

5. Diehl (1983), "Effect of the peso devaluation on Texas border cities," and Prock (1983), "The peso devaluations and their effect on Texas border economies."

6. San Diego Dialogue (1994), *Who Crosses the Border? A View of the San Diego/Tijuana Metropolitan Region*, and San Diego Dialogue, Centro Estudios Económicos del Sector Empresarial de Mexicali, A.C., and Universidad Autónoma de Baja California (1998), *Survey of Border Crossers: Imperial/Mexicali Valley.*

7. Papademetriou and Meyers (2001), "Overview."

1. According to the Mexican census bureau, in 2000, 28.8 percent of Tijuana's economically active population worked in manufacturing. By comparison, the figures for San Diego and the United States were 9.9 and 13.0 per-

cent, respectively. See U.S. Bureau of Labor Statistics (n.d.), *State and County Employment* and *National Employment*.

2. The most recent eruption was in 1935; geologic evidence points to eruptions as long as 10,000 years ago.

3. Though not located on the border, it is the largest city in a border county and so is included in the U.S. border region data set.

4. Wages in Mexico are generally measured as multiples of the minimum wage. Official census data are gathered and reported for the share of the population earning no wages, less than one times minimum wage, one to two times minimum wage, two to five times minimum wage, and more than five times minimum wage.

5. Public Affairs Office (2005), "Southern New Mexico regional history before 1945."

6. U.S. Bureau of Transportation Statistics (2006), *TranStats—The Intermodal Transportation Database*.

7. Arreola (2002), *Tejano South Texas: A Mexican-American Cultural Province*, 156.

8. Ramirez (2001), "Unions, collaboration and labour conditions in Mexican maquiladoras."

CHAPTER 2

1. Rural Terrell and Hudspeth counties in Texas and Camargo, Tamaulipas, all had negative population growth in the years 1950–2000.

2. These areas included Tijuana and Tecate in Baja California, Agua Prieta in Sonora, Ciudad Juárez in Chihuahua, Ciudad Acuña in Coahuila, and Yuma in Arizona.

3. Rural is defined as no town with more than 2,500 people.

4. These agglomerations were San Diego–Tijuana, Imperial County–Mexicali, El Paso–Ciudad Juárez, Webb County (Laredo)–Nuevo Laredo, Cameron County (McAllen)–Reynosa, and Hidalgo County (Brownsville)–Matamoros.

5. See Schultz (1974), *Fertility Determinants: A Theory, Evidence and Application to Policy Evaluation*, and Pritchett (1994), "Desired fertility and the impact of population policies," among many others.

6. Martin (2003), "Mexico-U.S. migration."

7. The data used here for population growth are the average growth rate for the decade ending in the year indicated. The natural percentage increase, however, is based on the number of births and deaths in that year.

8. Wilson (1993), "We seek work where we can: A comparison of patterns of out migration from a rancho in Jalisco and of internal migration into a Mexicali squatter settlement."

9. Authors' calculation based on data from INEGI.

10. Mexico has three minimum wages, depending on the region. They do not differ much.

11. World Bank (2005), *Doing Business 2005.*

12. Terminology is important. Many Mexicans and some Americans are offended by the use of the term "illegal immigrant," reasoning that people can commit illegal acts but cannot be illegal in themselves. Although this may seem like a useless piece of political correctness, we have avoided using the term. In place of "illegal" we offer "unauthorized" and "undocumented."

13. Massey, Durand, and Malone (2003), *Beyond Smoke and Mirrors: Mexican Immigration in an Era of Economic Integration.*

14. Meyers (2005), "U.S. border enforcement: From horseback to high-tech."

15. The estimate for migrant remittances in 2003 was $12 billion, and for 2005 it was $20 billion. There is considerable dispute about the size of the remittance flows, but everyone agrees it is in the billions and growing.

16. During the 1980s and 1990s, despite gains in Mexican labor productivity, real minimum wages and manufacturing wages fell. See Hufbauer and Schott (2005), *NAFTA Revisited: Achievements and Challenges,* for a discussion of labor productivity, wages, and the debates surrounding them.

CHAPTER 3

1. Hall (1994), "Bush links future of state to Mexican trade."

2. *New York Times* (1994), "Alamo? What Alamo? Texans want to get closer to Mexico."

3. Hall (1994), "Brownsville seeks rights to 'NAFTA Home Port' tag."

4. Rodriguiz and Hagan (2001), "Transborder community relations at the U.S.-Mexico border: Laredo/Nuevo Laredo and El Paso/Ciudad Juárez."

5. According to 2000 census data, Mexicali had 764,602 residents, while Imperial County had 142,362. The U.S. border city Calexico, which adjoins Mexicali's urban area, had only 27,109 residents. In addition, Mexicali is the capital of the state of Baja California and as such is a bustling city with government offices, universities, hotels, and other urban amenities.

6. Del Castillo (2001), "Between order and chaos: Management of the westernmost border between Mexico and the United States."

7. Jordan (1984), *Texas: A Geography.*

8. Wright (1940), "The making of cosmopolitan California: An analysis of immigration, 1848–1970."

9. Sandos (2000), "Because he is a liar and a thief: Conquering the residents of old California, 1850–1880." Sandos gives a good description of the fate of the residents of the state at the time of the Gold Rush. Although the Treaty of Guadelupe Hidalgo recognized the land rights as recorded in Mexican land grants, the need to prove title and to determine precise boundaries drove many

into bankruptcy. What the courts began, droughts and floods in the 1860s finished.

10. Martínez (1988), *Troublesome Border*, and Larralde and Jacobo (2000), *Juan N. Cortina and the Struggle for Justice in Texas*.

11. Arreola (2002), *Tejano South Texas: A Mexican American Cultural Province*.

12. Jordan (1984), *Texas: A Geography*.

13. This observation is based on data from the 1990 census.

14. A deficiency in English language skills has an economic cost in the United States. Numerous researchers have noted this, for example, McManus, Gould, and Welch (1983), "Earnings of Hispanic men: The role of English language proficiency." Their study and many others relied exclusively on male samples to measure the wage loss of workers who are deficient in English, but Mora and Dávila (1998), "Gender, earnings, and the English-skill acquisition of Hispanic workers," show that women suffer a smaller penalty. It also appears the wage loss is similar in the Spanish-friendly border region, implying that the economic incentive to learn English is no less strong in the border region. See Dávila and Mora (2000), "English skills, earnings, and the occupational sorting of Mexican Americans along the U.S.-Mexico border."

15. Similarly, other measures of concentration are consistent with this analysis. For example, the Gini coefficient for concentration of the Latino population (share of population relative to share of Latinos) is 0.298 in Texas and 0.195 in California, again using the 1990 census.

16. Rodriguez and Hagen (2001), "Transborder community relations," 107.

17. NALEO (National Association of Latino Elected Officials) (2002), *National Directory of Latino Elected Officials*.

18. In 2000, Texas exported goods and services to Mexico that were equivalent to 6.6 percent of its gross state product; Michigan's exports to Canada were 5.9 percent. See U.S. Bureau of Economic Analysis (n.d.), *Gross State Product*, and U.S. International Trade Administration (n.d.), *TradeStats Express*.

19. The U.S. Department of Commerce measures state exports from the point at which a good begins its movement abroad as an export, and not at its point of production. In certain cases this causes bias, as when shipments are consolidated at one point before being declared as exports. See: U.S. International Trade Administration (n.d.), *Guide to State Export Data*." More sophisticated analysis by the Census Bureau for manufactured goods alone (omitting agricultural commodities) shows that Texas exports the second greatest quantity of manufactured goods overall, behind only California ($70 billion versus $43 billion in 2001). See U.S. Census Bureau (2004), *Exports from Manufacturing Establishments*. Hence, regardless of the accuracy of the state export data, a large number of jobs and a significant share of goods production in Texas depend on its trade with Mexico.

20. For example, in the wake of U.S. concerns about a rising Japan, Congress passed the Omnibus Trade and Competitiveness Act of 1989. This bill

sought to bolster U.S. competitiveness, for example by funding Centers for International Business Education and Research. This is only one example, but it illustrates the general, nationwide discovery of "competitiveness" and international markets.

21. California used the direct initiative process to pass Proposition 187, denying social services to undocumented immigrants; Proposition 209, ending affirmative action; and Proposition 227, eliminating bilingual education in public schools. Proposition 187, the most objectionable, was determined to be unconstitutional and was never implemented. Nevertheless, the ability of an opportunistic politician (a governor fighting for reelection) to mobilize and split the electorate by blaming Mexicans for the state's woes points to the harmful way in which the migration issue can be used.

22. GATT is an agreement on tariffs that remains in force. With the completion of the Uruguay round of GATT negotiations, the agreement came under the umbrella of the World Trade Organization, which began life in 1995.

23. Gerber (2002), "Different states, similar responses: California, Texas, and NAFTA."

24. In 1987, manufacturing jobs began to expand in Texas, and between that date and 1999, Texas added 166,000 manufacturing jobs. Gerber (2002), "Different states."

25. Solunet (2001), *The Complete Twin Plant Guide*. Maquiladoras are export-oriented firms that operate under a special Mexican tax provision. Most of them are U.S. owned, and they are concentrated in electronics, auto parts, and to a lesser degree apparel.

26 Hanson (1996), *U.S.-Mexico Integration and Regional Economies: Evidence from Border City Pairs*; Hanson (1997), "The effects of offshore assembly on industry location: Evidence from U.S. border cities."

27. U.S. International Trade Administration (2003), *State Exports*.

28. Ibid.

29. Papademetriou and Meyers (2001), "Overview."

30. Purchasing power parity exchange rates take into account price differences. For example, the $9,500 in per capita GDP in the border municipios of Tamaulipas means that an average income in those border municipios will buy a basket of goods and services that would cost $9,500 in the United States. The ratios are based on county and municipio equivalents of GDP per person. This is a measure of the total value of all goods and services produced during a year.

31. Papademetriou and Meyers (2001), "Overview."

CHAPTER 4

1. The five gateway ports with the largest value of shipments are, in descending order, the Port of Los Angles (water), JFK International Airport (air), Detroit (land), the Port of New York and New Jersey (water), and the Port

of Long Beach (water). Laredo is the sixth most important port for overall U.S. trade, while El Paso is fourteenth and San Diego (Otay Mesa) is twenty-fifth. U.S. Bureau of Transportation Statistics (2006), *America's Freight Transportation Gateways.*

2. INEGI (Instituto Nacional de Estadística, Geografía e Informática) (2005), *Banco de Información Económica.*

3. In 2005, Canada purchased 23.4 percent of U.S. manufactured exports; Mexico and China (ex-Hong Kong) purchased 13.3 percent and 4.6 percent, respectively (Hong Kong purchased 1.8 percent). The United States imports more from China than from Mexico, but it exports so much more to Mexico that its total trade, exports plus imports, is greater with Mexico. In 2005, total trade with Mexico was $290 billion (exports plus imports, merchandise only), while trade with China was $285 billion. Extrapolating past rates of change, China was expected to pass Mexico as the number two trading partner (after Canada) in 2006. These figures omit services trade, which still favors Mexico. U.S. International Trade Administration (2005), *Foreign Trade Highlights.*

4. Foreign direct investment involves the purchase of real assets such as businesses, machinery, or real estate. Intra-firm trade occurs when the exporting firm and the importing firm are the same. If Toyota, for example, sends parts from one side of the border to a plant it owns on the other side, it shows up as international trade, in both the United States' and Mexico's national accounts.

5. Shatz and López-Calva (2004), *The Emerging Integration of the California-Mexico Economies.*

6. U.S. International Trade Administration (2003), *State Exports.* It is worth reiterating the caveats of Chapter 3 with respect to state export data: The U.S. Commerce Department measures state exports from the point at which a good begins its movement abroad as an export, and not at its point of production. This probably biases upward the absolute figures for state export totals from border states to Mexico, since warehousing and other trade services may be concentrated near the border. Nevertheless, as pointed out in Chapter 3, more sophisticated analysis does not undermine the qualitative results showing Texas and California to be the most significant state exporters to Mexico, and accounting for a disproportionately large share of overall U.S. exports to Mexico. U.S. Census Bureau (n.d.), "State export data series."

7. INEGI (2005), *Banco de Información Económica.*

8. See, for example, Little, Scitovsky, and Scott (1970), *Industry and Trade in Some Developing Countries: A Comparative Study;* Bhagwati (1978), *Foreign Trade Regimes and Economic Development: Anatomy and Consequences of Exchange Control Regimes;* Krueger (1978), *Foreign Trade Regimes and Economic Development: Liberalization Attempts and Consequences;* Balassa (1980), "The process of industrial development and alternative development strategies"; and Bruton (1998), "A reconsideration of import substitution."

9. For empirical evidence, see Krugman and Livas Elizondo (1995), "Trade policy and the Third World metropolis."

10. U.S. Census Bureau (n.d.), *Trade with Mexico.*

11. INEGI (2005), *Banco de Información Económica.*

12. U.S. Bureau of Economic Analysis (2004), *State and Local Personal Income*, and INEGI (2005), *Banco de Información Económica.*

13. The word *bracero* is derived from the Spanish *brazo*, or arm, indicating that the workers in the Bracero Program were meant to be manual laborers. A similar program was implemented during World War I. Many participants in the Bracero Program are alive today, and many are U.S. citizens or permanent residents, so that the memory of this experience has not completely faded into history.

14. Chapter 98 of the Harmonized Tariff System (HTS), sections 9802.00.60 through 9802.00.90, details so-called "production sharing" arrangements. See U.S. International Trade Commission (1999), *Production Sharing: Use of U.S. Components and Materials in Foreign Assembly Operations, 1995–1998.* These provisions are not exclusive to goods from Mexico, and a number of countries qualify to use this part of the U.S. tariff code.

15. See Grunwald and Flamm (1985), *The Global Factory.*

16. INEGI (2005), *Banco de Información Económica.*

17. Gruben (2001), "Was NAFTA behind Mexico's high maquiladora growth?" and Gerber and Mundra (2003), "Is the downturn in maquiladora employment cyclical or structural?"

18. External economies imply that average production costs decline as industry size increases. Marshall's work on industrial districts is an early statement. Marshall (1919), *Industry and Trade.*

19. Regional agglomeration effects also explain the processes behind Hollywood as a site for movie production, or Silicon Valley for software and computer equipment.

20. Gereffi and Tam (1998), "Industrial upgrading through organization chains: Dynamics of rent, learning and social mobility in the global economy," and Bhagwati (2002), *Free Trade Today*, discuss the concepts of industrial upgrading and the ladder of comparative advantage.

21. Carrillo and Hualde (1996), "Third generation Maquiladoras: The case of Delphi–General Motors."

22. Brown and Domínguez (1989), "Nuevas tecnologías en la industria maquiladora de exportación"; Carrillo and Ramírez (1990), "Modernización, tecnológica y cambios organizacionales en la industria maquiladora"; Wilson (1992), *Exports and Local Development*; Carrillo (Ed.) (1993), *Condiciones de Empleo y Capacitación en las Maquiladoras de Exportación en México*; and Contreras (2000), *Empresas Globales, Actores Locales: Producción Flexible y Aprendizaje Industrial en las Maquiladoras.*

23. Lara Rivero (1998), *Aprendizaje Tecnológico y Mercado de Trabajo en las Maquiladoras Japonesas*; Barajas Escamilla (2000), *Global Production*

Networks in an Electronics Industry: The Case of the Tijuana–San Diego Region; and Carrillo (2001), "Maquiladoras de exportación y la formación de empresas Mexicanas exitosas."

24. Gerber and Carrillo (2003), "Competitividad al debate: la experiencia de las maquiladoras mexicanas." Their estimates are based on survey data from El Colegio de la Frontera Norte. See COLEF, Facultad Latinoamericana de Ciencias Sociales-Mexico and Universidad Autónoma Metropolitana (2002), "Aprendizaje Tecnológico y Escalamiento Industrial: Perspectivas para la Formación de Capacidades de Innovación en las Maquiladoras en México."

25. Comisión Nacional de Inversiones Extranjeras (2006), *Informe Estadístico Trimestral sobre el Comportamiento de la Inversión Extranjera Directa en México.*

26. U.S. International Trade Administration, Office of Automotive Affairs (1999), *Fifth Annual Report to Congress Regarding the Impact of the North American Free Trade Agreement upon U.S. Automotive Trade with Mexico.* Among other motivations, they cite: (1) the formation of strategic alliances between U.S. and Mexican firms; (2) product specialization, for example when U.S. automakers decide to concentrate production of certain vehicle models in Mexico; (3) a decision to maintain or increase vertical integration by concentrating supply lines within the firm rather than purchasing inputs from outside suppliers; (4) the opposite of vertical integration, in which a firm chooses to seek alliances with an outside contractor; and (5) the advantages of regional manufacturing centers and the agglomeration or scale economies they offer. For example, U.S.-based Whirlpool and Mexico-based Vitro formed a strategic alliance in 1989 to produce and distribute small refrigerators in North and Central America and Asia, while the U.S.-based Johnson Controls formed a partnership with Varta AG and Grupo Isma SA to supply car parts throughout North America while other car manufacturers reduced the number of different vehicle models produced in Mexico while simultaneously developing specialized product lines for their Mexican factories. U.S.-based textile firms have integrated vertically in some cases and contracted out in others. Vertical integration and its opposite—contracting out—are choices facing every firm. The optimal strategy depends on a wide variety of factors, including technology, property rights, cost structure, and others. The theory is covered in any standard industrial organization textbook. See also Bair (2001), "The maquiladora industry and development in Mexico."

27. Dunning (1981), *International Production and the Multinational Enterprise.*

28. INEGI (2005), *Banco de Información Económica.*

29. Iglesias Prieto (1997), *Beautiful Flowers of the Maquiladora: The Life Histories of Women Workers in Tijuana.*

30. Intermediate inputs are goods that are incorporated into the final product. They include parts and assemblies that are built into a final product, such

as a car engine which is itself made up of many parts but which is bolted into a car. Factories that make cars do not also make engines but rather install the engine, which is obtained from a separate plant and may be imported.

31. INEGI (2005), *Banco de Información Económica.*

CHAPTER 5

1. Hufbauer and Schott (1993), *NAFTA: An Assessment;* U.S. Trade Representative (1992), *Review of U.S.-Mexico Environmental Issues;* Sierra Club (1993), *Funding Needs Associated with the North American Free Trade Agreement.*

2. Daly (1993), "The perils of free trade"; Bhagwati (1993), "The case for free trade."

3. The environmental Kuznets curve is named after Simon Kuznets, the noted economist who hypothesized a similar relationship between income inequality and income levels. See Kuznets (1955), "Economic growth and income inequality." Kuznets thought that most countries initially went through a process of worsening inequality with rising incomes, followed by improvements in inequality after a threshold income level was reached. The environmental Kuznets curve is directly analogous.

4. Neumeyer (2001), *Greening Trade and Investment: Environmental Protection Without Protectionism;* Stern (1998), "Progress on the environmental Kuznets curve?"; Gallagher (2004), *Free Trade and the Environment: Mexico, NAFTA, and Beyond.*

5. Gerber and Carrillo (2006), "The future of the maquiladora: Between industrial upgrading and competitive decline." ISO refers to the International Standards Organization, a nongovernmental organization recognized as an independent, best practices, standard-setting body in more than 140 countries. Standards 14001 and 14002 refer to their environmental control systems standards.

6. U.S. Environmental Protection Agency (2006), *U.S.-Mexico Border 2012 Framework.*

7. Ibid.

8. Over the same period, the number of passenger vehicles entering the United States rose from 62 million (1995) to 91 million (2004). U.S. Bureau of Transportation Statistics (2006), TranStats

9. Goldrich and Carruthers (1992), "Sustainable development in Mexico? The international politics of crisis or opportunity."

10. Hecht, Whelan, and Sowell (2002), "Sustainable development on the U.S.-Mexican border: Past lessons, present efforts, future possibilities."

11. Saldaña (1999), "Tijuana's toxic waters."

12. INEGI (Instituto Nacional de Estadística, Geografía e Informática) (1990–1992), *XI Censo General de Población y Vivienda, 1990;* ibid. (2001), *XII*

Censo General de Población y Vivienda, 2000. The accuracy of these numbers depends on an accurate count of people living in the new colonias on the
periphery of urban areas.

13. Cooney (2001), "The Mexican crisis and the maquiladora boom: A
paradox of development or the logic of neoliberalism?"; Public Citizen (2000),
"Deals for NAFTA votes II"; and Saldaña (1999), "Tijuana's toxic waters," favor
the pollution haven hypothesis, along with many others. Rugman and Verbeke
(1998), "Corporate strategy and international environmental policy," provide
the counterargument.

14. Hecht, Whelan, and Sowell (2002), "Sustainable development."

15. Ibid.

16. Hernandez (2004), "Mexico's maquiladora expansion during the 1990s:
An environmental assessment."

17. Tomaso and Alm (1990), "Economy vs. ecology: Mexico's drive for
growth eclipses concerns about toxic wastes from border plants."

18. McEnany and Young (2005), "A través de la frontera: Land use visioning—ICF/TSDF, Tijuana watershed."

19. The location of the border became contentious when the Rio Grande
shifted its position, causing conflicts and confusion.

20. Mumme (1987), "State and local influences in transboundary environmental policy making along the U.S.-Mexican border." SEDUE and other Mexican environmental agencies have changed names several times. The current
counterpart to the U.S. EPA is SEMARNAT, Secretaría de Medio Ambiente y
Recursos Naturales.

21. U.S. Government Accountability Office (1999), *U.S.-Mexico Border:
Issues and Challenges Confronting the United States and Mexico,* p. 35.

22. Peach and Williams (2003), "Population and economic dynamics on the
U.S.-Mexico border: Past, present, and future."

23. Papademetriou and Meyers (2001), "Overview."

CHAPTER 6

1. Labor force data for the United States and Mexico are from both countries' censuses, supplemented where necessary with information from the U.S.
Bureau of Labor Statistics and INEGI (Instituto Nacional de Estadística, Geografía e Informática), *Banco de Información Económica.*

2. Martin reduces Mexican employment by the number of workers laid
off and expecting recall, and by the number waiting to start a job within four
weeks. He also adjusts the labor force by subtracting unpaid family workers. In
his words, this is probably an overadjustment. He also notes that the 1.1 percent
upward adjustment in Mexico's unemployment rate is probably an "overadjustment." See Martin (2000), "Employment and unemployment in Mexico in the
1990s."

3. U.S. Bureau of Labor Statistics (n.d.), *State and County Employment.*

4. The U.S. Bureau of Labor Statistics uses a methodology known as the Local Area Unemployment Statistics (LAUS). LAUS instructs state and county labor offices on how to combine information taken from the CPS, the decennial census, new unemployment insurance claims, agricultural labor survey data, and other information sources to come up with a consistent set of state and local unemployment estimates. See Schamedick (2004), "Unemployment statistics: Is there a border bias?" for a detailed explanation and a critique of the BLS methodology.

5. PREALC (1981), *Sector Informal: Funcionamiento y Políticas.*

6. See Anderson (1988), "Causes of growth in the informal labor sector in the Mexican northern border region"; De Soto (1989), *The Other Path;* idem (2000), *The Mystery of Capital;* International Labor Organization (1972), *Employment, Incomes and Equality;* Otero (1989), "Rethinking the informal sector"; Palmade (2005), "Why worry about rising informality?"; Pozo (1996), *Exploring the Underground Economy;* and Schneider (2002), "Size and measurement of the informal economy in 110 countries around the world," among others, for additional discussion of the informal sector.

7. De Soto (1989), *The Other Path;* idem (2000), *The Mystery of Capital.* In de Soto's view, rural-to-urban migration began in many developing countries during the 1940s; consequently, in historical terms, the informal economy is a relatively new phenomenon.

8. World Bank (2005), *Doing Business, 2005.*

9. Fields (1990), "Labour market modeling and the urban informal sector: Theory and evidence."

10. Palmade (2005), "Why worry about rising informality?"; de Soto (2000), *The Mystery of Capital.*

11. INEGI (2005), *Banco de Información Económica;* Schneider (2002), "Size and measurement of the informal economy in 110 countries around the world."

12. Government employees have a separate but parallel set of benefits.

13. Anderson and Dimon (1999), "Formal sector job growth and women's labor sector participation: The case of Mexico."

14. On the other hand, men tend to accept a wife's or daughter's informal sector activities, such as selling, doing take-out sewing, or performing domestic work, as extensions of the woman's homemaker role. For a discussion of the issue of women workers in the maquilas, see Fernandez Kelly (1983), *For We Are Sold, I and My People: Women and Industry in Mexico's Frontier;* Tiano (1990), "Maquiladora women: A new category of workers"; Ward (1990), "Introduction and overview"; and Beneria and Roldan (1987), *The Crossroads of Class and Gender: Industrial Homework, Subcontracting, and Household Dynamics in Mexico City.*

15. Hansen (1981), *The Border Economy.*

16. Although mining has been the dominant activity in some Mexican municipios (Cananea, for example) during some periods, its share of the border region labor force is dwarfed by agriculture.

17. Gruben (2001), "Was NAFTA behind Mexico's high maquiladora growth?" and Gerber and Balsdon (2001), "The impact of the U.S. business cycle on Mexico's maquiladora industry." Both papers show that a 1 percent decrease in U.S. industrial production is associated with a 1.25 percent decrease in maquila employment.

18. INEGI (2005), *Banco de Información Económica.*

19. San Diego Dialogue (1994), *Who Crosses the Border?*

20. Patrick and Renforth (1996), "The effects of the peso devaluation on cross border retailing."

21. Patrick and Renforth (1996), "Effects of the peso devaluation on cross border retailing," studied Brownsville, McAllen, Laredo, and El Paso. See also Prock (1983), "The peso devaluations and their effect on Texas border economies," and Diehl (1983), "The effect of the peso devaluation on Texas border cities."

CHAPTER 7

1. World Bank (2005), *World Development Indicators, 2005.*

2. Heston, Summers, and Aten (2002), *Penn World Table Version 6.1.*

3. The estimated PPP exchange rate changes over time since the relationship between market exchange rates and domestic prices does not remain constant. Hence the 44 percent difference between Mexican income at market rates and at PPP rates is only the case for 2002.

4. UNDP (2004), *Human Development Report, 2003.*

5. Economists have pointed out that the years from 1950 to 1973 constituted the fastest period of economic growth in history, both in the United States and in the rest of the world. See Maddison (1989), *The World Economy in the 20th Century.* There does not appear to be a consensus explanation for the high rates of economic growth or for the subsequent slowdown.

6. Peach (1997), "Income distribution along the United States border with Mexico: 1970–1990." The actual years for the data are the years prior to the census taking: 1969, 1979, 1989, and 1999.

7. Ibid.

8. Gerber (2004), "Explaining low income and high unemployment in Imperial County"; Fullerton (2001), "Educational attainment and border income performance." Arellano and Fullerton (2005), "Educational attainment and regional economic performance in Mexico," show a similarly large potential income gain in Mexico from increased educational attainment.

9. Mexico has three minimum wages. Each applies to a different part of the country, and all are loosely based on regional differences in living costs.

The border area is in the highest zone. The differences in the three wages, again, are not reflective of actual differences in the cost of living, other than in the sense that the ranking of minimum wages is consistent with the ranking of living costs.

10. Peach and Molina (2002), "Income distribution in Mexico's northern border states."

11. Fujii (1995), "La distribución del ingreso en México, 1984–1992."

12. Peach and Molina (2002), "Income distribution." This survey began in 1992, two years before the signing of NAFTA, and has continued every even-numbered year since then.

13. Sandez Perez (2006), *Estructura Social y Distribución del Ingreso.*

14. Anderson, Clement, and Shellhammer (1980), *Economic Importance of the U.S. Southwest Border Region;* Stoddard and Hedderson (1989), *Patterns of Poverty Along the U.S.-Mexico Border;* Dillman (1983), "Border urbanization"; Pick and Butler (1990), "Socioeconomic inequality in the U.S.-Mexico borderlands: Modernization and buffering."

15. Unfortunately, U.S. and Mexican definitions are not equivalent, and therefore we were unable to make cross-border comparisons of poverty rates.

16. Centro de Estudios del Trabajo (1986), *Salario Minimo y Canasta Basica,* pp. 25–26.

17. Ranfla et al. (2001), "An exploratory study of urban marginality in Baja California," also use the proportion below two minimum wages as a measure of poverty for 1990.

18. Gonzalez de la Rocha (1986), "Los Recursos de la Pobreza," and Anderson and de la Rosa (1991), "Economic survival strategies of poor families in the U.S.-Mexico border region." The Latin American pattern is described in De Ferranti, Perry, Ferreira, and Walton (2004), *Inequality in Latin America: Breaking with History?*

19. De Ferranti et al. (2004), *Inequality in Latin America.*

20. Birdsall and Londoño (1997), "Asset inequality matters: An assessment of the World Bank's approach to poverty reduction."

21. U.S. Department of Commerce (2002), *Regional Economic Information System.*

22. In general, a nation's or a region's gross product is greater than its personal income primarily because the former includes output not received by individuals, such as capital depreciation and indirect business taxes. Gross product rather than personal income must be used in order to create consistency between the U.S. county and Mexican municipio estimates.

23. Gilmer (1995a), "Gross regional product: Another view of Houston's economy"; idem (1995b), "Driven by differences: GRP of Houston and Dallas." This assumption may overstate regional product in counties where there are proportionately fewer businesses and indirect business taxes make up a smaller share of total economic activity. However, since income is but one

of three components of the index, and all counties are aggregated when we construct the overall border index, the bias on the Border Human Development Index is likely to be small.

24. Heston, Summers, and Aten (2002), *Penn World Table* Version 6.1.

25. Fullerton and Coronado (2001), "Restaurant prices and the Mexican peso."

26. A more complex question relates to regional price variations within each country. That is, prices along the U.S. border are not adjusted for local price differences between U.S. regions. Similarly, prices along the Mexico border are not adjusted for differences between Mexican municipios. To our knowledge, there is no way to make such adjustments.

CHAPTER 8

1. Secondary school is the equivalent of junior high school or middle school in the United States.

2. This story is based on three interviews conducted in Tijuana in 1985, 1986, and 1987 by Joan Anderson and Martin de la Rosa.

3. Anderson and de la Rosa (1991), "Economic survival strategies of poor families in the U.S.-Mexico border region."

4. In 1950, Mexican data on housing lacking a sewer connection were not collected.

5. The median dwelling size for the border region is calculated as a weighted average of the median house size for each border county, weighted by the total number of dwellings in each county. Note that this includes not only houses but also apartments and condos.

6. Regional Task Force on the Homeless (2004), "Regional homeless profile, July 2004."

7. Sharp (1998), *Bordering the Future: Challenge and Opportunity in the Texas Border Region*, p. 92.

8. Sharp (1998), *Bordering the Future*, pp. 92–93.

9. Lindert (2004), *Growing Public: Social Spending and Economic Growth Since the Eighteenth Century.*

10. In Mexico, high schools are called *preparatoria*, or "preparatory schools." Mexico also offers vocational or technical schools to its high school age students, in lieu of attending a preparatoria, which is more academic. A high school diploma is called a *bachillerato;* "bachelor's degree" is obviously a false cognate.

11. Santibañez, Vernez, and Rasquin (2005), *Education in Mexico: Challenges and Opportunities.*

12. The data were never available at the local level, only for the border states.

13. Anderson (1996), "Trends in poverty in the post-war period in the U.S.-Mexico region."

14. Mier celebrated its 250th anniversary in 2003.

15. Smaller, more rural municipios tend to have lower percentages of education beyond elementary school.

16. The Mexican census data on education report the data for the population aged fifteen years and older, while the U.S. census data report for the population aged twenty-five years and older.

17. UABC also added a campus in Ensenada, which is not in our sample because it does not touch the border.

18. Piñera (1999), "Higher education along the northern border of Mexico: A historical approximation," is a good historical treatment of the subject.

19. Bracho (2000), "Poverty and education in Mexico, 1984–1996."

20. Federal expenditures rose from 16.9 percent of the budget in 1950 to 34.6 percent in 1970; during the debt crisis of the 1980s, education expenditures fell to 20 percent of the federal budget, but rose to 37.5 percent in 1990 and 36.6 percent in 2000. Authors' calculations based on INEGI data of Mexican federal government expenditures.

Chapter 9

1. UNDP (2004), *Human Development Report, 2003*. See also Haq (1995), *Reflections on Development*, and Sen (1999b), *Human Development as Freedom*.

2. INEGI (2006), *Regiones Socioeconómicas de México*; Consejo Asesor del Informe Nacional sobre Desarrollo Humano (2004), *Informe Sobre Desarrollo Humano México 2004*.

3. Haq (1995), *Reflections of Development*; Sen (1999a), "Assessing human development"; idem (1999b), *Human Development as Freedom*.

4. UNDP (2001), *Human Development Report, 2000*, pp. 147–150. The current year's report as well as previous editions are available online at http://hdr.undp.org.

5. For a description of the methodology used in estimating per capita GDP, see Chapter 7 and the technical appendix to that chapter.

6. UNDP (2001), *Human Development Report, 2000*, p. 269.

7. The discrepancy in youngest age is due to the difference in the data as reported in the U.S. and Mexican censuses. Since the enrollment is divided by population over the same age range, it was felt that the year's difference in starting age would not cause a large bias. Basically, the U.S. data start with kindergarten and the Mexican data start with first grade.

8. The type of data gathered by a country's census is highly influenced by the level of its economic development. The differences in development levels between the United States and Mexico add to the difficulties in getting compatible data.

9. UNDP (2001), *Human Development Report, 2000*, p. 143.

10. Sen (1999a), "Assessing human development."

11. Morley (2001), *The Income Distribution Problem in Latin America and the Caribbean,* p. 55.

CHAPTER 10

1. In 2003, Immigration and Customs Enforcement, formerly the Immigration and Naturalization Service, spent 4 percent of its budget on employer enforcement programs. See U.S. Government Accountability Office (2005), *Immigration Enforcement: Preliminary Observations on Employment Verification and Worksite Enforcement Efforts.*

2. Schumpeter coined this term to refer to change within an industrial, capitalist economy; we use it here in a slightly different sense to refer to the historical transformation of an economy.

3. Massey, Durand, and Malone (2003), *Beyond Smoke and Mirrors: Mexican Immigration in an Era of Economic Integration,* estimate that Western Europe's transition lasted nine to ten decades, during which time the region was a high-emigrant region. More recently, South Korea passed through the same transition in three to four decades.

4. Work visas were required to work legally, but anyone from Mexico could cross into and stay in the United States without a visa. The Bracero Program that began in 1942 required visas because Mexican nationals were brought to the United States to work. Deportations of Mexicans and Mexican Americans in the 1930s were either illegal or physically and psychologically coerced under a thin layer of legality.

5. Massey, Durand, and Malone (2003), *Beyond Smoke and Mirrors.* These and subsequent data on migrant characteristics are based on data collected since 1980 in a binational project of the University of Guadalajara and the University of Pennsylvania, known as the Mexican Migration Project. A detailed description of the data is available on the Mexican Migration Project Web site (http://mmp.opr.princeton.edu/).

6. Meyers (2005), "U.S. border enforcement."

7. In fiscal year 2005, the United States reported 450 deaths. See Meyers (2005), "U.S. border enforcement."

8. Massey, Durand, and Malone (2003), *Beyond Smoke and Mirrors,* p. 131.

9. SANDAG (2005), *Economic Impacts of Border Wait Times at the San Diego–Baja California Border Region.*

10. U.S.-VISIT is an attempt to track all holders of U.S. visas and to limit the documents that U.S. citizens must show to legally reenter the country. In a phased implementation, it will require visas to include biometric identifiers (digital photographs and fingerprints) and checks on outgoing traffic. It will also require U.S. citizens to use passports for reentering the United States.

These checks will significantly increase the amount of time it takes to cross the U.S. border, although policy makers in the Bush administration have argued that there are technological means to speed things up. The Secure Border Initiative is a program to provide greater interagency and international cooperation in customs inspection and immigration control, along with new technologies for interdiction and inspection.

11. U.S. Department of Homeland Security (2005), "DHS announces long-term border and immigration strategy."

12. Ibid.

13. As shown in Chapter 9, the Border Human Development Index in 2000 was 0.74 in the Mexican border region and 0.90 in the U.S. border region (difference = 0.16). Nationally, comparably constructed indexes were 0.72 in Mexico and 0.93 in the United States (difference = 0.21), or about one-third larger.

14. This gap is smaller than the national gap between the United States and Mexico, where U.S. GDP per capita exceeds the Mexican level by more than 3.5 times.

15. Birdsall and Londoño (1997), "Asset inequality matters: An assessment of the World Bank's approach to poverty reduction."

16. U.S. Census Bureau (2000), *Census 2000 Summary File 3 (SF 3): Sample Data.*

17. Mexico clearly supports increased and more open migration for its citizens wanting to enter the United States; however, it has no clearly stated policy toward migrants entering its territory from Central America, and it often behaves in ways every bit as brutal as the treatment some of its migrants receive when entering the United States.

18. There is no evidence that undocumented migrants are more likely to engage in illegal activities. Coronado and Orrenius (2003), "The effect of undocumented immigration and border enforcement on crime rates along the U.S.-Mexico border," provide analysis as well as a survey of several studies. They conclude that undocumented immigrants are more likely than average to be victimized and that the people smugglers (coyotes) they associate with are more likely to commit crimes.

19. As noted earlier, the average trip length to the United States for a migrant from Mexico has increased to 8.9 years in the post-IRCA era, with a probability of returning in a given year of around 0.10.

20. This is the expression coined by Galbraith (1998), *The Affluent Society.*

REFERENCES

Alegría, T. (2002). Demand and supply of Mexican cross-border workers. *Journal of Borderlands Studies*, 17, 37–55.

Anderson, J. B. (1988). Causes of growth in the informal labor sector in the Mexican northern border region. *Journal of Borderlands Studies*, 3, 1–12.

———. (1996). Trends in poverty in the post-war period in the U.S.-Mexico border region. Paper presented at a meeting of the Association of Borderlands Scholars, Reno, NV, April 17–20.

Anderson, J. B., Clement, N. C., and Shellhammer, K. (1980). *Economic Importance of the U.S. Southwest Border Region*. San Diego, CA: California Border Area Resource Center, San Diego State University.

Anderson, J. B., and de la Rosa, M. (1991). Economic survival strategies of poor families in the U.S.-Mexico border region. *Journal of Borderlands Studies*, 6, 51–68.

Anderson, J. B., and Dimon, D. (1998). Married women's labor force participation in developing countries: The case of Mexico. *Estudios Económicos*, 13, 3–34.

———. (1999). Formal sector job growth and women's labor sector participation: The case of Mexico. *Quarterly Review of Economics and Finance*, 39, 169–191.

Anderson, J. B., and Gerber, J. (2004). A human development index for the United States–Mexico border. *Journal of Borderlands Studies*, 19, 1–26.

Arellano, A., and Fullerton, T. M. (2005). Educational attainment and regional economic performance in Mexico. *International Advances in Economic Research*, 11, 231–242.

Arreola, D. (2002). *Tejano South Texas: A Mexican American Cultural Province*. Austin: University of Texas Press.

Balassa, B. (1980). *The Process of Industrial Development and Alternative Development Strategies*. Essays in International Finance 141. Princeton, NJ: Department of Economics, Princeton University.

Bair, J. (2001). The maquiladora industry and development in Mexico: Lessons from the textile and apparel industries. Paper presented at a meeting, "Export Promotion, Economic Development, and the Future of Mexico's Maquiladora Industry," Mexico, DF, June 14–15.

Barajas Escamilla, M. (2000). *Global Production Networks in an Electronics Industry: The Case of the Tijuana–San Diego Binational Region.* PhD diss., University of California, Irvine.

Beneria, L., and Roldan, M. (1997). *The Crossroads of Class and Gender: Industrial Homework, Subcontracting, and Household Dynamics in Mexico City.* Chicago: University of Chicago Press.

Bhagwati, J. (1978). *Foreign Trade Regimes and Economic Development: Anatomy and Consequences of Exchange Control Regimes.* A Special Conference Series on Foreign Trade Regimes and Economic Development XI. New York: National Bureau of Economic Research.

———. (1993). The case for free trade. *Scientific American,* 269, 5.

———. (2002). *Free Trade Today.* Princeton, NJ: Princeton University Press.

Birdsall, N., and Londoño, J. (1997). Asset inequality matters: An assessment of the World Bank's approach to poverty reduction. *American Economic Review,* 82, 32–37.

Border Environment Cooperation Commission—North American Development Bank. (2005). *Joint Status Report.* http://www.nadbank.org/Reports/Joint_Report/status_eng.pdf (retrieved May 1, 2006).

Bracho, T. (2000). Poverty and education in Mexico, 1984–1996. In F. Reimers (Ed.), *Unequal Schools, Unequal Chances* (pp. 249–284). Cambridge, MA: Harvard University Press.

Brown, F., and Domínguez, L. (1989). Nuevas tecnologías en la industria maquiladora de exportación. *Comercio Exterior,* 39, 215–223.

Brownell, P. (2005). The declining enforcement of employer sanctions. *Migration Information Source.* http://www.migrationinformation.org (retrieved June 5, 2006).

Bruton, H. J. (1998). A reconsideration of import substitution. *Journal of Economic Literature,* 36, 903–936.

Cahill, M. B. (2002). Diminishing returns to GDP and the human development index. *Applied Economics Letters,* 9, 885–887.

Cantlupe, J. (2005). Cleanup of toxic waste at Tijuana site is praised. *San Diego Union-Tribune,* August 6.

Carrillo, J. (Ed.). (1993). *Condiciones de Empleo y Capacitación en las Maquiladoras de Exportación en México.* Tijuana, Mexico: Secretaría del Trabajo y Previsión Social and El Colegio de la Frontera Norte.

Carrillo, J. (2001). Maquiladoras de exportación y la formación de empresas Mexicanas exitosas. In E. Dussel Peters (Ed.), *Claroscuros: Integración exitosa de las pequeñas y medianas empresas en México* (pp. 157–208). Mexico: Jus/CEPAL/CANACINTRA.

Carrillo, J., and Hualde, A. (1996). Third generation maquiladoras: The case of Delphi–General Motors. *Journal of Borderlands Studies,* 13, 79–97.

Carrillo, J., and Ramírez, M. A. (1990). Modernización, tecnológica y cambios organizacionales en la industria maquiladora. *Estudios Fronterizos*, 23, 55–76.

Catanzarite, L. M., and Strober, M. H. (1993). The gender recomposition of the maquiladora workforce in Ciudad Juárez. *Industrial Relations*, 32, 133–147.

Centro de Estudios del Trabajo, A.C. (1986). *Salario Minimo y Canasta Basica*. México, DF: Centro de Estudios del Trabajo.

Chenery, H., and Syrquin, M. (1975). *Patterns of Development, 1950–1970*. Oxford: Oxford University Press.

Clement, N. (Ed.). (2002). *The U.S.-Mexican Border Environment: U.S.-Méxican Border Communities in the NAFTA Era*. San Diego, CA: San Diego State University Press and Southwest Center for Environmental Research and Policy.

COLEF (El Colegio de la Frontera Norte), Facultad Latinoamericana de Ciencias Sociales-México, and Universidad Autónoma Metropolitana. (2002). *Aprendizaje Tecnológico y Escalamiento Industrial: Perspectivas para la Formación de Capacidades de Innovación en las Maquiladoras en México*. Proyecto Conacyt No. 36947-s.

Coleman, M. T. (1993). Movements in the earnings-schooling relationship, 1940–1988. *Journal of Human Resources*, 28, 660–680.

Consejo Asesor del Informe Nacional sobre Desarrollo Humano. (2004). *Informe Sobre Desarrollo Humano México 2004*. UNDP México. http://saul.nueve.com.mx/estadisticas/index.html (retrieved September 10, 2005).

Contreras, O. F. (2000). *Empresas Globales, Actores Locales: Producción Flexible y Aprendizaje Industrial en las Maquiladoras*. México, DF: El Colegio de México.

Cooney, P. (2001). The Mexican crisis and the maquiladora boom: A paradox of development or the logic of neoliberalism? *Latin American Perspectives*, 28, 55–83.

Coronado, R., and Orenius, P. (2003). The effect of undocumented immigration and border enforcement on crime rates along the U.S.-Mexico border. Working Paper 0303. Federal Reserve Bank of Dallas. http://www.dallasfed.org/research/papers/2003/wp0303.pdf (retrieved April 4, 2006).

Council on Foreign Relations. (2005). *Building a North American Community: Report of an Independent Task Force*. New York: Council on Foreign Relations.

Daly, H. (1993). The perils of free trade. *Scientific American*, 269, 5.

Dávila, A., and Mora, M. T. (2000). English skills, earnings, and the occupational sorting of Mexican Americans along the U.S.-Mexico border. *International Migration Review*, 34, 133–157.

De Ferranti, D., Perry, G., Ferreira, F., and Walton, M. (2004). *Inequality in Latin America: Breaking with History?* Washington, DC: World Bank.

De Leon, A. (1983). *They Called Them Greasers: Anglo Attitudes Toward Mexicans in Texas, 1821–1900*. Austin: University of Texas Press.

De Soto, H. (1989). *The Other Path: The Invisible Revolution in the Third World.* New York: Basic Books.

———. (2000). *The Mystery of Capital: Why Capitalism Triumphs in the West and Fails Everywhere Else.* New York: Basic Books.

Del Castillo V., G. (2001). Between order and chaos: Management of the westernmost border between Mexico and the United States. In D. G. Papademetriou and D. W. Meyers (Eds.), *Caught in the Middle: Border Communities in an Era of Globalization* (pp. 117–164). Washington, DC: Carnegie Endowment for International Peace.

Diehl, P. N. (1983). The effect of the peso devaluation on Texas border cities. *Texas Business Review,* 57, 120–125.

Dillman, C. D. (1983). Border urbanization. In E. Stoddard, R. L. Nostrand, and J. P. West (Eds.), *Borderlands Sourcebook: A Guide to the Literature on Northern Mexico and the American Southwest* (pp. 237–244). Norman: University of Oklahoma Press.

Dunning, J. H. (1981). *International Production and the Multinational Enterprise.* Boston: Allen and Unwin.

Elorduy, E. (2003). Interview. *San Diego Union Tribune,* March 9.

Fernandez Kelly, M. P. (1983). *For We Are Sold, I and My People: Women and Industry in Mexico's Frontier.* Albany: State University of New York Press.

Fields, G. (1990). Labour market modeling and the urban informal sector: Theory and evidence. In D. Turnham, B. Salone, and A. Shwarz (Eds.), *The Formal Sector Revisited.* Paris: OECD.

Fleck, S., and Sorrentino, C. (1994). Employment and unemployment in Mexico's labor force. *Monthly Labor Review,* 117, 3–31.

Fujii, G. (1995). La distribución del ingreso en México, 1984–1992. *Investigación Económica,* 211, 147–165.

Fullerton, T. M. (2001). Educational attainment and border income performance. *Economic and Financial Review, Third Quarter, 1–10.* Dallas, TX: Federal Reserve Bank of Dallas. http://dallasfed.org/research/efr/2001/efr0103a.pdf (retrieved April 7, 2006).

Fullerton, T. M., and Coronado, R. (2001). Restaurant prices and the Mexican peso. *Southern Economic Journal,* 68, 145–155.

Galbraith, J. K. (1998). *The Affluent Society, 40th Anniversary Edition.* Boston: Houghton Mifflin.

Gallagher, K. (2004). *Free Trade and the Environment: Mexico, NAFTA, and Beyond.* Stanford, CA: Stanford University Press.

Gerber, J. (1999). The effects of a depreciation of the peso on cross-border retail sales in San Diego and Imperial Counties. San Diego Dialogue. www.sandiegodialogue.org/pdfs/tax_paper.pdf.

———. (2002). Different states, similar responses: California, Texas, and NAFTA. In E. J. Chambers and P. H. Smith (Eds.), *NAFTA in the New Millennium* (pp. 147–166). San Diego, CA: Center for U.S.-Mexican Studies, and Edmonton, AB: University of Alberta Press.

———. (2004). Explaining low income and high unemployment in Imperial County. In K. Collins, P. Ganster, C. Mason, E. Sánchez Lopez, and

M. Quintero-Núñez (Eds.), *Imperial-Mexicali Valleys: Development and Environment of the U.S.-Mexican Border Region* (pp. 99–112). San Diego, CA: San Diego State University Press.

Gerber, J., and Balsdon, E. (2001). The impact of the U.S. business cycle on Mexico's maquiladora industry. Paper presented at a meeting of the First NOBE/REF International Research Forum, "The U.S-Mexico Border Economy in the XXI Century," El Colegio de la Frontera, Tijuana, Mexico, June 22–23.

Gerber, J., and Carrillo, J. (2003). Competitividad al debate: La experiencia de las maquiladoras mexicanas. *Revista Latinoamericana de Estudios de Trabajo,* 16, 7–30.

———. (Forthcoming). The future of the maquiladora: Between industrial upgrading and competitive decline. In V. Miller (Ed.), *NAFTA and the Maquiladora Program: Rules, Routines, and Institutional Legitimacy.* El Paso: Texas Western Press.

Gerber, J., and Mundra, K. (2003). Is the downturn in maquiladora employment cyclical or structural? Paper presented at a meeting of the Dallas Federal Reserve, El Paso Branch, "Maquiladora Downturn: Structural Change or Cyclical Factors?" South Padre Island, TX, November 21.

Gerber, J., and Patrick, M. J. (2001). Shopping on the border: The Mexican peso and U.S. border communities. Presented at a meeting of the Association for Borderlands Studies, Reno, NV, April 23.

Gereffi, G., and Tam, T. (1998). Industrial upgrading through organizational chains: Dynamics of rent, learning, and mobility in the global economy. Paper presented at the 93rd annual meeting of the American Sociological Association, San Francisco, CA, August 21–25.

Gibson, C., and Jung, K. (2002). Historical census statistics on population, totals by race, 1790 to 1990, and by Hispanic origin, 1970 to 1990, for the United States, regions, divisions, and states. Working Paper Series 56. Washington, DC: Population Division, U.S. Census Bureau. http://www.census.gov/population/www/documentation/twps0056.html (retrieved July 15, 2004).

Gilmer, B. (1995). Driven by differences: GRP of Houston and Dallas. *Houston Business.* Dallas, TX: Federal Reserve Bank of Dallas.

———. (1995). Gross regional product: Another view of Houston's economy. *Houston Business.* Dallas, TX: Federal Reserve Bank of Dallas.

Goldrich, D., and Carruthers, D. (1992). Sustainable development in Mexico? The international politics of crisis or opportunity. *Latin American Perspectives,* 19, 97–122.

Gonzalez de la Rocha, M. (1986). *Los Recursor de la Pobreza: Familias de Bajos Ingresos de Guadalajara.* Guadalajara, México: El Colegio de Jalisco A.C.

Graziani, A. (1978). The Mezzogiorno in the Italian economy. *Cambridge Journal of Economics,* 2, 355–372.

Griswold del Castillo, R. (1985). Tejanos and California Chicanos: Regional variations in Mexican American history. *Mexican Studies / Estudios Mexicanos,* 1, 134–139.

Gruben, W. (2001). Was NAFTA behind Mexico's high maquiladora growth? *Economic and Financial Review, Third Quarter,* Dallas, TX: Federal Reserve Bank of Dallas. http://www.dallasfed.org/htm/pubs/pdfs/efr/efr0103b.pdf (retrieved March 30, 2003).

Grunwald, J., and Flamm, K. (1985). *The Global Factory: Foreign Assembly in International Trade.* Washington, DC: Brookings Institution.

Hall, K. G. (1994a). Bush links future of state to Mexican trade. *Journal of Commerce,* November 23.

———. (1994b). Brownsville seeks rights to "NAFTA Home Port" tag. *Journal of Commerce,* December 6.

Hanoch, G. (1967). An economic analysis of earnings and schooling. *Journal of Human Resources,* 2, 310–329.

Hanson, G. (1996). *U.S.-Mexico Integration and Regional Economies: Evidence from Border-City Pairs.* Cambridge, MA: National Bureau of Economic Research.

———. (1997). The effects of offshore assembly on industry location: Evidence from U.S. border cities. In R. Feenstra (Ed.), *The Effect of U.S. Trade Protection and Promotion Policies* (pp. 297–322). Chicago: University of Chicago Press, and New York: National Bureau of Economic Research.

Hanson, N. (1981). *The Border Economy: Regional Development in the Southwest.* Austin: University of Texas Press.

Haq, Mahbub ul (1995). *Reflections on Human Development: How the Focus of Development Economics Shifted from National Income Accounting to People-Centred Policies.* New York: Oxford University Press.

Hecht, A. D., Whelan, P., and Sowell, S. (2002). Sustainable development on the U.S.-Mexican border: Past lessons, present efforts, future possibilities. In P. Ganster (Ed.), *The U.S.-Mexican Border Environment: Economy and Environment for a Sustainable Border Region: Now and in 2020* (pp. 15–54). SCERP Monograph Series 3. Southwest Center for Environmental Research and Policy. San Diego, CA: San Diego State University Press.

Hernandez, P. (2004). Mexico's maquiladora expansion during the 1990s: An environmental assessment. *Ecological Economics,* 49, 163–185.

Heston, A., Summers, R., and Aten, B. (2002). *Penn World Table Version 6.1.* Center for International Comparisons at the University of Pennsylvania (CICUP), Philadelphia.

Hufbauer, G. C., Esty, D. C., Orejas, D., Rubio, L., and Schott, J. J. (2000). *NAFTA and the Environment: Seven Years Later.* Policy Analyses in International Economics 61. Washington, DC: Institute for International Economics.

Hufbauer, G. C., and Schott, J. J. (1993). *NAFTA: An Assessment.* Washington, DC: Institute for International Economics.

———. (2005). *NAFTA Revisited: Achievements and Challenges.* Washington, DC: Institute for International Economics.

Iglesias Prieto, N. (1997). *Beautiful Flowers of the Maquiladora: Life Histories of Women Workers in Tijuana.* Translated by Michael Stone with Gabrielle Winkler. Austin: University of Texas Press.

International Labour Organization (ILO). (1972). *Employment, Incomes and Equality: A Strategy for Increasing Productive Employment in Kenya.* Geneva: ILO.

Jordan, T. G., with Bean, J. L., Jr., and Holmes, W. M. (1984). *Texas: A Geography.* Boulder, CO: Westview Press.

Jusidman de Bialostozky, C. (1992). *The Informal Sector in Mexico.* Occasional Paper Series on the Informal Sector 1. México, DF: Secretaría del Trabajo y Previsión Social de Mexico, and Washington, DC: U.S. Department of Labor.

Krueger, A. O. (1978). *Foreign Trade Regimes and Economic Development: Liberalization Attempts and Consequences.* A Special Conference Series on Foreign Trade Regimes and Economic Development. Vol. X. New York: National Bureau of Economic Research.

Krugman, P., and Livas Elizondo, R. (1995). Trade policy and the third world metropolis. *Journal of Development Economics,* 49, 137–150.

Kuznets, S. (1955). Economic growth and income inequality. *American Economic Review,* 45, 1–28.

Lara Rivero, A. (1998). *Aprendizaje Tecnológico y Mercado de Trabajo en las Maquiladoras Japonesas.* México, DF: Miguel Ángel Porrúa-UAM Xochimilco.

Larralde, C., and Jacobo, J. R. (2000). *Juan N. Cortina and the Struggle for Justice in Texas.* Dubuque, IA: Kendall Hunt Publishing Co.

Lindert, P. H. (2004). *Growing Public: Social Spending and Economic Growth Since the Eighteenth Century.* New York: Cambridge University Press.

Little, I.M.D., Scitovsky, T., and Scott, M. (1970). *Industry and Trade in Some Developing Countries: A Comparative Study.* London: Oxford University Press.

Lorey, D. E. (1993). *United States-Mexico Border Statistics since 1900: 1990 Update.* Los Angeles: UCLA Latin American Center Publications.

Maddison, A. (1989). *The World Economy in the 20th Century.* Paris: Development Centre of the Organization for Economic Co-operation and Development.

Marshall, A. (1919). *Industry and Trade: A Study of Industrial Technique and Business Organization, and of Their Influences on the Conditions of Various Classes and Nations.* London: Macmillan.

Martin, G. (2000). Employment and unemployment in Mexico in the 1990s. *Monthly Labor Review,* 123, 3–11.

Martin, P. (2003). Mexico-US migration. Washington, DC: Institute for International Economics. http://www.iie.com/publications/papers/nafta-migration.pdf (retrieved March 20, 2005).

Martínez, O. J. (1988). *Troublesome Border.* Tucson: University of Arizona Press.

Massey, D. S., Durand, J., and Malone, N. J. (2003). *Beyond Smoke and Mirrors: Mexican Immigration in an Era of Economic Integration.* New York: Russell Sage Foundation.

McEnany, A., and Young, E. (2005). A través de la frontera: Land use visioning—ICF/TSDF, Tijuana watershed. Funders Network Publication 48–51. San Diego, CA: International Community Foundation.

McManus, W. S., Gould, W., and Welch, E. (1983). Earnings of Hispanic men: The role of English language proficiency. *Journal of Labor Economics*, 1, 101–130.

Meyers, D. W. (2005). U.S. border enforcement: From horseback to high-tech. *Insight*. 7. Migration Policy Institute. http://www.migrationpolicy .org (retrieved May 5, 2006).

Mincer, J. (1974). *Schooling, Experience and Earnings*. Cambridge, MA: National Bureau of Economic Research.

Mora, M. T., and Dávila, A. (1998). Gender, earnings, and the English-skill acquisition of Hispanic workers. *Economic Inquiry*, 36, 631–644.

Moran, T. (2002). *Beyond Sweatshops: Foreign Direct Investment and Globalization in Developing Countries*. Washington, DC: Brookings Institution.

Morley, S. (2001). *The Income Distribution Problem in Latin America and the Caribbean*. Santiago, Chile: Economic Commission for Latin America and the Caribbean.

Mumme, S. (1987). State and local influence in transboundary environmental policy making along the U.S.-Mexico border: The case of air quality management. *Journal of Borderlands Studies*, 2, 1–16.

Murphy, K., and Welch, F. (1992). The structure of wages. *Quarterly Journal of Economics*, 107, 285–326.

NALEO (National Association of Latino Elected Officials). (2000). *National Directory of Latino Elected Officials*. Los Angeles: NALEO Educational Fund.

Neumeyer, E. (2001). *Greening Trade and Investment: Environmental Protection without Protectionism*. London: Earthscan.

Nevins, J. (2002). *Operation Gatekeeper: The Rise of the "Illegal Alien" and the Making of the U.S.-Mexico Boundary*. New York: Routledge.

New York Times. (1994). Alamo? What Alamo? Texans want to get closer to Mexico. November 27.

Otero, M. (1989). Rethinking the informal sector. *Grassroots Development*, 13, 3–8.

Palmade, V. (2005). Why worry about rising informality? The biggest and least well understood impediment to economic development. Unpublished working paper. http://rru.worldbank.org/documents/discussions/ palmade.doc (retrieved November 2005).

Papademetriou, D. G., and Meyers, D. W. (2001). Overview, context and vision for the future. In D. G. Papademetriou and D. W. Meyers (Eds.), *Caught in the Middle: Border Communities in an Era of Globalization* (pp. 1–41). Washington, DC: Carnegie Endowment for International Peace.

Pastor, R. (2001). *Toward a North American Community: Lessons from the Old World for the New*. Washington, DC: Institute for International Economics.

Patrick, J. M., and Renforth, W. (1996). The effects of the peso devaluation on cross border retailing. *Journal of Borderlands Studies*, 11, 25–41.

Peach, J. (1997). Income distribution along the United States border with Mexico: 1970–1990. *Journal of Borderlands Studies*, 12, 1–16.

Peach, J., and Molina, D. J. (2002). Income distribution in Mexico's northern border states. *Journal of Borderlands Studies*, 17, 1–13.

Peach, J., and Williams, J. (2003). Population and economic dynamics on the U.S.-Mexico border: Past, present, and future. In P. Ganster (Ed.), *The U.S.-Mexican Border Environment: A Road Map to a Sustainable 2020* (pp. 37–72). SCERP Monograph Series 1. San Diego, CA: San Diego State University Press.

Pick, J. B., and Butler, E. W. (1990). Socioeconomic inequality in the U.S.-Mexico borderlands: Modernization and buffering. *Frontera Norte*, 2, 31–62.

Piñera, D. (1999). Higher education along the northern border of Mexico: A historical approximation. *Journal of Borderlands Studies*, 14, 93–112.

Pozo, S. (Ed.). (1996). *Exploring the Underground Economy.* Kalamazoo, MI: W. E. Upjohn Institute for Employment Research.

PREALC. (1981). *Sector Informal: Funcionamiento y Políticas.* Santiago, Chile: PREALC.

Pritchett, L. H. (1994). Desired fertility and the impact of population policies. *Population and Development Review*, 20, 1–55.

Prock, J. (1983). The peso devaluations and their effect on Texas border economies. *Inter-American Economic Affairs*, 37.

Psacharopoulos, G., and Patrinos, H. A. (2004). Returns to investment in education: A further update. *Education Economics*, 12, 111–134.

Public Affairs Office, White Sands Missile Range. (2005). Southern New Mexico regional history before 1945. http://www.huntel.com/~artpike/history.htm (retrieved February 12, 2006).

Public Citizen. (2000). Deals for NAFTA votes II: Bait and switch. http://www.citizen.org/publications/release.cfm?ID=6825 (retrieved February 2, 2006).

Ranfla G., A., Toudert, D., Alvarez de la T., G., and Ortega V., G. (2001). An exploratory study of urban marginality in Baja California. In P. Ganster (Ed.), *Cooperation, Environment, and Sustainability in Border Regions* (pp. 125–145). San Diego, CA: Institute for Regional Studies of the Californias, San Diego State University Press.

Ramirez, C. Q. (2001). Unions, collaboration and labour conditions in Mexican maquiladoras. Matamoros, Mexico: Colegio de la Frontera Norte, Dirección regional de Matamoros. http://www.isanet.org/archive/ramirez.html (retrieved July 2, 2004).

Raymond, R., and Sesnowitz, M. (1975). The returns to investments in higher education: Some new evidence. *Journal of Human Resources*, 10, 139–154

Regional Task Force on the Homeless. (2004). Regional homeless profile, July 2004. http://www.rtfhsd.org/index_profile.html (retrieved September 5, 2005).

Rodriguiz, N., and Hagan, J. (2001). Transborder community relations at the

U.S.-Mexico border: Laredo/Nuevo Laredo and El Paso/Ciudad Juárez. In D. G. Papademetriou and D. W. Meyers (Eds.), *Caught in the Middle: Border Communities in an Era of Globalization* (pp. 88–116). Washington, DC: Carnegie Endowment for International Peace.

Rugman, A. M., and Verbeke, A. (1998). Corporate strategy and international environmental policy. *Journal of International Business Studies*, 29, 819–831.

Sachs, J. (2005). *The End of Poverty: Economic Possibilities for our Time.* New York: Penguin Press.

Saldaña, L. (1999). Tijuana's toxic waters. *NACLA Report on the Americas*, 33, 31–35.

San Diego Dialogue. (1994). *Who Crosses the Border? A View of the San Diego/Tijuana Metropolitan Region.* San Diego: University of California, San Diego.

San Diego Dialogue, Centro Estudios Económicos del Sector Empresarial de Mexicali, A.C., and Universidad Autónoma de Baja California. (1998). *Survey of Border Crossers: Imperial/Mexicali Valley.* Unpublished manuscript.

SANDAG (San Diego Association of Governments). (2005). *Economic Impacts of Border Wait Times at the San Diego-Baja California Border Region.* San Diego, CA: SANDAG. http://www.sandag.org/index.asp?projectid=253&fuseaction=projects.detail (retrieved March 16, 2006).

Sandez Perez, A. (2006). *Estructura Social y Distribución del Ingreso: Un Estudio Transversal de las Disparidades en el Nivel de Vida de los Hogares: El Caso de Mexicali, Baja California, 2004.* PhD diss., El Colegio de la Frontera Norte (COLEF), Tijuana, México.

Sandos, James A. (2000). "Because he is a liar and a thief": Conquering the residents of "Old" California, 1850–1880. In K. Starr and R. J. Orsi (Eds.), *Rooted in Barbarous Soil: People, Culture, and Community in Gold Rush California* (pp. 86–112). Berkeley and Los Angeles: University of California Press.

Santibañez, L., Vernez, G., and Razquin, P. (2005). *Education in Mexico: Challenges and Opportunities.* RAND Corporation Document Briefing. Santa Monica, CA: RAND Corporation. http://www.rand.org/pubs/documented_briefings/DB480/ (retrieved January 10, 2006).

Schmaedick, G. (2004). "Unemployment statistics: Is there a border bias?" NOBE/REF U.S.-Mexico Border Economic Indicators Workshop (2004). El Paso: University of Texas at El Paso and El Paso Branch of the Dallas Federal Reserve Bank, August 6. http://www.nobe-ref.org/pdf/Conferences/2004/Paper_Schmaedick.pdf.

Schultz, P. T. (1974). *Fertility Determinants: A Theory, Evidence and Application to Policy Evaluation.* Santa Monica, CA: RAND Corporation.

Schneider, F. (2002). Size and measurement of the informal economy in 110 countries around the world. Doing Business Website. Washington, DC: World Bank. http://www.doingbusiness.org/Methodology/EconomyCharacteristics.aspx (retrieved March 16, 2006).

Sen, A. (1999a). Assessing human development. In M. ul Haq (Ed.), *Human*

Development Report, 1999. New York: United Nations Development Program.

———. (1999b). *Development as Freedom.* New York: Knopf.

Sharp, J. (1998, July). *Bordering the Future: Challenge and Opportunity in the Texas Border Region.* Publication 98–599. Austin: Texas Comptroller of Public Accounts.

Shatz, H., and López-Calva, L. F. (2004). *The Emerging Integration of the California-Mexico Economies.* San Francisco: Public Policy Institute of California.

Sierra Club (1993). *Funding Needs Associated with the North American Free Trade Agreement.* Washington, DC: Sierra Club.

Sklair, L. (1989). *Assembling for Development. The Maquila Industry in Mexico and the United States.* Boston: Unwin Hyman.

Solunet (2001). *The Complete Twin Plant Guide.* El Paso, TX: Solunet.

Souza, P. R., and Tokman, V. E. (1976). The informal urban sector in Latin America. *International Labor Review,* 114, 335–365.

Sreeramamurty, K. (1986). *Urban Labour in the Informal Sector.* Delhi: B.R. Publishing Corporation.

Stern, D. (1998). Progress on the environmental Kuznets curve? *Environment and Development Economics,* 3, 176–196.

Stoddard, E. R. (1987). *Maquila: Assembly Plants in Northern Mexico.* El Paso: Texas Western Press.

Stoddard, E. R., and Hedderson, J. (1989). *Patterns of Poverty Along the U.S.-Mexico Border.* Borderlands Research Monograph Series No. 3. Las Cruces, NM: Joint Border Research Institute, New Mexico State University.

Tiano, S. (1990). Maquiladora women: A new category of workers? In K. Ward (Ed.), *Women Workers and Global Restructuring* (pp. 193–223). Cornell International Industrial Labor Relations Report No. 17. Ithaca, NY: ILR Press, Cornell University.

Todaro, M., and Smith, S. C. (2003). *Economic Development,* 8th ed. Boston: Addison Wesley.

Tomaso, B., and Alm, R. (1990). Economy vs. ecology: Mexico's drive for growth eclipses concerns about toxic wastes from border plants. *Transboundary Resources Report,* 4, 1–4.

UNDP (United Nations Development Program). (2001). *Human Development Report, 2000.* Oxford, England: Oxford University Press.

———. (2004). *Human Development Report, 2003.* New York: United Nations.

Ward, K. (1990). Introduction and overview. In K. Ward (Ed.), *Women Workers and Global Restructuring* (pp. 1–22). Ithaca, NY: ILR Press, Cornell University.

Wilson, P. A. (1992). *Exports and Local Development: Mexico's New Maquiladoras.* Austin: University of Texas Press.

Wilson, T. (1993). We seek work where we can: A comparison of patterns of out migration from a rancho in Jalisco and of internal migration into a Mexicali squatter settlement. *Journal of Borderlands Studies,* 8, 33–58.

World Bank. (2005). *Doing Business 2005.* Washington, DC: World Bank.

―――. (2005). *World Development Indicators, 2005*. Washington, DC: World Bank.

Wright, D. M. (1940). The making of cosmopolitan California: An analysis of immigration, 1848–1970. *California Historical Society Quarterly*, 19, 323–343.

Zarsky, L., and Gallagher, K. P. (2004). NAFTA, foreign direct investment and sustainable industrial development in Mexico. IRC Americas Program Policy Brief. http://americas.irc-online.org/briefs/2004/0401mexind_body.html (retrieved June 6, 2005).

GOVERNMENT SOURCES

Mexico Census

Coordinación General de los Servicios Nacionales de Estadística, Geografía e Informática. (1982). *X Censo General de Población y Vivienda, 1980*. México, DF.

Dirección General de Estadística. (1952–1953). *Séptimo Censo General de Población, 6 de Junio de 1950*. México, DF.

―――. (1964). *VIII Censo General de Población, 1960, 8 de Junio de 1960*. México, DF.

―――. (1972). *IX Censo General de Población, 1970, 28 de Enero de 1970*. México, DF.

INEGI (Instituto Nacional de Estadística, Geografía e Informática). (1990–1992). *XI Censo General de Población y Vivienda, 1990*. Aguascalientes, México.

―――. (2001). *XII Censo General de Población y Vivienda, 2000*. Aguascalientes, México.

OTHER MEXICO

Comisión Nacional de Inversiones Extranjeras. (2006). *Informe Estadístico Trimestral sobre el Comportamiento de la Inversión Extranjera Directa en México*. Enero-Marzo. http://www.economia.gob.mx/index.jsp?P=1164 (retrieved June 12, 2006).

INEGI (Instituto Nacional de Estadística, Geografía e Informática). (2005). *Banco de Información Económica*. http://www.inegi.gob.mx.

―――. (2006). *Regiones Socioeconómicas de México*. http://www.inegi.gob.mx/est/default.asp?c=1413.

UNITED STATES CENSUS

U.S. Bureau of the Census. (1952). *U.S. Census of Population: 1950*. Washington, DC: U.S. GPO.

―――. (1961). *U.S. Census of Population: 1960*. Washington, D.C.: U.S. GPO.

―――. (1973). *1970 Census of Population: Characteristics of the Population*. Washington, DC: U.S. GPO.

———. (1983). *1980 Census of Population: volume 1, Characteristics of the Population*. Washington, DC: U.S. GPO.

———. (1992). *1990 Census of Population: General Population Characteristics*. Washington, DC: U.S. GPO.

———. (1993). *1990 Census of Population: Social and Economic Characteristics*. Washington, DC: U.S. GPO.

———. (2000). *Census 2000 Summary File 1 (SF 1) 100-Percent Data*. Washington, DC. http://www.census.gov/main/www/cen2000.html.

———. (2000). *Census 2000 Summary File 3 (SF 3) Sample Data*. Washington, DC. http://www.census.gov/main/www/cen2000.html.

OTHER UNITED STATES

U.S. Bureau of Economic Analysis. (n.d.). *Gross State Product*. http://www.bea.gov/bea/regional/gsp.htm.

———. (n.d.). *State and Local Personal Income: Local Area Annual Estimates*. http://www.bea.gov/bea/regional/statelocal.htm.

U.S. Bureau of Labor Statistics. (n.d.). *Local Area Unemployment Statistics*. http://www.bls.gov.

———. (n.d.). *State and County Employment*. http://www.bls.gov.

———. (n.d.). *National Employment*. http://www.bls.gov.

U.S. Bureau of Transportation Statistics. (2006). *America's Freight Transportation Gateways*. http://www.bts.gov/publications/americas_freight_transportation_gateways/.

———. (2006). *TranStats—The Intermodal Transportation Database*. Washington, DC: Bureau of Transportation. http://www.bts.gov.

U.S. Census Bureau. (2001). *Time Series of State Population Estimates*. http://www.census.gov/popest/archives/2000s/vintage_2001/ST_2001EST_-1.html.

———. (2002). *2002 Census of Governments: Government Organization*. Washington, DC. Available: http://www.census.gov/prod/2003pubs/gc021x1.pdf.

———. (2004). *Exports from Manufacturing Establishments: 2001*. http://www.census.gov/mcd/exports/ar01.pdf.

———. (n.d.). State export data series. *Foreign Trade Statistics*. http://www.census.gov/foreign-trade/aip/elom.html.

———. (n.d.). *Trade with Mexico*. Foreign Trade Division, Data Dissemination Branch. Washington, DC. http://www.census.gov/foreign-trade/balance/c2010.html#top.

U.S. Department of Commerce. (2002). *Regional Economic Information System*, Washington, DC. http://fisher.lib.virginia.edu/reis/.

U.S. Department of Homeland Security. (2005). DHS announces long-term border and immigration strategy. Press release, November 2. http://www.dhs.gov/dhspublic/interapp/press_release/press_release_0795.xml.

U.S. Department of Labor. (1992). *The Underground Economy in the United States*. Occasional Paper Series on the Informal Sector, No. 2. México,

DF: Secretaría del Trabajo y Previsión Social de México, and Washington, DC: U.S. Department of Labor.

U.S. Environmental Protection Agency. (2006). *U.S.-Mexico Border 2012 Framework.* http://www.epa.gov/usmexicoborder/intro.htm.

U.S. Government Accountability Office. (1999). *U.S.-Mexico Border: Issues and Challenges Confronting the United States and Mexico.* GAO/ NSIAD-99-190. http://archive.gao.gov/f0902b.

———. (2005). *Immigration Enforcement: Preliminary Observations on Employment Verification and Worksite Enforcement Efforts.* GAO-05-822T. http://www.gao.gov/new.items/d05822t.pdf.

U.S. International Trade Administration. (2003). *State Exports.* Washington, DC: U.S. Department of Commerce. http://www.ita.doc.gov/td/ industry/otea/state/.

———. (2005). *Foreign Trade Highlights.* Washington, DC: U.S. Department of Commerce. http://ita.doc.gov/td/industry/otea/usfth/index.html.

———. (n.d.). *Guide to State Export Data.* http://www.ita.doc.gov/td/ industry/otea/state/technote.html.

———. (n.d.). *TradeStats Express.* http://tse.export.gov/.

U.S. International Trade Administration, Office of Automotive Affairs. (1999). *Fifth Annual Report to Congress Regarding the Impact of the North American Free Trade Agreement upon U.S. Automotive Trade with Mexico.* Washington, DC: USITA, Department of Commerce. July.

U.S. International Trade Commission. (1999). *Production Sharing: Use of U.S. Components and Materials in Foreign Assembly Operations, 1995–1998.* USITC Publication 3265, December, Investigation 332–237. Washington, DC: USITC.

———. (2001). *Examination of U.S. Inbound and Outbound Direct Investment.* Staff Research Study 26, Office of Industries, USITC Publication 3383, January. Washington, DC: USITC.

U.S. Trade Representative. (1992). *Review of U.S.-Mexico Environmental Issues.* Washington, DC: Office of the U.S. Trade Representative.

INDEX

Note: Italic page numbers refer to figures, maps, photographs, and tables.

and cross-border integration,
223–226; and cross-border relations, 2–3, 70, 210; historical trajectory of, 12; and income gap,
139; and migration, 5, 60–61, 62;
and migration policies, 34, 54,
210, 211–215, 219–222, 225–226;
national capitals as focus of, 2;
and priorities of border region,
100, 215–216, 225–226; and trade
policies, 83–85, 216; and water
supply, 107
U.S. VISIT, 216, 242–243n10

wages: and demographic transition,
46; differentials in, 55, 58, 89;
and education levels, 174; and
English as a second language,
230n14; and exchange rates, 10;
and export-processing zones, 88;
and income inequality, 150; and
labor productivity, 62, 229n16;
and maquiladora industry, 94,
95; measurement of Mexican
wages, 20, 228n4; and migration,
5, 54, 55, 56, 58, 217; minimum
wages in Mexico, 152–153, 153,
155, 229n10, 238–239n9; and
women's employment, 133; and
youth dependency ratios, 49
War of North American Invasion, 14
wastes: and environmental issues,
7; industrial wastes, 7, 103, 106,
109–110; and population growth,
103, 106; and sewage disposal,
7, 106–107; and water quality,
108–109. See also industrial
wastes
wastewater treatment, 103, 107–
108, 109, 114
water quality, 7, 8, 103, 108–109,
190

water supply: and border environmental institutions, 111; in Chihuahua, 22; and environmental
issues, 7, 106, 107–108; and living standards, 166; and maquiladora industry, 95, 99, 103
Waterton Lakes National Park,
111
Webb County, Texas, 67, 125, 151
White Sands Missile Range, 23
wildlife preservation, 7, 103,
110–111, 116
Wilson, Pete, 63
Wilson, Tamar, 49
women's employment: and demographic transition, 46; and fertility rate, 45; and household sector
work, 122–123, 132; and informal economy, 132, 237n14; and
labor force participation rate,
120, 121, 122, 122, 123, 131–133;
in maquiladora industry, 99,
122, 131–133, 132, 133
World Bank, 129, 139, 141
World Bank Doing Business Index,
56
World Trade Organization, 89, 90,
231n22
World War II, 17, 19
Wright, D. M., 66

youth dependency ratios, 46–47, 48,
48, 150
Ysleta, Texas, 23
Yuma, Arizona, 19, 228n2
Yuma County, Arizona, 126

Zapata, José Antonio, 30
Zapata, Texas, 30
Zapata County, Texas, 195
Zedillo, Ernesto, 83, 84